ANDY BLANKENBUEHLER

Also available in the series:

MICHAEL JOHN LACHIUSA
by Joshua Robinson

ANDY BLANKENBUEHLER

A CRITICAL COMPANION

Amanda Jane Olmstead

methuen | drama
LONDON • NEW YORK • OXFORD • NEW DELHI • SYDNEY

METHUEN DRAMA
Bloomsbury Publishing Plc, 50 Bedford Square, London, WC1B 3DP, UK
Bloomsbury Publishing Inc, 1359 Broadway, New York, NY 10018, USA
Bloomsbury Publishing Ireland, 29 Earlsfort Terrace, Dublin 2, D02 AY28, Ireland

BLOOMSBURY, METHUEN DRAMA and the Methuen Drama logo are trademarks of Bloomsbury Publishing Plc

First published in Great Britain 2026

Series cover design by Holly Capper
Cover image © Rachel Papo

A catalogue record for this book is available from the British Library.

A catalog record for this book is available from the Library of Congress.

ISBN: HB: 978-1-350-52435-4
PB: 978-1-350-52434-7
ePDF: 978-1-350-52437-8
eBook: 978-1-350-52436-1

Series: Musical Theatre Critical Companions

Typeset by Integra Software Services Pvt. Ltd.
Printed and bound in Great Britain

For product safety related questions contact productsafety@bloomsbury.com.

To find out more about our authors and books visit www.bloomsbury.com and sign up for our newsletters.

For Andy—whose work and brilliance remind us that we all have a story to tell.

CONTENTS

FIGURES

ABOUT THE AUTHOR

Dr. Amanda Jane Olmstead (she/her) is a faculty member in the Theatre Arts Department at the University of Pittsburgh and in the School of Drama at Carnegie Mellon University in Pittsburgh, USA. She received her PhD in Theatre and Performance Studies from the University of Pittsburgh, her MA in Performance Studies from New York University, and her BA in Theatre with a minor in Dance from the Indiana University of Pennsylvania. Olmstead is also a choreographer for local Pittsburgh schools and the Pitt Stages Theatre Arts Department. Her publications include an article titled "Développé: Katherine Dunham's Diasporic Dance" in the *Studies in Musical Theatre Journal* and a chapter titled "Dance as Narrative: Storytelling Through the Ensemble Body" for the collection titled *Dance in Musical Theatre: A History of the Body in Movement.*

ACKNOWLEDGMENTS

In the early stages of this project, back in 2018, I cast a wide net amongst the Broadway industry to see what performers I could get in touch with that had worked with Andy Blankenbuehler. Little did I know my inquiries would make their way to Andy himself. Just four hours after defending my PhD Prospectus I received an email, "hello, andy blankenbuehler here." Andy, I cannot thank you enough for reaching out to me and transforming my project in a way I could have never imagined. Your invitation to observe the audition process of *Only Gold* in New York was personally life changing. Watching you create and jam about your process opened fundamental doors for my exploration—not to mention, it was a complete dream come true. Your continued support and celebration of my work, your desire to share your story with students and young artists, your collaborative spirit in every avenue of your life is beyond inspiring.

To Stephanie Klemons, Michael Balderrama, Luis Salgado, Morgan Marcell, Ben Darmanin, Betsy Struxness, Shonica Gooden, Antwan Bethea, David Guzman, Karla Puno Garcia, and all of the other incredible associates, assistance, and performers who generously took the time to answer my questions and shed light on the critical work of the ensemble bodies on Broadway, from the bottom of my heart, thank you.

I also owe a debt to Deborah Kaufman, founder of Words on Dance, for inviting me to attend the talk featuring Andy Blankenbuehler and Sarah L. Kaufman. Being able to witness Andy explain his philosophies while demonstrating choreography with performers—followed by more wonderful conversation—took my project to the next level. Without Words on Dance the notion of the ensemble as the lens of a piece may not have been nearly as clear.

Additionally, I would like to express my deepest and sincerest gratitude to my mentor Michelle Granshaw. Your dedication, positive energy, and extraordinary capacity for knowledge is absolutely inspiring. Thank you for perpetually challenging me to consider different angles, possibilities, and philosophies. Furthermore, I am eternally grateful for your constant encouragement to trust and uplift my own voice in my work. And to professors Cynthia Croot, Kathleen George, and Cindy García for guiding me throughout my scholarship and writing. I also owe great thanks to Dom O'Hanlon for entrusting me with this responsibility and granting me the opportunity of a lifetime.

Finally, to my friends, I would not be where I am today without your unwavering compassion. There are not enough words in the world to properly thank you all. My beloved husband Michael, thank you for being so incredibly patient and pushing me to keep going. To my family, Grandma Jane, Nona, Papa, Pap, Gram, Alyssa, Andrew, Mom, and Dad, you have each given me more than I will ever know, more than words will ever be able to express gratitude for. You are my rock. I'll love you forever and always.

PREFACE

Andy Blankenbuehler's choreography of the chorus/ensemble in the musicals on which he has worked have fundamentally altered the landscape of musical theatre forever. How dance looks, how choreography world builds, and how the chorus/ensemble functions have become essentially nuanced due to his innovations. Through years of deep diving into Blankenbuehler, I have theorized conceptions of an "ensemble body"—to be defined more thoroughly later in this piece—that he activates, allowing for the individual performer and their purpose inside the world of the show to function in tandem with one another. It is undeniable that he prioritizes character and storytelling, activating the individual ensemble bodies to communicate complex social meaning as opposed to utilizing performers to simply showcase spectacle and virtuosity. Is the uniquity of Blankenbuehler's pieces about a curated style or an efficacious process? Moreover, how has his work turned into a methodological practice that subsequent productions and artists have adopted?

On September 18, 2024, I had the immense privilege of seeing a tour production of *Hamilton* in Pittsburgh, Pennsylvania, at the Benedum Center for the Performing Arts with Andy Blankenbuehler himself. Until that show, I had actually never seen *Hamilton* in person—but I had analyzed every inch of the Disney+ and any other piece of footage that existed publicly. At intermission, he asked me if it was everything I expected it to be. I paused. Then, I cautiously replied, "It is both expectedly and unexpectedly very different watching new bodies take on these choreography scores." To which he responded, "This is a very young and clean cast." He continued to explain that it was only their third city on the tour, so they still had a lot to learn about activating their individual perspectives.[1] A flood of thoughts rushed through me. Everything I had argued about his work and how he creates was coming to life in a new way. Yes, his choreography is unique. Yes, it prioritizes the individual over virtuosity. Yes, it frames the production through the bodies of the ensemble. But, the new conundrum becomes, how does that spirit live on when he is no longer the main point of instruction for these young casts who are freshly learning the material? What happens when the company does not have months to develop alongside the creators, but instead only has a few short weeks with associate or resident choreographers and directors to get it together and head out on tour?

The following day, I observed Blankenbuehler lead a rehearsal with this cast, conveying the (what would become ten typed) pages of notes he wrote down in his notebook during the show we watched the night before. Eleven out of twenty-two notes on the first page concerned character, point of view, and being "less clean." In the opening of rehearsal notes, he explained, "People need truth, and they need connection … ultimately it's not about execution … we want to experience the world through you."[2] Blankenbuehler is undeniably dedicated to and passionate about the process—the storytelling process, the emotional process, the creative process, the research process, and the connection process. How do we tell stories? How do we make our vision clear to others? How do we bring the audience into our journey? How and why does our process matter when a product emerges? It is an honor to shine a light on Andy Blankenbuehler's processes for artists, scholars, students, and fans. It is a humbling privilege to do so alongside Andy. After all, it is always important to remember the question: who lives, who dies, who tells your story?

INTRODUCTION

> There are very few times when I really want the audience to look at dance … Dance is just meant to be a framing device that matches emotionally what I want the audience to feel.
>
> Blankenbuehler, *Hamilton: the Revolution*

> The ensemble MUST be the lens of the piece. The ensemble MUST focus the principal storyline so that no matter where your eye goes in the show, you see refracted back what the principal is going through.
>
> Blankenbuehler, "Fresh Steps"

In 2016, Lin-Manuel Miranda and Jeremy McCarter put together *Hamilton: the Revolution*, "the complete libretto of the Broadway musical with a true account of its creation, and concise remarks on hip-hop, the power of stories, and the new America."[1] *Hamilton* is an entirely sung-through musical. Consequently, the musical is nearly danced-through. In the chapter "On 'Non-Stop,' both The Song and The Way of Life, as Manifest by Andy Blankenbuehler and the Public Theater's Props Department," Miranda and McCarter point out:

> When *In the Heights* came around, [Andy] knew he had to choreograph the salsa-and-hip-hop show, even though—as he admitted to Tommy [Kail] and Jeffrey [Sellers]—he didn't know anything about salsa or hip-hop. They thought he had a knack for telling stories, so they hired him anyway. To prepare for the show, he moved to Los Angeles, took four hip-hop classes a day, soaked up the rhythm of salsa, and devised a hybrid style of his own. It won him a Tony Award.
>
> For *Hamilton,* he needed another new vocabulary. Beyond several varieties of hip-hop dance, you can see little traces of Gene Kelly and Justin Timberlake in the result. When Andy himself dances it, you see a lot of Jerome Robbins. But the movement of *Hamilton,* in its totality, reaches far beyond conventional dance steps, of any tradition. Andy

> devised a language of what he calls "stylized heightened gesture." It includes everything from the way a chair is moved, to how a shoulder pops, to the bows at the curtain call.[2]

It is without doubt that Blankenbuehler's utilization of a hybrid dance style, merging jazz, ballet, hip-hop, and stylized pedestrian gesture, has been pivotal to his success. However, it is how his choreography engages and actuates specific bodies on stage that is particularly noteworthy. Of course, his choreography style and current methodology did not come to him overnight.

Andy Blankenbuehler followed a relatively traditional Broadway performer career path before landing an opportunity that would change his life. As a young child, Blankenbuehler studied ballet, jazz, and tap. He began his professional career performing for the Walt Disney Company, in regional theatre productions such as *A Chorus Line* (1991) and *West Side Story* (1991), and then debuted on Broadway in *Guys and Dolls* (1992). Additional highlights of his Broadway dance career include *Fosse* (1999), *Saturday Night Fever* (1999), and *Contact* (2000). Blankenbuehler began his entrance into the world of choreography around 2002 eventually gaining recognition for his work with Andrew Lippa's *A Little Princess* (2005), Jerry Bock and Sheldon Harnick's *The Apple Tree* (City Center Encores, 2005 and Broadway revival transfer, 2006), and Frank Wildhorn's *Waiting for the Moon* (2006). He was two big numbers into Paper Mill Playhouses' production of *It's A Wonderful Life* (2006) when he got a call that he had booked *In the Heights*. Blankenbuehler recalls:

> I got *In the Heights* at the same time as the *Apple Tree*. So then, all of a sudden, I had no jobs and now I had two big jobs at the exact same time … And so there I was with all these balls in the air which was, in a way, good because I just had to trust my instincts I had going into *In the Heights* and not do ten versions, but do the one that is speaking to me. I didn't take a day off for months. I was working so hard, opened the *Apple Tree* on Broadway, and then *In the Heights* opened off Broadway a month and a half later and so everybody thinks *In the Heights* was my first show but actually *Apple Tree*.[3]

Although *The Apple Tree* was chronologically first, *In the Heights* marked a precise moment of transition for his choreographic practice. Continuing, he reflects,

> Ultimately, once I did *Heights,* I felt a familiar fulfilment to what I had felt before working on shows like *Fosse.* I felt I could do something good because it's hard when you're doing a show where all things aren't in sync—it just doesn't always feel fulfilling. Then, I made mistakes after that. It didn't all go great, but at least I felt like I had started a new chapter.[4]

In the Heights challenged Blankenbuehler to learn entirely new genres of dance to keep up and innovate alongside the changing landscape of Broadway. Influenced by predecessors such as Jerome Robbins and Bob Fosse and building on the complex history of the chorus's role and the chorus member's body in a musical, he activates the individual bodies cast in these supplemental roles so that they each affectively operate within the production.[5] His work on *Heights* would ignite a foundational transition toward "ensembleizing" an entire chorus—prioritizing intentional, individual characterizations over superfluous, ambiguous background characters. To ensembleize effectively means the precedence is placed upon uniquity over uniformity within the collective group. Historically, in musical theatre, the chorus member has been scripted and staged as an anonymous entity, supplemental to the milieu of a show. Relatively unmediated by specified characteristics regarding personality or biography, those in the chorus have been subject to generalized groups such as townsfolk repudiating any sense of individuality or uniquity. Although he has worked on more traditional-style productions such as *9 to 5* (2009), *Annie* (2012), and *Cats* (2016), where he does implement choreographic practices that sustain "the chorus," his work with *In the Heights* (Off-Broadway, 2007; Broadway, 2008), *Bring It On: The Musical* (2012), and *Hamilton* (The Public, 2015; Broadway, 2016) would help him curate a choreographic style that prioritizes the ensemble and the ensemble body as a fundamental production element. Through the use of a hybrid dance genre that melds pedestrian movement with hip-hop, jazz, and ballet, he promotes dance and the dancing body as communication tools to connect the audience to sociological metanarratives that surround the productions on which he works.

At a talk for Words on Dance at Symphony Space in 2019, Blankenbuehler proclaimed, "The ensemble MUST be the lens of the piece. The ensemble MUST focus the principal storyline so that no matter where your eye goes in the show, you see refracted back what the principal is going through."[6] His prioritization of the ensemble as crucial to understanding the action within a show consequently positions the ensemble body as an indispensable element through which the audience gains vital (sub)text. As a result, his choreography has become distinctly different from his predecessors and

Figure 1 A master at work. Photo by David Korins.

peers. In *Hamilton: the Revolution* (2016), Blankenbuehler is quoted saying, "There are very few times when I really want the audience to look at dance … Dance is just meant to be a framing device that matches emotionally what I want the audience to feel."[7] By utilizing the ensemble body as a lens of a piece and dance as a framing tool, Blankenbuehler's choreography coordinates what information the audience receives and how.

Blankenbuehler emphasizes, "It is easy to over choreograph and show off … I am not interested in spectacle […] it's important to remind yourself when you don't need movement."[8] He emphatically contends that the choreography needs to serve the story and not one's ability as a choreographer. Dance should only be implemented when it is real and character-motivated. Therefore, dance is his frame. It is not a vital component to see, but it can add structure, information, or support. To see, in order for the dance to obtain any level of significance, he needs his lens, the ensemble. It is the ensemble, and thus the ensemble bodies, doing the dancing that is fundamental in providing clarity for the audience.

Reflecting on his time with *9 to 5*, directed by Joe Mantello, Blankenbuehler discusses the significance of "buttons" in a musical. A button is traditionally the final beat, pose, or moment of a scene or song. When considering processes of collaboration with directors and writers, he often muses about how dance can support such significant moments of storytelling. After all, the end of a moment contains a fundamental dialogue with an audience. Blankenbuehler elaborates on the expectations of a button:

> You can't just expect the audience to clap because a song ended. There has to be an emotional accumulation to button a song and then, there's an emotional release because something was accomplished. Sometimes songs button and you've accomplished nothing. That's a problem. That's a dramaturgical problem and is going to add up through the course of the night.
>
> If a moment doesn't build to a button, the audience doesn't have a release. They don't have closure. They don't have a new mindset going into the next scene. It's not just the button makes a bigger applause—yes, the button makes a bigger applause—but, it's accomplishing a lot of emotional things.
>
> So, for me as a choreographer, I try to figure out how to bring the number to an accumulative ending … but adding dance might to that moment might not make the show better, it might actually make the show worse.[9]

His comprehension of when dance is necessary to support a moment versus when it is overwhelming and can distract from a vital emotional beat is something he has become more attuned to throughout his career. He asserts, "I can over-choreograph things all of the time. It's important to remind yourself when you don't need movement … Movement is just a scale. Sometimes you gotta go all the way to the right and all the way to the left so you can figure out what the possibilities are."[10] As will be thoroughly explored throughout this book, Blankenbuehler has garnered an incredibly intimate understanding of storytelling necessities and modalities.

In musical theatre, dance is one of the acknowledged languages for expression. The audience enters the theatre, suspending their disbelief and accepting that the characters in a musical will use song, speech, and in many cases, dance to communicate dialogue, feelings, thoughts, and abstract ideas. Additionally, the style of dance can provide the audience with information. Ballet, jazz, tap, social, and hip-hop dance suggest specific meaning based on sociohistorical connotations. In their article, "Dance in Musical Theater," Stacy Wolf and Liza Gennaro generated a list of functions for how dance operates as a storytelling modality within musical theatre productions:

> (1) dance to reveal a character's psychology; (2) dance to tell a piece of the story; (3) dance to express an unspoken aspect of the libretto; (4) dance to transition to another scene; (5) dance to allow the characters to express themselves; and (6) dance to present an idea or feeling metaphorically or abstractly. In many cases, a specific dance functions in more than one way.[11]

This book seeks to build on their work and expand such analysis of the functions of dance in musical theatre also to consider the functions of the ensemble within musical theatre. In using Wolf and Gennaro as a steppingstone, I am able to move beyond dance alone, as Andy Blankenbuehler has, as the primary site of analysis and interrogate the ensemble as being fundamental to the productions on which he has worked. The dance allows bodies to speak even when they have no "text" and helps create the ensemble body as doing and being within the world of a production. For Blankenbuehler, the dance provides ensemble bodies with structure or vocabulary by which they can speak. It aggrandizes their potential. It is the individual bodies themselves who then contextualize the dance and communicate the meaning, emotions, ideas, etc. to the audience.

To this end, the ensemble body becomes a fundamental dramaturgical element of the storytelling, and thus, a necessary component of Blankenbuehler's choreographic methodology. In order to understand the significance of how bodies can function or be analyzed dramaturgically, it is valuable to first apprehend a clear and concise meaning of "dramaturgy" as both a practice and a philosophy. According to Dennis Waskul and Phillip Vannini's conceptions of bodily impression, "From a dramaturgical perspective, bodies are *necessarily* performative—which is to say that bodies are always in motion and, hence, a perpetual site of action—the fundamental unit of dramaturgical analysis and the most essential element of any drama."[12] Epistemologically, the concept can be split into two factions, being and doing. The *being* of dramaturgy considers "the proprietary structure of a play or a body of work … the skeleton of the work."[13] Jonathan Borrows's *A Choreographer's Handbook* similarly suggests that dramaturgy "describes the thread of meaning, philosophic intent, or logic, which allows the audience to accept and unite the disparate clues you give them into a coherent whole, connecting to other reference points and contexts in the larger world."[14] Therefore, the body itself, rich with storytelling components, is dramaturgical.

Often credited with coining the term "dramaturgical body," Waskul and Vannini set up to their piece "The Performative Body: Dramaturgy, the Body, and Embodiment," positing:

> Everywhere, and at all times, bodies are actively inscribed with any one or more of the physical markers of powerful social institutions including age, gender, race, ethnicity, sexuality, and religion … the body is clearly the site of enormous expressive and impressive appearance management as well as a focal point for significant ritual activity—two dynamics that are, without question, foremost to dramaturgical analysis.[15]

A viewer can see and read this body, gathering clues to connect or draw conclusions regarding said body to broader contexts outside of itself. Still, their defining of terms rests on the concept of *doing* dramaturgy. They continue to argue that because the body is produced, manipulated, and presented in accordance with such socially constructed situations, "people do not 'have' a body so much as people actively *do* a body."[16] The body is moving, operative, efficacious, productive, energetic, dynamic, and indispensable. Assessing the dramaturgical body considers race, ethnicity, class, gender, sex, sexuality, and athleticism. The dramaturgical body is emotional, experienced, and authentic. The dramaturgical body *is* and *does.* However, what happens when this dramaturgical body performs or becomes a character? What happens when this dramaturgical body is acknowledged rather than erased or detached from its social moorings as is the case with traditional uses of bodies within a musical theatre chorus? Blankenbuehler honors an ensemble body's interiority and activates it as a vital storytelling device. The ensemble body *is,* but it also *does.*

Chapters 2, 3, and 4 of this book deeply analyze key choreographic moments throughout Blankenbuehler's work on *In the Heights, Bring It On: The Musical,* and *Hamilton,* respectively. Utilizing thick descriptions, I detail how the choreographic moments look. Then, to interrogate and dissect each movement or phrase and how the corresponding ensemble body(ies) affect the audience's understanding at that moment, I consider the following:

1. What does the ensemble (body) represent at this point in the story? Is it individual, or is it collective?
2. What is the ensemble body's relationship to the narrative and milieu of the show?

3. What is the choreography's relationship to the narrative and milieu of the show?
4. How does the choreography shape X function? (Filling in Wolf and Gennaro's functions of dance in musical theatre)
5. How does the ensemble body shape X function?
6. How does the vocabulary of the choreography frame the ensemble body?[17]

In short, I employ basic stage directing and dance vocabulary to describe how the dance and choreography look. A goal of mine was to make the dance as legible to as wide of an audience as possible. To do this, I activate footnotes whenever any technical dance term requires further explanation. Moreover, I rely on Jonathan Burrows's *A Choreographer's Handbook* to define choreographic principles. In his opening, he illuminates, "A principle is a way to make a map where no map exists. The landscape is there already, but a map might help you decide where to go."[18] As the ensemble body functions as communication, transition, metaphor, spectacle, and most importantly, lens, I use my questions above, Burrows's principles, ethnographic and archival information, alongside philosophical and theoretical scholarship to explore the unwritten potential of the ensemble (body).

There are a multitude of factors that come into play when writing, dancing, enjoying, and examining choreography. The very notion that audience members can and will interpret dance differently regardless of the choreographer's intent is important to acknowledge here. As I read, dictate, and translate Blankenbuehler's choreography throughout my investigation, I rely as much as I can on his words, words of the performers, and scholarship to provide the most conscientious analysis possible. This book is both an illumination of Andy Blankenbuehler's creative process and an investigation into how that process comes to life. While Part 1, "Becoming Blankenbuehler" introduces readers to Blankenbuehler's career and road to developing his unique, creative methodology, Part 2, "Extended Choreographic Analysis," provides a deeper look into Blankenbuehler's choreographic score in conversation with the ensemble body(ies) doing the dancing. The book weaves interludes throughout—augmenting moments of pause for personal and theoretical reflection leading to Part 3, "Continued Practice," which briefly highlights his career beyond work with Lin-Manuel Miranda, and points to future projects and a continued influence on the Broadway landscape.

PART 1
BECOMING BLANKENBUEHLER

CHAPTER 1
WORDS WITH ANDY: THE CREATIVE PROCESS

A wall adorned with intricate collages of black-and-white photos, vibrant splashes of color, typed quotes, and scattered hand-written Post-its curate an affective space for world-building and storytelling in the home studio of choreographer Andy Blankenbuehler. Images of moving bodies, piercing eyes, striking architecture, and moody lighting offer conceptual inspiration for his upcoming projects. The studio is a blend of history and creativity, featuring exposed pre-war wooden beams, stunning brick, floor-to-ceiling mirrors, black Marley floor, and large windows framing the garden terrace—an open invitation for collaboration with past, present, and future. Blankenbuehler's studio space offers him a place to become completely and intimately steeped in the worlds of his ideas while balancing the delicate nature of a tumultuous industry with his ever-important home life.

> It's hard because now, business and creativity are two different things. Yesterday, my body was a mess. I hadn't worked out for three days. So, I was like, I have to work out. I have to work out. But I ended up in business for four straight hours and didn't work out and I obviously wasn't creative. I was just doing business. And it's difficult … I'm at my most creative when I'm physical. And so just to have an hour and a half every morning is not easy. I like to walk the dog, but I can't walk the dog and have an hour and a half in the morning. I also can't walk the dog two days in a row or my knee is a mess. Like, I have to work out before I walk, literally. That balancing act is only getting harder …
>
> In a weird way, the kids are easier, but the kids are not easier because they remember everything now. You want to be there for every meal. So, that is actually more demanding time-wise than when they were five, six years old and I was working constantly. And I hated being away, but it did not feel as dire then as it is now to be around … It's tricky. I don't have such a hard time with motivation, but ultimately, I am at my happiest when I'm actually making something. When I'm

planning something and envisioning something, I can get not so great to be around. But, when I'm making something, I'm happier. I'm more productive.

Part of it for me is realizing that to work at the level I want to work at, just for me personally, I'm going to spend a lot of time walking in circles, warming up, thinking, experimenting, throwing it away, listening to music. And, when I am busy, I realize that I can get things done a lot faster. Then, it's about pushing a rock up a hill or juggling so many different things because you just don't know what's going to happen.

The reason I'm doing *Never Alone* now is just because I need the choreography now. I need to. I don't have anything right now. So, I need to make something up. I need to choreograph.[1]

During the September 18, 2024 tour performance of *Hamilton*. Blankenbuehler was sure to call home between our dinner and the start of the production. Throughout our meetings in New York, he was either checking in upstairs or checking in at home through his phone or through his assistant, Ben Darmanin. His reflections on the tensions between business, creativity, and personal relationships, responsibilities, and joys unapologetically highlight the humanity that is often lost when we look at successful artists in the industry. It is easy to lose sight of the hustle they, too, need to navigate to make their dreams a reality.

Blankenbuehler has an intimate relationship with research and has curated dynamic ways of immersing himself into the worlds of his upcoming pieces. He reflects, "The first part of the rehearsal process is understanding the world. Do I like the world, does the world speak to me, and what's special about the world—the fashion, the social climate, political climate?"[2] From understanding movement vocabulary to music to imagery, he spends a great deal of time in pre-production finding where and how the story fits within the body.

1.1 On Imagery

I see things in color, meaning when I'm working on a piece, I see the piece in a color. So everything I wore when I made *Hamilton* was maroon and black. I just saw maroon. I don't know why, but that was sort of my comfort zone. And so, in that way my "Method-y"- self kind of took over.

Blankenbuehler

In a 2016 interview regarding *Hamilton*, Andy Blankenbuehler recalls,

> In many ways, I saw the readings and wondered if I needed to choreograph it. Like, was it better just sitting on a chair and saying the words … We needed to stay out of the way of the words … I always see choreography, but especially with *Hamilton*, as an Impressionistic painting, where the surround of bodies has to inform what you are supposed to be looking at.[3]

Blankenbuehler's keen eye and affinity for imagery are particularly heightened during his pre-production process. From his use of physical and digital vision boards to the comprehension of worlds and moments in his mind, the significance of color, shapes, and stories from images is a profound point of discussion as he creates.

> I was in a café in Boston. And, whenever I was on tour as a performer, I'd always find local cafes, and I would write like ten pages a day or in my journal or draw. I did a lot of drawing. And, so I was at this café in Little Italy in Boston, and I was going through some angst breakup or something, and I was writing, and this guy comes in covered in oil paint, like hair sticking up, crazy Italian artist, like oil paint all over his clothes. He had obviously had just taken a break from painting, and comes into the café, never sits down, orders his, you know, espresso, and he's talking to the Italian guy behind him. And the guy's hair was sticking straight up like Einstein. And I was like, my God, this guy's amazing. And I wrote about him in my journal. And then I was back in that same city maybe five years later, and I go to the same café, amazing sunlight in the afternoon, and I'm writing in my journal, and a guy comes in wearing a black suit, sophisticated looking, hair slicked back, and goes to the counter. He orders an espresso, he's talking to the barista. I'm writing, and I look over at the guy, and he has one drop of oil paint on his shoe. It's the same guy.
>
> But all that craziness had somehow laser-beamed in. But one drop gave him away, and he was still the same painter. And so that's when they do this (demonstrating a move from *Hamilton*'s "My Shot" where the left hand is at the waist, begins with the fingers close, and flicks downward as if dropping something to the ground) on [the word] "scrappy." That's the image in my head of, like, these bombastic kids, but when it comes down to it, they have the ability to be laser-sharp.

> They just don't know it yet. And so, that my-shot-ness is the crazy guy. It's not until the second act that he's the five years later guy—the specificity of it. But, that's what I think we try to do in theatre, is take this huge picture, but then push it into a laser beam. And I think that's maybe kind of unique to my work a little bit, about the lasery kind of stillness. But if we don't get the thing right that is the laser, you're lead astray. You still have to get the image completely right.[4]

In "My Shot," the notion that Alexander Hamilton is young, scrappy, and hungry is such an essential theme to the entire production. Blankenbuehler's allegorical connection between Hamilton and the painter he encountered in Boston showcases such layered storytelling within one gesture, one movement that takes a breath to complete—but is riddled with meaning.

Reflecting once again on inspiration drawn from art, in his 2019 talk for Words on Dance, he discusses Michelangelo's *Moses*: "I remember reading a thing about Michelangelo and he said he could not start the carving until he knew the exact instant that he was trying to capture."[5] When he and his wife went to see *Moses* at San Pietro in Vincoli, Rome, he remembers:

Figure 2 In the studio with Andy. Photo courtesy of Andy Blankenbuehler.

> Moses is sitting … with his [left] foot back … And the intense look is because this is the instant before he stands up and changes the world. His leg is like that because … there's weight on his big toe … The strength of the sculpture is that he knows action is about to happen. So, in that moment, I realized that I have to choreograph in fourth position for the rest of my life. Because characters who take action are the heroes.[6]

He elaborates:

> I was never impressed by *Moses* as a young person. I was always into *David*. Until, I really started to understand the stuff behind this *Moses* … He's pushing his weight into his toe, but his hand is so soft. There is a contradiction of, like, he's holding these stone tables that are so heavy, but there is no strain in his hand ….He's looking on this downstage left angle as opposed to the downstage right because he knows how difficult it's going to be. That's the angle of maturity and cynicism as opposed to aspiration and idealism. This (the downstage left) is Angelica's angle while the other is Eliza's angle. So, all of "Satisfied" turns to this angle.

As mentioned earlier, Blankenbuehler continues to philosophize about the difference between second and fourth position and how the activations of each have changed throughout his career and can be activated throughout a show based on a character's objectives and journey.

> There is so much fourth position in *Hamilton*. For example, when he leaves "Nonstop" through the remainder of the show. Now, "My Shot" starts in second position. That's where the whole theme is set, in second position. "Right Hand Man" is in second position—because nobody knows anything yet. They're just kids ….But if you look at *In the Heights*, it is so in second position. But, *Hamilton* is more of an adult show. The messaging is, what really is worth fighting for.[7]

Shedding some more context on his use of Pinterest boards and mental imagery he muses:

> There are different things to help my brain get into the zone of what I see in my head. And I have maybe 3—images on a Pinterest board.

(Showing me a board full of monochromatic images for a new work called *Bone Music* he is developing) This is an unrefined board for *Bone Music.* I set images around me all the time to remind myself of the show that I want to make. Obviously, this is a show that happens in a black void. There's not a lot of scenery. There's a harsh light about it, because it's a harsh world of collectivism. And there's a lot of teenage angst that is young people wanting to be exuberant and joyful, but having to face really harsh circumstances. So I start to understand the tone. And I frankly start to imitate light cues. I'll have images on my boards where I know that's an image that's interesting. And like anything else for me, when something sticks around, I know it's worth making. When something doesn't stick around, it was just a step in the process …

The thing that has staying power, I just have to find a way to be honest about it, to say that's the thing that I'm interested in. So, even if something like *Bandstand,* where it's 1942, if something's staying with me that's a really contemporary image, that's the thing that's staying with me. One of the most powerful things in *Bandstand* that everybody talked about was the soldiers on each other's backs, and then the soldiers pushing the piano. And that image was so clear in my head, and it kind of made no sense. And I said to the men that morning we were rehearsing, this is gonna sound strange, but this is what we're gonna try to do. And they were so wholeheartedly behind it, because it just organically made sense to everybody. I just realized now that I have to pay attention to those things that seem random.

The same thing happened in *In the Heights,* when everybody in the blackout hits the floor at the same time. I had an image so clear in my head, and the first time I did it and we set it, the company, I mean, everybody loved it. It was hard to execute, but it was a really stunning moment. And so that's what kind of happens on my collage boards …

And so, that's a big part of my prep process, is just being completely steeped in the world. Because ultimately, I'm going to come up with ideas that that are so detailed, and they take so long to make, but I can't be imprisoned by those ideas. But if you're so steeped in the world, then you can actually improvise and roll with it.

I remember the summer when I did *Nine* (2024), I had this image in my head for the little boy, and he was going to be on a chair, and he was being tortured emotionally by, on one hand, this woman who was a prostitute, affecting him in one way that he couldn't understand, and his mother, on the other hand reprimanding him and torturing him.

So, he felt tortured emotionally between his sexual yearning, which he didn't understand, and the repercussions of structure, which his mother in the church represented. And I had this image in my head of him laying sideways on a chair, and his body being wrung out like a towel.

And instantly, the body could not do it. He wasn't equipped to understand what I was doing. Understandably so, he was nine. As an adult, I could make that moment work, but he couldn't make that moment work … I tried it and it lasted about one minute. And after one minute, I made up another option. And we did it immediately. It worked immediately. And somebody said to me after rehearsal, "I've never been around somebody who can throw away their stuff so quickly or can improvise something. Like, they have ten things planned already. Did you have that planned?" And I said no, I didn't have it planned. But I just knew. I knew him. I knew the world. I knew the situation. Because I had spent so long analyzing the situations that then you can roll, you can riff. And so, that's in the prep process for me, in the research part of the process. It's just getting to know the world.[8]

1.2 On Style

In a talk at Symphony Space in Upper West Side Manhattan, through an organization called Words on Dance, Andy Blankenbuehler spoke to a small crowd of dance, choreography, and musical theatre enthusiasts. Reflecting upon his development as a performer, he said, "Through imitation, you can meet and be mentored by icons."[9] He asserts he had a sponge-like ability to learn the dances of Gene Kelly, Fred Astaire, Jerome Robbins, Bob Fosse, and Michael Jackson, among others, which allowed him to be "taught" by some of the most renowned performers in the history of the industry. He explained how their impact influenced him to make later choices in his career, citing the notion that there is Astaire, Robbins, Fosse, and Jackson in *Hamilton*. Blankenbuehler discussed two key lessons that propelled his creative process—both lessons are notably learned from Jerome Robbins. Reflecting on *West Side Story* (1957), he explained how, in the "Prologue," the character Riff has a moment of standing with both arms and legs in second position.[10] He notes that this second position is a stance for believing in something. Riff sees the world's possibilities in front of him, but there is no action behind it. Immediately following, Riff turns upstage and decides to go and fight for the turf that "belongs" to the Jets. He then turns back around in fourth position and goes to make his next move.[11] The fourth position allows the character to take action, to progress forward. Blankenbuehler recalls choreographing in second position for nearly ten to fifteen years because it was presentational, showy, and frankly, what was done most commonly in musicals before him. But changing his choreography to fourth position turned it into action, beyond believing and toward doing.

When Blankenbuehler saw *Jerome Robbins Broadway* in 1989, he learned the second lesson that he would carry with him through his career. While watching "New York, New York" from *On the Town,* he began to learn about the depths of storytelling through the body. He later named these depths the body's "three engines:" intellect, heart, and gut. Knowing how the story affects us in these different places at different times informs where the movement emanates. At the top of "New York, New York," the men dock in the city for twenty-four hours and anything is possible. Robbins gives us this information by having the dancers travel upstage left to downstage right diagonal using a series of grand sautés with their arms reaching over the top of their heads and their chests puffed outward.[12] Blankenbuehler observed that the heart leads the body down a long diagonal, informing the audience of the open-eyed belief that anything is possible.[13] He continues:

> Raising the arms over the head must mean something. In real life, we don't often reach our arms over our head. If in dancing you are going to do a huge sauté and reach for the sky, whatever you are reaching for, better be important—and for those men who are used to dying, now they have ultimate freedom even just for twenty-four hours .... Moments can be heighten-able if what you're reaching for is actually valid; if it is not honest, then we are seeing musical theatre and dance that we have all seen before that we don't believe in. It is just entertaining—definitely a world where that is valid, but that becomes a different type of dance.[14]

Blankenbuehler prioritizes the meaning and impetus behind each movement of his choreography over entertaining dance spectacle to make moments more honest and believable.

Through his now decades of work, Blankenbuehler has theorized in and around the performers, directors, and choreographers who have preceded him to create his unique choreographic style and methodology. But he reminds us about the tricky nature of being inspired or influenced by those who have come before:

> I actually don't want to make steps that people recognize. It's the same way if you see a show and it's a Beyoncé song, do you start to think about the Beyoncé music video? Your brain leaves the show. There have been times where the Sons of Liberty [in *Hamilton*] have a bit of liberty in the scene after the wedding and they're kind of grooving, but they're not allowed to groove with like, The Running Man. They can't groove to a step you know. Because it goes back to Musical Theatre 101. There's no music playing. We're living a musical existence that emotional situations get so heightened that it blooms into music. It blooms into movement. But there's no music playing.
>
> There can't be existing dance steps because then you're doing a real dance step. It has to be a step that is just life taking a different form. And so, in that way, I've always been opposed to copying steps. Even a shuffle-ball-change. I don't want to do a jazz square. I mean, I do all the time, but I don't want to do steps that people know. In my prep process, I always start that way. I start with steps and then the steps go away because what I'm trying to do is be honest to people, to the people in the show.[15]

Blankenbuehler's articulation of the tensions between steps and honesty go hand in hand with a long-standing conundrum in the field of dance history: virtuosity versus storytelling. Dance scholar Susan Leigh Foster identifies two essential ideas when discussing the body in relation to dance: the notions of the body's autonomy and interiority as well as the body's virtuosity. The first suggests the ability to produce feelings and reproduce those feelings for a viewer. The latter is the mastery of a technique, the capacity to exhibit the choreographer's vision. As scientific developments began to increase since the codification of ballet in the 1600s, dance practitioners tested the limits of the body's capabilities; thus, the importance of virtuosity began to triumph over autonomy and interiority. Foster points out that the dancing body became "detached from its social moorings and objectified through scientific investigation."[16] The operative word here is "detached." If the dancing body has indeed been detached from any previously cultivated sense of self in favor of virtuosity, the identifications associated with that body have arguably not disappeared. Social conscriptions on the body can be ignored, but they cannot be escaped.

Furthermore, Foster's book *Choreographing History* questions how body-history, writing, and research work in tandem to create a methodology for reading dance. Foster argues:

> A body, whether sitting writing or standing thinking or walking talking or running screaming, is a bodily writing. Its habits and stances, gestures and demonstrations, every action of its various regions, areas, and parts—all these emerge out of cultural practices, verbal or not, that construct corporeal meaning. Each of the body's moves, as with all writings, traces the physical fact of movement and also an array of references to conceptual entities and events.[17]

Her conception of "a bodily writing" correlates directly with the notion of the dramaturgical body. How can acknowledging the construction of corporeal meaning through sociocultural identifications in conjunction with the performing body affect the ways in which we read, write, and apprehend that body in a production? My analysis of Blankenbuehler's work and process considers the multiple layers of corporeality within the ensemble and considers how choreography can influence the comprehension of the ensemble body by an audience. Foster's epistemology regarding choreography proves to be vital in developing an analysis of the body, ensemble, and dance.

Additionally, Foster posits, "Objectivist dance focuses on the body's movement, allowing any references to the world to accrue alongside the dance as a by-product of the body's motion."[18] Objectivist types of dance have a specific set of conventions that tells the body what to do rather than what to say. For example, in the *Nutcracker,* the Sugar Plum Fairy begins her number in tendu devant with an elegant pas de bourée moving into an arabesque allongé, passé back through the arabesque.[19] She then completes a series of piqué battements.[20] These movements are a specific set of codified conventions that articulate to the dancer how their body is supposed to move. These movements alone do not convey any form of narrative structure or emotional suggestion. When the dancer executes these movements, the movements suggest to the viewer: "look at this aesthetic," rather than "interpret and read my story." An objectivist choreography often tends to athletic ability and precision in training. The goal is to show off the mastery of a skill.

Juxtaposed to objectivist choreography, Foster argues, is reflexive choreography. A reflexive choreography tends to the meaning of a piece, the mood, the frame, the mode of representation, style of delivery, or vocabulary of the piece.[21] An assumption made by the audience (and on behalf of the choreographer) that certain movements suggest meaning. For example; a dancer does the combination balancé, balancé, balancé en tourant, balancé en tourant, balancé de côte, balancé de côte, chaînés, chaînés, grande ronde de jambe, and plié, the light feet in the rocking steps of the balancés, small turns throughout, and a slow poised ending (executed in a ¾ time signature—similar to that of a waltz) could provide the mood of love or delight.[22] The movements are not overly exerted regarding weight or intensity, suggesting exuberance or anger, and the slow ending promotes a softer tone. If the dancer places their hands on their heart throughout the turns, this further encourages the love narrative. However, if the arms were to reach out as if they were begging or yearning for something on one side and then the other, and the ending was more of a collapse than a slow, graceful descent, then perhaps the mood of desperation, longing, or loss could be imposed upon the combination. Blankenbuehler firmly advocates that his work tends to the meaning of a piece first—reflexive choreography—and the virtuosity of a piece second—objectivist choreography.

> Young people do need to learn what a passé is. They need to learn what a straight leg is. They need to know what a plié is. You have to learn the steps to then break them. And obviously there are famous quotes, you have to learn the rules before you bend them or break them. You know what a plie feels like to then torque your body in a melting transition. But, it happens all the time where I'm auditioning and hiring these young people and I can't get the steps out of them. I can't get them to be real.[23]

As Blankenbuehler theorizes about his work and his style, he presents a dichotomy between activating a curated style or vocabulary of his own and allowing the world of show itself to bring about the style that it needs:

> You have to pay attention to the DNA of what the show is. To me, that's very clear in rhythm. Some things are rhythmic, some things are not. Some things are syncopated and some things are not … I say all the time that people (as characters in *Hamilton*) are always on the count before the beat, because I want these active characters who are anxious to move forward to try to figure out a situation. So, I'm always on this sort of ball change that's moving forward ahead of the

beat. I'm always slightly ahead of the beat. Some of that comes from, just people I respect. Like, that's in Robbins's choreography, that's in Fosse's choreography. But when I made my debut in *Guys and Dolls Guys* (1992), Chris Chadman, wasn't so much ahead of the beat. But, he once said in rehearsal, you can't start the movement before the beat, but you have to finish it by the beat. So, it's like we were moving so fast on the front side of the movement, and that became very much my style.

I move fast, slightly ahead of the beat, and then there's a bit of a Halley's Comet behind me. So, there's this diminuendo of speed, a slight pause behind my action. And I think it's interesting. I don't think they analyze it, but they notice it. And that's why a lot of really cool hip-hop stuff is like that too. They move so quickly and then they freeze. But, it also functions as sort of close-up camera work, where there's a bit of a pause. In that pause, people's eyes are able to focus on something, and that image goes to their brain. Where, if it's legato all of the time, you only take in energy waves, as opposed to pictures. And I like to make pictures that resonate. Even when I'm dancing to lyrical music, I'm still moving fast. If I can't move fast to a slow song, it's not going to go well. And I've done that before. I've done things that are lyrical and it's not great work. Other people are great at it, but I'm not great at it. And, I'm also not that interested in it. So, that part of the prep process is really big to me, about understanding the thing. And where that usually happens for me is, once story beats start to come together, then I can start improvising.[24]

1.3 On Music

I see things in movement, and the next part of the process for me, then, is understanding what the structures are, and I see that first rhythmically. So, my Spotify playlists start to teach me what kind of pace people move in and what kind of syncopations people move in … And, sometimes I let go of entire projects if I feel the rhythms aren't appealing to me. If they're not syncopated, if they're not really interesting rhythmic worlds, rhythmic characters, then I'm bored by the piece, I'm bored by the characters. And some shows, the music should be square. The music should move forward in a way that is not so unexpected or so agitated. And those shows can still be good. I just find that I don't really want to make them. And it took me a really long time to figure that out ...

Researching something like *In the Heights,* for me, was literally just saturating myself in music. It was, frankly, musical styles that I knew, but wasn't my comfort zone. And so, I all of a sudden had a completely different playlist on my iPod. Everything was hip-hop, everything was Latin music, just so that I could feel what I connected to, feel what moved me, tried to point my finger to, oh, Lin is writing for this story, beat, and this is the emotional response I get out of the music ... Of music, of dance, of people's journeys, and what was really interesting to hear Lin talk about was how he'd walk down the street in Washington Heights, and out of every door, out of every window, you would hear a different kind of musical style. It really was a melting pot, where people just loved different things. You walk onto the subway platform, and this person has a jam box, and it's this kind of music, but it's this kind of a dance. Like, there wasn't necessarily music that matched only people—that neighborhood plays that kind of music, this kind of neighborhood. It was kind of just a hodgepodge in a really exciting New York American way ...

My first part of research was saturating myself in music, everywhere I went. You know, the treadmill at the gym, the commute to the gym, the dance studio, my warm-up, all my music changed for about a year straight. And my clothes changed. I'm very method, so totally different wardrobe, became slightly a different person in the way I was carrying my body. But I didn't have to research the history of the location, because it was Manhattan right then.[25]

1.4 On Documentation

In addition to his Pinterest boards, his collage boards, and his Spotify playlists. Blankenbuehler also has a carefully curated, and albeit somewhat chaotic, way of documenting and tracking his immense breadth of ideas as he is in development or pre-production for a project. This system involves Word documents, video recording, Dropbox, and charts.

I have Word documents for everything ... I videotape everything ... As soon as I find a groove that really works, and it might be quoting something I've done before, I'd name everything. So, for example "one,

Figure 3 Blankenbuehler takes a look at the monitors while filming *Cats* (2019). Photo by Ben Darmanin.

two, three break" is a step. And I have a heading that says "steps" and then I'll write "one, two, three break." But, then, when I'm improvising, that "one, two, three break" is nothing like the actual one, two, three. And so, I'll have these video files that are sometimes ten seconds long, sometimes they're three minutes long. And then I'll go through the file, and then I'll find sixteen counts or four counts or whatever it is. And then, on the next occasion, I'll do that and see what it turns into. So, slowly that 'one, two, three break' turns into something … Not a lot of those steps make it into the show. They're just my method …

When it comes to the Word documents, the first thing I do is I have a general document that I always call "Working Notes." It might start as simple as top of show, scene one, end of show. It's general mile markers where I write down ideas. Then, when I have collaborators, I'm writing down my thoughts on their ideas. "This scene feels like a repetition." It's thoughts. It's notes/ Maybe it's the first time a person sees the person they're going to fall in love with. And, I have an image in my head of maybe how that moment could be. I'll just write the image down.

For example, I had a great image in the ballet I was working on a couple of weeks ago (*Never Alone*) where the men are pushing against the walls of the submarine. There was another moment I was watching a rehearsal, and somebody slid to the floor. And I had an image of all the men just seeping like water to where the floor met the wall as if you were a broken prisoner in solitary confinement feeling where the wall hits the floor, memorizing every corner. And all of a sudden, I knew that had to exist in the show. I knew that the moment had to exist where everybody was on the floor feeling the corners of their spaces. And so, I said to myself, where does that go? Oh, that goes in part three. So on the Word document, I'll just write that image. I have another document that just always says "images." With the ballet … I probably have eighty ideas and I don't know where they go, but they just feel like people. Then, in that main document, "Working Notes," it gets more and more delineated. Scene one becomes this, Scene two becomes this …

Then, because I choreograph in transition, the transitions become titles because I think there's always really good storytelling to be had linking one moment to the next … if you watch plot point A happen, your brain is saying, "what are the repercussions of that?" If he kisses her in this scene, what is on his mind? What is on her mind? What is on her boyfriend's mind? So, if the audience is starting to think that, I like to tease in the transition with either something that they're leaning toward or something they didn't think about at all.

And so, because of that, the transitions become mini scenes. I note all the transitions in my document. A tricky thing for me is if something's not a dance narrative, eventually the writer has to really take ownership. So, I try not to go too deeply into my ideas because somebody else is going to write the script, which is a whole other thing that is difficult. But once a piece exists, that document just gets thicker. And then each paragraph, like scene one, might end up being five more paragraphs on the Word document. And each of those paragraphs becomes something, a movement. The first paragraph is the introduction. The second paragraph is the verse.

The sentences, often I'll write something like, "he's banging his head into the wall," meaning he can't find the answer. That's a piece of choreography. So, then I put an open bracket "[piece of choreography banging head against the wall]." Then, now that I know the song for that moment, I'm improvising in the morning. Let me experiment now with what it feels like to bang your head against the wall. And, there'll be ten versions of that. And sometimes that will make it into the show. But many times that's just the process. It's not really banging head against the wall. But, banging head against the wall is almost the same as feeling like you can't breathe in a way. So maybe the imagery turns into something else. By me saying banging my head against the wall, it gives me a place to start … I have to ask myself, "how does this idea become choreography?" …

(opening up his Dropbox for *Never Alone*)

Part one. Obviously, if something's in red, it's a problem. If something's in yellow, it's I wanna do it. So when I highlight something that's yellow, as soon as I have dancers, that's the thing I'm gonna try to do first. So this is, "first man steps out of the peaceful solitude"—those are going to become dance steps. Now, these are, I should … because these are not choreographed, there's no open brackets. But here, there's all open brackets. Because those are things I know I have to do … Whenever I make anything in blue, it's for the music department. For example, new timing of the bass beat drops or find time for the next time passage.

This section says "wipe the sweat." The idea of the dance is gonna be about wiping the sweat off. The idea is gonna be about the blinders, meaning concentrate on only one thing. And then, it's interesting. I work with people a long time. So this step I have the "Morgan split"—like Morgan Marcel. Here it says "six pack up," it's about the men's abs. So the step is six packs up to inflate the chest. But I also have a video where I make that into a step. When a note is done, I've crossed it out. Then, I'll write that as a normal paragraph. So, I do this for awhile …

The next thing I do is I do my staging charts. I'll have a footprint of the stage, the set. And then I have the cast on the side and I'll chart out the number. Any given number, I'll have maybe forty charts. And by looking at all the Xs and Os, I can then see the number in my head and visualize what the pattern is going to be. As I'm drawing the patterns and stuff, I'm realizing I don't have a step to make that pattern happen, then I'll go back into here. The number really takes shape when I'm making my charts.[26]

PART 2
EXTENDED CHOREOGRAPHIC ANALYSIS

CHAPTER 2
EN WASHINGTON HEIGHTS: STAGING AUTHENTICITY THROUGH THE INDIVIDUAL ENSEMBLE BODY

Imagine a hot summer morning in Washington Heights. The neighborhood bodega owner begins his day chasing away a young vandal from his shop. A metro worker dawdles on his way to the train. A man bops to the sound of his boombox, nodding "sup" to another who is strolling down the street going who knows where. As the piragüero gently pushes his cart down the sidewalk, a young woman struts past him, waving "hello." Another woman pauses to dig through her purse for money to buy her lottery ticket. Others pop into the bodega to purchase water, coffee, or a magazine. On balconies, people shake out rugs and hang their clothes on the line. Some begin their day by taking a jog, hailing a cab, or gossiping with a colleague on their way to work. This scene could depict an average Tuesday morning in uptown Manhattan or the opening of the 2008 Tony Award-winning musical *In the Heights*. As associate choreographer Stephanie Klemons puts it, "Other choreographers build portraits … Andy's experience is like a 3-D Imax fresco."[1]

Creator Lin-Manuel Miranda "wanted to create something that shows Latinos in the everyday mode [he's] used to, and not just in gangs."[2] A review for *Newsday* reported that the production had "the authenticity of the immigrant stories" but with "a heartening minimum of stereotypes."[3] In other words, it was in contrast to something like *West Side Story* (1957). *In the Heights* has been praised for being the first Broadway musical about Latinx stories created by Latinx artists. Conversations about casting practices, reaching new audiences, cultural hybridity, and "authenticity" have surrounded the production since its inception some twenty years ago when Miranda was a young student writing its first iterations. Miranda's mission to diversify Broadway—its aesthetics, stories, and soundscape—created a unique set of challenges for aspiring choreographer Andy Blankenbuehler. In order to choreograph Miranda's vision of showcasing Latinxs in "everyday mode," he would need to learn the accompanying movement and music styles (hip-hop, salsa, merengue, etc.) not traditionally incorporated into musical theatre productions or even his personal vocabulary. Then, Blankenbuehler would have to negotiate a choreographic score that would highlight the dancers who were, frankly, more skilled than he was in these diverse genres while also blending in "traditional" Broadway dancers trained in Euro-centered movement aesthetics (ballet, modern, and jazz).

In a 2008 interview promoting *In the Heights*, Blankenbuehler remarked, "It's all about communication … the performance of dance, not the showing off in a studio … is about translating the kernel of an emotional idea to the audience … it comes from understanding life. If you don't understand life, you can't understand what you are trying to communicate through dance."[4] Believing that lived experience is essential to successfully communicating a story or idea allowed him to capture the performer's body itself as a storytelling apparatus. In this way, the body as a tool could establish an environment on stage that a viewer may identify as being "authentic."

Jayzel Samonte's article for *Movmnt Magazine,* "Heightened Exposure: In the Heights," reports, "Choreographer Andy Blankenbuehler didn't cast dancers with traditional dance backgrounds. Blankenbuehler's talent of conveying a dance landscape seemingly true to the streets required dancers whose abilities interpreted these gyrations authentically. It's that authenticity from every level of the creative team that makes Heights such a captivating evening."[5] Many critics and artists similarly hail the production as presenting Latinx authentically. Such praise begs the question, what exactly is the relationship between *In the Heights* and dramaturgical, choreographic, or embodied authenticity? Authenticity suggests that something is real, bona fide, genuine. If something is labeled "authentic," it is supposedly based on facts, giving it a heightened level of authority or believability. Western tourist culture, in particular, thrives on notions of authenticity: certificates of authenticity, authentic cuisine, or authentic experiences.

Associating *In the Heights* with such a promise of authenticity can become problematic when considering the relationship between authenticity and commodification. Although selling access to a culture/cultural product not typical to the Broadway audience (who is, more often than not, middle to upper class and white) is not a new phenomenon, *In the Heights* is the first Latinx show (created by Latinx artists) to do so. Samonte's identification of the *In the Heights* dance landscape demanding dancers whose abilities could interpret movements authentically, in particular the gyrations, suggests that not every *body* can execute such activity "correctly," perhaps not even Blankenbuehler's body. Such an insinuation that there are right and wrong bodies to execute dance movements specific to Latinx culture risks essentializing both the performers and the form. Because of the production's call for a dramaturgy attuned to "Latinos in the everyday mode," the *In the Heights* creative team manufactured a world in which the characters become displays of staged authenticity—codified within a story for repeated audience consumption. Similarly, situating Latinx-rooted dance movements as requisite to staged Washington Heights's daily activities creates an illusion of an unmediated encounter with a cultural entity.[6]

The tension between authenticity and commodification is incredibly complex in any situation, but especially in theatricalized settings where audiences are to suspend ideas of disbelief and give in to the notion that what they are witnessing is, in essence, a reality. Audiences often expect an "authentic" performance. Where does this notion of authenticity lie? What are the inherent problems with attempting to produce and manufacture authenticity? How does staged authenticity, replicated for potentially thousands of audience members, impose a false or stereotyped identity on a culture?

To begin, Andy Blankenbuehler is a white choreographer tasked with choreographing a show about a community of color—predominantly Latinx—using movement styles of which he did not necessarily have previous experience. In a personal interview with Blankenbuehler, he said, "My comfort zone is in 50s and 60s jazz, but most people don't do this anymore, so you have to adapt and evolve."[7] For him to adapt and evolve, he would have to learn dance styles previously unfamiliar to him. In Lyn Cramer's book *Creating Musical Theatre,* he reflected on this learning process:

> I had never done salsa or hip-hop. I grew up rhythmic, dancing tap and swing. It's not dissimilar. I started taking everyone's classes and watching whose work I liked … I surrounded myself with very smart people. I studied many videos, attended competitions, and I learned enough salsa to provide a slow building process to form a number. With the hip-hop, I decided I needed to be able to do it, actually dance the style. So, once I could see the number in my head, I would start to choreograph it on my own. Sometimes my work would look like a tap step, and sometimes it would look like a Jack Cole step. Then I would bring these fierce hip-hop dancers into the room, and I would say, "How can this be better? How can this look like a real hip-hop step?" We would take my steps and convert them. I just needed help.[8]

Blankenbuehler elaborated on his engagement with hip-hop and his research process in an interview with me in December, 2024:

> I made the early decision to not stylize anything that was in Latin dance. Besides a little bit of "Paciencia y Fe," there was never a time where I was taking Latin steps, like a salsa step or a merengue step and turning it into storytelling. In the opening number, yes, there was some footwork that felt like it could be social dance or cultural dance, but I wasn't going to break it and turn it into something else. But, I felt differently about hip-hop-based stuff because I felt that hip-hop was already, in so many ways, an amazing evolution of so many prior styles …
>
> The first thing I did was a lot of hip-hop research. I made the decision that I was going to use hip-hop vernacular in style, not in steps, but in theory, to tell the story in an impressionistic way. And I remember, I went to LA for a while and I was taking five or six classes a day just to learn as many things as I could, just to understand what my take on it was. I was choreographing mid-century jazz that's often based out of tap and tap rhythms. So, in a way, people's hip-hop was comfortable to me, because tap, like so many amazing styles, came out of the African American experience. And I was lucky enough to have trained in swing dancing and tap dancing and jazz dancing that had their roots in African American studies and culture.
>
> So, one day in a hip-hop class in LA, this guy did a turned-out passé into something else. And I just kind of stopped in class, and I was like, this isn't a hip-hop step. There's nothing that's hip-hop about what he's teaching right now. Then it just really struck me that it was a mood, it was an energy, it was a take on life, it was a way to approach life. There was a hip-hop mentality. Of course there are hip-hop steps. There are steps from the 70s, from the 80s, from the 90s, that are vernacular, that people made up. But, I also made the decision early on, I didn't want to try to quote anything. I didn't want to quote steps, because I kind of … it wasn't that I didn't feel like I had permission to, but I wasn't steeped in the world enough to say, I'm going to live in this way. What I wanted to do was take that hip-hop style, that sort of energy, and apply it to real people.
>
> So, if a real person is stressed out about work, and they're walking to the subway, and they're going to be late, how does their body shift in a way that feels like if you're playing a hip-hop groove, it matches? So,

> it wasn't ever an attempt to match steps, because frankly, I knew that I hadn't lived that experience, so I couldn't really do that.[9]

Nevertheless, since *In the Heights,* he has absorbed hip-hop dance aesthetics into his toolbox of movement possibilities curating a hybrid-dance and choreography style he would come to use in every subsequent production he has choreographed, making him a three-time Tony Award-winning choreographer. If Blankenbuehler himself does not claim to have such expertise in hip-hop specifically, or Latinx social dance forms for that matter, how did he produce choreography hailed as "authentic," propelling him into a space of notoriety? The answer is found in the incredible community of artists around him. Through collaboration with other dancers and assistant or associate choreographers, he successfully developed his uniquely hybrid-dance genre. This correspondence occurs within the rehearsal process, rather than just between performer and audience member. The exchanges of labor develop a collective, embodied understanding of a cultural product. By actively seeking instruction or input from artists proficient in styles he feels less connected to physically and culturally, he can deepen the connection between his body and the choreographic intent of said styles. Conversely, through such collaboration, he can embrace and implement the skills of those within the production to generate a textured and diversified choreographic score.

This chapter focuses on how Blankenbuehler's choreography for *In the Heights* creates staged authenticity by making visible the diversity of lived experiences of the individuals shaping the choreography. Because the ensemble in musical theatre has not previously had such augmented individualization, the ensemble body becomes a foundational entity in creating the world of the musical. The ensemble body is the lens through which the audience gains access into a layered, complex social world that is staged Washington Heights. Through collaborative creation and emphasis on action over spectacle, this ensemble body is choreographed in performance to frame the society from their individual perspectives transporting the audience into a heterogeneous world that might have otherwise been seemingly superficial. The emphasis on individualized choreographic scores in the musical numbers "In the Heights" and "Carnaval del Barrio," for example, produce sociological milieus specific to their respective purpose within the narrative. Blankenbuehler's choreography positions the bodies of the performers in *Heights* to bring people with different ethnic, race, gender, sexuality, and socioeconomic backgrounds in relation to one another and adapt dance into a variety of social and physical environments necessary for staged Washington Heights.

2.1 Luis Salgado: On Collaboration and Connection

In an article for *Playbill*, assistant choreographer Luis Salgado (billed as the "Latin Assistant Choreographer") said this about *In the Heights*,

> My very first journey with this show was an explosion of pride through its movement as I worked next to Andy Blankenbuehler enhancing the choreographic authenticity in numbers like 'Carnaval' and the "Club" among others [...] "the process" has been the priority on every step of the journey, allowing a unique ownership of the character and community moments in the show.[10]

Salgado aided in the manufacturing and editing of Latinx dance styles throughout the production.

Regarding his own start in dance and the world of storytelling through movement, Salgado reflected:

> When anybody asks me about start, I think about public school and dirt, because I literally did not grow up in a space where we had a dance space right, with mirrors or anything like that. So, my teacher in fifth grade—his name is Jose Javier Rivera—we call him Pepito. He just was magnificent—got us up just running and learning and all we had was the patio. We would be doing first position, demi pliés, jazz, and splits in the grass. Our uniform was like green jeans and a yellow shirt, and my jeans would come home brown from just doing splits and rolling all over the yard. So, that is kind of special. It's a special memory for me to think about that ... but like the "Carnaval del Barrio" already manifesting, right? Like the desire that—I'm going to cry just thinking about it—that with whatever you have available, you can still make a fiesta. You can still grow. You can persist, not give up.[11]

As Salgado grew older, he became beyond eager to learn more. Eventually moving to New York City and falling in love with musical theatre, he began attending classes at Broadway Dance Center where he would come to meet and learn from Michéle Assaf, Richard Pierlon, Rhapsody James, Joshua

Bergasse, and Andy Blankenbuehler. The first Broadway show Salgado ever saw was *Fosse*—a show featuring now-famed Tony-award-winning Sergio Trujillo and Blankenbuehler. He remembers this show feeling like an odd "first" experience with Broadway due to its black box nature with its black costumes. But, as he progressed as an artist he began to reflect on the nuances of that show and the value in how choreography would come to function as a storytelling component of a musical.

Oddly enough, Salgado's first encounter with Blankenbuehler was before he had even taken a class with him. He recalls:

> The joke is, this is kind of a cool story, that I had not stepped into his class. And one day, he pulled me aside and said, "Hey. I see you around a lot. Can I have your resume?" And I was like, okay. So, he was working on *Man of La Mancha* and he was going to go away to do something else. And, he was trying to recommend people that could replace his track. I don't know in what class he had seen me, or maybe I had taken one of his classes, but it was an honor and crazy that he randomly was asking me for my resume. So, that was the first interaction I ever really one-on-one had with Andy. And, of course, it left a memory because it's somebody already sort of looking out for you to have an opportunity.

This moment would ultimately lead to their partnership with *In the Heights* and a lifelong friendship. In several meetings with Blankenbuehler, he insisted that I talk to Salgado about his experiences.

Reflecting more specifically on *In the Heights*, Salgado elaborates:

> Truly, because of Andy, the whole scope of what an ensemble means … my whole life changed with the perspective of what an ensemble means because of him … There's people who get it. There's people who don't get it. The ensemble is the lead character of the show for me. And that's because of *In the Heights* … what I experience being in the ensemble is that [Usnavi] is a narrator. The story, really, the lead role will follow Nina Rosario. But the story is about the title of the show—*In the Heights*. So *In the Heights* is created by everybody that lives there. And therefore, the ensemble being included, and Nina, and everybody else—it's the story that is the lead role.
>
> And then, I think what was really smart about getting the truth that I brought in, that Nina Lafarga brought in, that the store brought

in—by getting the truth of the ensemble and allowing our physical and live story, our truth to resonate through the characters we were creating … that's a luxury. Cause who gets that opportunity? Oftentimes you come in and got to wear a shoe … it's a very different thing to have to fit into something … the perspective of the ensemble is the greatest tool you have to tell a story, you know? … The ensemble is the buttons of a complete arc of a story. And, that changed with me the day I started working on *Heights.*

Heights meant everything and it also gave me everything. I got to contribute a lot of synergies … I'm in the room with Andy Blankenbuehler trying to figure out what "Carnaval del Barrio" is and I get to bring all this history and passion and respect and knowledge for what it is. We actually even say "Vega Alta," which is my hometown. It's in the scripts, in the song, because Lin's family was also from the same town—the synergy there. So, in the club number, I'm able to talk to Andy and be like, "Hey, there's this book I love called *La Carreta* (by René Marqués, 1953) that has this character named Luis. And Luis goes to work into the industries in the United States and leaves his land and leaves the farmer idea." So, I get a very deep relationship between Kevin Rosario, my father was a farmer, his father was a farmer, and then Luis in *La Carreta* leaving to go for a better future. When I connect those dots from my history, if he lived in New York in the sixties and seventies, when salsa was evolving, I mean, Kevin Rosario, who's now working his butt off to pay his family's future, might have actually learned to dance salsa too.

So, everything that we do for the club … Lin or Usnavi and Nina and Benny, all of these characters, it's not like they are going to go and dance salsa just because, who are they learning salsa from? Probably they're learning salsa in the living room of Kevin Rosario first. And if Kevin Rosario is dancing the salsa on the two, they are able and capable of dancing the salsa on the two … there's the three-two clave, and the two-three clave … so dancing on the two means you're dancing on that clave rhythm and it changes the style of the entire scope of movement. So, we build the entire club number around that theory, you know? To be able to contribute that to Andy's brain and then to have his brain do what his brain does. It's incredible, you know you're a part of something …

The Latin steps are all around the show … but it really starts with coffee. It starts with Bustelo coffee, really. And the idea of the opening number, none of these humans get to move without having their café ... life doesn't seem the same way until you have your taste of coffee to go about your day and the difficulties of your day. So that moment that you have your sip of coffee, the Latin step begins. You just walk you're just, whatever. The moment you have your coffee, there's a circle step. There's a basic salsa step. So, then, if we do that in the opening number, how does it carry forward?

Sometimes when I'm directing the show, I talk to my cast about the history of Latin influence in four eight counts in "Carnaval del Barrio," when we're doing a plena, which is folklore [and] was an influence for La Salsa, and we do the three-two clave, which is the first step of salsa development. Then we go to a rumba. It could go into other Latin American countries outside of the Puerto Rico influences. It gets sort of like folklore hybrid. And then we go and you're scoffing into hip-hop. So, the way that we're doing the development of our history in basically four eight counts, the audience, will they know that? No, but we know that that's the DNA that we constructed that through and what it creates in the spatial atmosphere is powerful, right? People resonate because you either are hooked to the plena or you're hooked to the salsa or you're hooked to the hip-hop, but in any form where we're sort of conquering the passion for the Latin movement in four eight counts. And we have little pockets of that kind of reality all through the show.[12]

2.2 "Blankenbuehlerizing" Choreography and Staging Authenticity

For the PBS *Great Performances* documentary on *In the Heights*, Blankenbuehler points out that nearly 75 percent of the cast was making their Broadway debut, many of whom had never even done a musical before.[13] Working with this novice cast provided him with the unique opportunity to train young dancers in his method of working. He did not have to readjust their way of doing traditional musical theatre choreography on Broadway—which was, in many ways, a hierarchical system that did not afford such dialogic relationships. As Salgado suggested, Blankenbuehler's collaborative proclivity allowed for a creative process that would open up the possibility for individual cast members to have agency over their characters and the development of community throughout the production. In fact, many of the performers from *Heights* would come to follow Blankenbuehler and work with him on future productions.

In his preparation, he films himself in his studio, improvising and creating dance steps. Then, he takes these clips to a few dancers in a studio and says, "This isn't the step, but the step feels like this."[14] Reflecting on his process, Blankenbuehler said, "Those dancers often have so much better style than I have. Then they immediately make it look so much more heightened than I can make it."[15] Much of these dance moves look more like pantomime before making it to the dancers and becoming the codified, technical, energized dance audiences see as the final version.

An interview with longtime associate choreographer Stephanie Klemons (who began as assistant dance captain and swing in *In the Heights*) sheds light on this collaborative process of creating choreography:

> He and I together can say we need something that swirls in the air for the last seven counts, but he and I are not going to sit in the studio and continue to choreograph that. For example, we are not going to choreograph lifts together because that is just not our bodies … and so we rely on other people who, we can say, "no, put her up this way, try putting her leg like this, maybe try putting her leg like that."[16]

Klemons also affirms that developing in the space with the cast can help fill in any "dead" moments where dance or bodies may be needed. Blankenbuehler, or Klemons, may say, "we need this moment to feel ominous," and the performers will create what that feels like for their specific body at that moment. Another technique they use in collaboratively creating is giving individual cast members predetermined choreography and allowing others to improvise at the same time.[17] As Susan Leigh Foster points out:

> People teach each other dances, and they also teach each other how to dance. In so doing they often repeat movements or phrases of movements, and they copy others' movements, transferring them into their own lived corporeality. They also inflect these movements with their own style or distinctive qualities, all the while retaining an apprehension of the movement's relation to its original articulation.[18]

The improvising ensemble body can promote instincts that add layers of nuance.

By bringing in multiple voices, embodied voices, to the creative process, Blankenbuehler's choreographic ideas can connect in a way far more personal to the specific bodies of the performers. It is common practice for the choreographer to precisely tell the dancer what the movement is and how it needs to look. Typical Broadway dancers are usually highly skilled in ballet, jazz, and tap dance. Ballet, in particular, requires the body to be much more upright than, say, hip-hop. For example, in a moment that involves breakdance, he might not include a dancer who is more rooted in ballet; it does not fit their body or training experience. Similarly, a hip-hop dancer may not have the "pretty" pointed toes and turn out required to do a particular lift. In blending all of these different dance genres, he can create a dance style and choreography that supports dancers of varying training backgrounds within one production. Rather than forcing a body to learn to move in a way that is not veridical to their personal corporeality, he is able to create a score that provides opportunities for individuals to show off their skill set through their embodied character.[19] He has opened up the potential for other storytelling modes through the body within musical theatre beyond the standard ballet, jazz, and tap. By allowing for the flexibility of individual interpretation, ensemble bodies can communicate lived experience. A dialectical relationship is created between Blankenbuehler's body, the performer's body, and their character's body. Such tangible corporeality through dance can lead to a viewer's perception of an authentic embodied presence—one that is manufactured and staged through this dialectical relationship and the codified product of choreographed musical theatre/ Latinx dance.

Supported by experienced practitioners such as Luis Salgado, the enaction of such socially and culturally identifiable movement by a diverse group of bodies attempts to bring the audience in contact with a locale in a way that resists generalization and promotes individuality. The performer has agency in how the staged authentic presentation of sociocultural movement is received by the audience. In other words, because of Blankenbuehler's collaborative creative process and emphasis on the individual's ability to communicate lived experience through dance, the performer is able to lightly manipulate the choreography, so it is derived from their individual ensemble body, producing a performance of an authentically dancing body.

As this chapter proceeds through a specific analysis of choreographically abundant numbers, the complication of perceived authenticity/staged authenticity becomes more conspicuous, particularly with "Carnaval Del Barrio." "Carnaval Del Barrio" rests on incorporating Latinx social dance, which engenders the audience to view the characters as (more) authentic. Commenting on dancers doing social dancing, Jane Desmond observes, "They are often taken as evidence of a 'character,' sometimes of a 'national character,' and often of 'racial character.' This is where the nonverbal aspect of dance or our general ignoring of movement as a meaningful system of communication reinforce popular beliefs about the supposed transparency of expressivity."[20] When social dance is staged, it often becomes a mere representation or essentialization of a cultural product and loses its attachment to social relevance. According to Desmond, "The pleasure aspect of social dancing often obscures our awareness of it as a symbolic system, so that dancers are often seen as 'authentic' unmediated expressions of psychic or emotional inferiority."[21] In "Carnaval Del Barrio," the community celebrates the assortment of countries they come from by waving their flags and dancing accompanying Latinx social dances. In this case, the dance is directly used to accentuate possible identifications of nationality and ethnicity. The dances in "Carnaval Del Barrio" are seemingly organic, almost improvised at times. There is little codified synchronous choreography. The individual doing the dancing shapes the choreography.

Staging Latinx social dance by a white choreographer not trained in these forms risks misappropriation and exoticization. Additionally, as Foster argues, when dance functions as a commodity, it can become "governed by the potential to profit from the money that is exchanged."[22] For *Heights,* the promise of "authenticity" promoted by reviewers of the production triggers the possibility of bringing in more audience members, thus more profit. However, the dialectics created between choreographer and performer, performer and character have the potential to intervene in these challenges. For example, when Blankenbuehler stages a moment of salsa, Luis Salgado is able to take his personal backgrounds make that moment his. Salgado does not dance Blankenbuehler's salsa; he has the freedom to use Blankenbuehler's idea and make it true to his body and his experience. Salgado's salsa combination may connect movements more fluidly than someone who is not well versed in the genre. He has the potential to more holistically create a salsa score and avoid a generalized interpretation.

It is critical to pause and acknowledge the risk of asserting that Salgado is "naturally" able to execute salsa more "authentically" than Blankenbuehler. The stereotypical connection between Latinness, one's "'naturally expressive body,'" and the "supposed genetic propensity for rhythmic movement" walks a fine line in this situation.[23] It is Salgado's embodied experience of being trained in Latinx social dance forms that heightens his legitimacy of executing such movements, not his racial or ethnic background. But, Mark Franko contends, "The necessary relation of the fleshy body to its markers of identity and subjectivity lends feeling its structure from experience, through performance, to interpretation."[24] Latinx social dance danced by a dramaturgically Latinx body does transmit a performed bodily discourse and narrative that enhances the audience's perception of an "authentic" encounter propagated by U.S.-based stereotypes. If the audience visually recognizes the body as Latinx—which can potentially rely on how individual audience members read, identify, and stereotype Latinx markers of identity—the body has the capacity to contribute and lend itself to performance. Still, Salgado has ownership over the movements he presents. Blankenbuehler's collaborative rehearsal environment opens up the opportunity for the individual ensemble body doing the dancing to use its actual lived experience rather than a socially homogenized idea of how something is *supposed* to look. When the individual ensemble body is linked explicitly to Latinx lived experience, like Salgado's, the conception of producing (staged) authenticity through Latinx social dance can become more affective.

The staging of social dance in this way resists commodification processes that make the dance a replicable product. Franko asserts that dance can be turned into social energy; therefore, as a product, dance has the potential to be considered as producing ideology rather than sensuous experiences.[25] If Blankenbuehler's choreography generates such social energy or social connection through the individual's shaping the movement on stage, it can communicate their beliefs or ideas and produce staged authenticity.

2.3 "In the Heights": Staging Community, Establishing Vocabulary

It is July 3rd—Sunrise.

(*A beat comes in. In the shadows,* GRAFFITI PETE *is revealed painting various walls in the neighborhood. Enter* USNAVI *from his stoop.*)

Usnavi Yo, That's my wall!

Graffiti Pete Pshh …

(**Graffiti Pete** *runs away.* **Usnavi** *turns to us.*)[26]

Figure 4 Andy and Lin. Photo by Josh Leher.

Now, let us imagine that moment again. It is July 3rd—Sunrise. Graffiti Pete is walking down the street to find his next target. He places his boom box on the ground, pauses to look at Usnavi's bodega, rubbing his hands together as he comes up with a plan. Pete pulls out his spray cans and pumps one into the air, followed by three backward steps on the beat shift into the next song on the radio, to the syncopated rhythm one, (pause) two, and three—analyzing the canvas he is about to develop. Electronic dance music (EDM) plays as he jumps into second position (a position of believing in something), shrugs his shoulders, and lunges right, lifting one spray can and looking at it—the creative juices are beginning to flow. Spinning the spray can in his left hand, he leans left, then jumps to cross his legs, and jumps out into second position once more with his arms out in the shape of a "T"—getting pumped up. He turns over his right shoulder, slowly drags his foot around as he looks left, then he looks back at the bodega—double-checking no one is around. Pete lunges to his right, alternating his arms: punch out with right/pull left into a bent elbow, palms are up with spray cans, switch, switch, switch (to the eight-note rhythm one, and, two, and)—the vision is almost prepared. Once more, he lunges, but this time it is forward into a fourth position (a position of action) before activating his cans behind him and completing a three-step turn toward the bodega storefront—the plan is in motion; the art is blossoming. He jumps into a backward lunge facing the bodega analyzing his work, and leaps back to the front to keep going before Usnavi comes outside and scares him away.

Graffiti Pete is the first character the audience sees in the world of *In the Heights.*[27] In the prologue-style opening, it would have been very simple to have the character walk out, spray a little paint, get caught by Usnavi, and then have the opening number "In the Heights" begin. It would have been just as easy not to have the character at all. Even so, what Blankenbuehler, and the creative team, did was make this moment heightened to dictate its importance. The moment itself is not necessarily the "important" part, though Pete does come back later in the show to paint a beautiful mural of Abuela Claudia. What is important is the idea that the body performing Graffiti Pete is unique, even though he is not a principal character. Pete's ensemble body dancing movements that fall, arguably, under the genre of hip-hop establish a vocabulary of the piece (which is notably different from Broadway shows at the time). This body says, *In the Heights* is going to move in this way. It informs the audience that bodies other than principal characters will be essential for creating the world of staged Washington Heights. From the very first movement, the ensemble—even if it is just one member—is choreographed as a lens for the audience to understand the show's milieu. The ensemble body is immediately set up as being essential to the dramaturgy of the world.

Charles Isherwood's review of *In the Heights* Off-Broadway on February 9, 2007, makes a note of "Andy Blankenbuehler's joyous choreography, which synthesizes street styles and Broadway athleticism, showcasing the fabulously elastic bodies of the ensemble. A particular standout is Seth Stewart, playing a sweet-hearted graffiti artist, who seems to have little springboards in his sneakers."[28] Isherwood's specific mention of Seth Stewart, who originated the role of Graffiti Pete, is noteworthy. Had this "elastic body" from the ensemble entered the space later in the show or in a group of synchronized dancers, would he have made such an impact? Stewart has an extensive dance background. From the ages of sixteen to eighteen, he began to take ballet classes and was welcomed into the Bachelor of Fine Arts program at Alvin Ailey. After about a year and a half, he left Alvin Ailey to pursue professional work. Stewart was a featured music video and concert dancer for performers such as Jay Z, Madonna, Jennifer Lopez, and Britney Spears. An online interview with Stewart discusses that he grew up with artists such as Michael and Janet Jackson and MC Hammer as his inspiration to be a dancer.[29] His very specific embodied experiences helped him to create the role of Graffiti Pete. The choice to heighten Pete's gestures in this opening picture offered Stewart the opportunity to show off his skill, guided by Blankenbuehler, while also adding to the overall atmosphere of *Heights.*

As Blankenbuehler was reflecting on his process of studying and learning hip-hop dance styles with Lyn Cramer, he noted, "The hip-hop that looked like pantomime was really interesting to me … I tried to make hip-hop dance a bit abstract, deconstructing it, so I could apply it to the way people would simply walk down the street."[30] He leaned into this idea of hip-hop dance, having the capacity to become a story language. In another interview for *Dance Teacher Magazine,* he added, "I always tried to make [the dance] look like the city in a very heightened way. If you look around, people always have rhythm about them—the way they push onto the subway or go up and down steps. There is really this natural syncopation to the way people move in the city."[31] The opening number "In the Heights" is an excellent example of how Blankenbuehler choreographs the idea of a city. By curating varied, individualized choreographic scores for each body in this number, staged Washington Heights comes to life; it gives a sense of impressionistic, staged authenticity.

After Usnavi chases away Graffiti Pete, he begins singing directly to the audience. As he narrates an introduction to Washington Heights through hip-hop-based music, the neighborhood comes to life around him. The number begins using quotidian movement to introduce the audience to the idea of the staged city and slowly incorporates abstract ideas within the choreography. A metro worker dawdling on his way to work walks from stage right past the piragüero, who is selling shaved ice, goes up the steps located center stage, and exits. As the city continues to wake up, other people begin to walk down the street, entering from stage left, stage right, or upstage center down the stairs. Throughout the number, there are little break-out scenes that introduce the audience to specific characters. For example, Abuela Claudia stops at Usnavi's bodega to pick up her lottery ticket, and they have a conversation about spoiled milk.

Following Abuela Claudia's exit from the bodega, dance movements begin to creep into the piece. While some pedestrians continue to walk down the street normally, others may add a turn, a syncopated step, or an arm flourish. Though still subtle in terms of "dance," each has an individual movement score that is molded to their character, to their bodies. A man upstage walks to the beat with a stack of newspapers before setting the stack down, pausing, and jumping up into second position to sell another paper. Each of these moments happens in concert with the syncopation of the claves in the percussion score. The piragüero bounces to the beat as he makes his way across the stage. A young woman casually walks at her own pace to stage left. No two people have the same movement pattern or objective; they are just characters living in (staged) Washington Heights.

Usnavi calls out the audience's potential privilege or ignorance regarding their probable lack of exposure to the Washington Heights neighborhood, saying, "You're prob'ly thinkin', 'I'm up shit's creek! / I never been north of ninety-sixth street.'"[32] As Usnavi explains Washington Heights's socioeconomic conditions, the entire ensemble moves synchronously for the first time. In a 2014 interview for the podcast *The Ensemblist,* Lin-Manuel Miranda said this about the importance of an ensemble:

> You need an ensemble because you are trying to immerse the audience in a world. And the richer the ensemble, the more immersive the world. You want the *oomph* … One of the times it's most important to use, to deploy your ensemble—right, because everything's a weapon, everything's a tool or a weapon depending on how you're feeling that day—Sondheim always says the trickiest thing about writing

> an ensemble number is what is something that everyone in this neighborhood is feeling at the same time ... they find unison lines to sing on that [idea] with *Heights* we made it about the grind. Everything is about, we get our coffee, we get our paper, we're all working our asses off to get through the day. And so, you find those communal moments and build ...[33]

The first moment of synchronized movement brings this idea of unison, of community into a visceral experience for the audience. Accompanying the simultaneous movement with Usnavi's lyrics suggests that the gentrification of the Heights is impacting all of them, even if we, the audience, cannot *hear* them discuss the matter. Although this section is communal, synchronistic choreography, the establishment of each individual ensemble member has not disappeared. From the top of the number through this moment, each individual enacts movements in their own way; no two bodies do a movement *exactly* the same. The dialectic between performer and character creates a textured experience that allows the audience to see a diverse (staged) Washington Heights through the ensemble. Rather than a generic, one-size-fits-all view, the audience can see individual characters being affected by a situation differently.

Wherever they are on the stage by the lyric, "our neighbors started packin' up," they pause.[34] The movement sequence here is full of small pauses. For Words on Dance at Symphony Space, Blankenbuehler discussed the importance of pauses in movement-based storytelling:

> In just a moment's time, the audience's eye [can] see something like a close-up or a freeze-frame ... even if it was just a sixteenth note, there would be a moment of pause. And in that moment of pause, the audience could learn a story ... If you're talking about a sixteenth note, you're forcing the audience to catch something that fast. Which actually, I think, makes them lean forward and pay more attention because they have to work harder.[35]

He acknowledges that this would become a staple for him as a choreographer.

In the second verse of "In the Heights," Blankenbuehler implements this notion of the quick pause to promote a crucial subtext regarding the neighborhood of (staged) Washington Heights. Usnavi sings all of the lyrics for this section center stage while the ensemble is spread around him sporadically. The choreography accompanying these lyrics starts out slow, holding each of the first two shapes for two counts. The movements become gradually faster by the end of the song. On "packin' up," facing whichever direction they are traveling, the ensemble leans back on their heels with both arms straight out in front of their chest, hands loose. It is as if they have been punched in the gut and are falling backward in slow motion. During the pause of "packin' up," this freeze-frame moment highlights the varied impacts gentrification has on the community. To elaborate, if an audience member is looking at Krysta Rodriguez, they will understand her situation to be a little less ominous. She is holding a purse in her right arm, and when she gets "punched in the gut," she only contracts slightly and only extends one arm, rather than both. On the opposite end of the spectrum is Afra Hines. Her torso is significantly more collapsed, causing her to lean further back on her heels with both arms extended parallel as if she has been forcefully knocked backward. The ensemble bodies hold this image, and on "and pickin' up," they lift their right foot, leaning forward onto the left foot—making an exaggerated shape of walking—while reaching fists down as if they are picking up suitcases. Some individuals, like Hines, are in a wide stance, closer to the ground. Some are in a closed stance, like Rodriguez, and therefore seeming to be shouldering less weight. Depending on whom the audience member is looking at, they may be receiving a story about someone who is in deep despair or someone who is still doing pretty well and was not as severely affected by the changes in the Heights.

Next, the ensemble places their right foot back down and plié into fourth position turning slowly over the right shoulder to face upstage on "and ever since the rent went up."[36] After a few quickly syncopated shoulder movements through the lyrics, "it's gotten mad expensive, / but we live with just," they throw their arms up and hop back onto the right foot, kicking out the left on the word "enough."[37] Following this sequence, they begin a stop-motion walk taking one step every two counts for four counts. Then, some return to an average walking speed, some remain slower but relaxed, some are seemingly in a hurry. Each little pause or holding of a movement, as well as the speeding up of the tempo of the movements in this verse, tells the story of getting knocked down by forces outside of one's control, fighting to pick oneself back up, and accepting that they are going to have to keep moving forward. Every individual handles the situation at various levels and accepts the challenge at different speeds. As the ensemble bodies engage in their personal choreographic scores, they create a layered and elaborate atmosphere. Although their movement is heightened and stylized beyond quotidian practices, the resistance to uniform synchronicity allows the audience to comprehend a more realistic world, a (staged) authentic world. Reflecting on the individuality within the ensemble, Miranda told *The Ensemblist*:

> You know I was in the show, so the first time that I saw the show, I was blown away by all the other plotlines that were happening that were purely visual. You know, with "96,000" [...] we have these individual lines of "well if I had the money I would do this," "if I had the money I would do this" and then you see it spread and spread and spread and you can slowly fold it until you don't even realize the entire company is now doing this crazy unison number. Because we kind of keep going into these solos and solos, and how much can we continue to build while doing a solo. And that was very much a group ... that thing was written by committee. It was, "All right, can we get away with this happening, and what can we build here?" And, "All right, so, Benny will solo over this while everyone's going woo." And like ... I worked very closely with Andy to find the way to make that build musically and physically at the same time.[38]

Although Miranda explicitly mentions the number "96,000," his reflection is equally true of "In the Heights." As we see with this analysis, the heightened-every day builds and builds into a fully developed dance as the number continues. The anonymous background actors walking around the stage become individual characters in Washington Heights with lives theoretically independent of the central storyline. Developing the "individual" within the ensemble of *Heights* allows for the creation of a community that promotes the sentiment of real life, of an authentic representation of the Washington Heights neighborhood.

As the staged social world of Washington Heights comes alive through the bodies of the performers/characters of the entire company, the dancing ensemble body becomes increasingly crucial to forming the idea of a milieu with a complex, layered history. While the principals' bodies are undoubtedly essential and engaging in telling through their corporality, the ensemble body is doubly performative, for it travels between being mediated and unmediated by text. Such relationships between the ensemble body and written text can be arguably broken into three ideas. First, there are moments throughout where the body moves independently of any spoken text. For example, it can move to the beat of the music underscoring dialogue. This means that the viewer can see the ensemble body as directly affected by the text/music and inherently connected to the story. Alternatively, similar to the beginning of "In the Heights," it can simply move while music is happening but not be in sync with that music. Or, the ensemble body can be seen by the viewer as a separate entity, not connected to the story but living in the same physical space; it is related to the world but perhaps not to the action. When you take a walk down the street, there are people who shape your walk. You pause to let someone walk past, you say "hello," or you ignore someone completely. Each of those people has their own story, but you are all connected by being in the same milieu at that moment. The same applied to staged Washington Heights. Incorporating this idea elevates the individuality of the ensemble body.

Second, as detailed by the section where Usnavi calls out the gentrification of the Heights, the body can move in sync with the lyrics, but it is not singing. Here, the ensemble bodies become physically connected within the milieu of (staged) Washington Heights. When they are collectively mediated by the text, it points to the notion that they have all been affected by the verbally communicated idea on some level. They may not be directly involved in the story at that moment, but as they subtly move in the periphery, it amplifies Usnavi's sentiments.

Moreover, there are choruses in the song when the ensemble joins in singing while they continue to move. The next section in the song is the first time when the ensemble sings the chorus. Yet, the unison singing is now the underscore for what can only be described as a constellation of movement sequences; the individual choreographic scores become palpable. Rather than imposing specific choreography on the entire ensemble and asking them to be completely in sync with one another as they sing this chorus, Blankenbuehler accommodates each performer's individuality. Throughout this section, his choreographic landscape breathes between brief moments of synchronization and moments of individuality to highlight the uniting principles of this group of people but acknowledge each performer/character's unique personalities. The linkage of movement, music, and text by the ensemble bodies during these moments of unity speaks to Miranda's point of "What is something that everyone in this neighborhood is feeling at the same time?"[39] The mediation of all of the bodies onstage is a point of connection. The fluidity of the ensemble body to move between mediated and unmediated phases creates a multiplexable environment that promotes the community atmosphere of Washington Heights as well as the sense of staged authenticity.

Blankenbuehler's implementation of individualized choreographic scores while the ensemble sings in unison helps generate a robust staged community environment. These lyrics act as a guide map for understanding the constellation of events that occur:

All (except NINA) In the Heights

Piragua Guy/Carla/Daniela/Others I flip the lights and start my day

All There are fights

Carla/Daniela/Women And endless debts

Kevin/Benny/Piragua Guy/Men And bills to pay

All In the Heights

Benny/Kevin/Piragua Guy/Others I can't survive without café

Usnavi I serve café

All 'Cuz tonight seems like a million years away! En Washington—[40]

Graffiti Pete enters upstage center with a boom-box executing a slow-motion walk. He sits on the railing for a moment, followed by a quick chaîné turn off upstage right between "pay" and "In."[41] The Piragua Guy enters upstage enter slowly pushing his cart toward stage left. On the stage deck, Krysta Rodriguez, ensemble, is stage right in the bodega. Rodriguez is upstage of the counter, paying Usnavi for a purchase. Then, she walks around to the front of the counter and stops, posing with one leg beveled and her back to the audience. Afra Hines, ensemble, begins a slow-motion walk toward the bodega from stage left. Her pace returns to normal on "day." She pauses to greet Luis Salgado on her way through the door, followed by a quick chaîné turn into the bodega with arms in a "touch down" shape (hands in fists) crossing in front of the counter between "pay" and "In." On the downbeat before "In," her arms flip so her fists are toward the ground, then back to touch down shape on "In" and back to the reverse with legs bent and back curved on "the." Ending the movement sequence in front of the counter, posing with one leg beveled and her back to the audience. They all pause by the end of the second "In the Heights."

Throughout the above choreography, the juxtaposition between quotidian and heightened everyday movement, synchronous and asynchronous movement frames the individual ensemble bodies within the community setting. When a moment becomes heightened, it attracts a viewer's attention to that body/those bodies. Movement of any kind can be one of the most powerful tools to draw focus onstage. In some instances, two or three bodies may be moving or gesturing in a similar, synchronized way to create embodied community amongst the characters. Jonathan Burrows argues, "The meaning or logic that arrives when you put things next to each other that accumulates into something which makes sense for the audience. This something that accumulates seems inevitable, almost unarguable. It feels like a story, even when there is no story."[42] When the heightened movement is set next to everyday movement, it suggests to the audience that they are semiotically related; the people living in this world move in both realist and abstract ways interchangeably.

Lin-Manuel Miranda remembers:

> With *In the Heights,* we were very much trying to convey a community. We wanted it to feel like you could follow that person down the block, and there's another musical happening with Nina Lafarga and Ricky Tripp as they exit stage right, and they do their own thing. And it's a credit to [Tommy Kail's] direction [and] Andy Blankenbuehler's choreography that it felt like that. It felt like this community.[43]

Let us take Miranda's suggestion and follow Nina Lafarga for the next part of the chorus. Lafarga, ensemble, is seen entering upstage center wearing a cropped, tight tank top and short skirt with her hair down. She walks directly to Rosie Lani Fiedelman, dressed in Bermuda shorts, a hooded crop top, and short hair. They exchange a few words; it is no coincidence that they meet on the word "fights." Luis Salgado has now left the bodega and crossed to Fiedelman, sending Lafarga into an evasively quick chaîné turn toward downstage right with arms in a "touch down" shape (hands in fists). On the downbeat before "In," her arms flip so her fists are toward the ground, then back to touch down shape on "In" and back to the reverse with legs bent and back curved on "the." Ending the movement sequence near Benny, posing with one leg beveled facing the audience, she pauses, looking back at Salgado and Fiedelman, who are now paired center. They salsa together straight down center stage on "I can't survive." As they salsa, everyone else onstage is in their point of pause, making them the only moving entity. On "café," Salgado and Fiedelman continue their duet, and the others onstage pick up where they left off.

Isolating these three ensemble members, allowing Lafarga's action to drive the plot, a love triangle arises. There may not be a story there, but it feels like a story. When this sequence becomes the focus, the movement (quotidian and danced) accumulates into a narrative completely separate from the central plot of *In the Heights*. If an audience member were to attach to this idea, they would later see Lafarga and Salgado in "The Club" scene dancing rather intimately with one another, propagating this fabricated story. The initially brief exchange between Lafarga and Fiedelman occurs upstage center, with little obstructing them from view. Such in-depth character development through choreography and the individual ensemble bodies further enhances the production's social world.

Just the same, Salgado and Fiedelman's salsa does not go unnoticed. The inclusion of Latinx social dance within the first three minutes sets up the fact that there will inevitably be Latinx social dance included throughout the show. Furthermore, the entire company's pause during Fiedelman and Salgado's salsa down the strongest path onstage (on the phrase "I can't survive without … ") indicates this style is something to pay attention to as it is a cultural practice fundamental to these characters and this social world. Because it is the opening number that institutes a vocabulary for the entire production, immediately establishing this concept is essential. In Burrows's book, he cites an email correspondence with choreographer Jerome Bel saying:

> The first seven minutes of a performance are for free, the audience can accept anything—after this is another problem, then they want what they have paid for—but during those first seven minutes, as choreographer, you have total freedom. You can try to attempt something else, to put the audience on a different track than the usual one for the rest of the performance. It's after those seven minutes that they start to yell at you.[44]

Inaugurating the vocabulary early on is crucial to get the audience on board, making a promise to them about what they are going to see and experience for the remainder of the production. For *Heights*, this means both hip-hop and salsa must be included from the beginning.

During the final line of the chorus, on the beats of the word "away," the ensemble on the stage deck (Salgado, Fiedelman, Lafarga, Hines, Rodriguez, Stewart, and a few others) complete a few synchronized shoulder pops with a foot flick followed by a sweeping arm motion that turns the body as if gesturing to a distant landscape. As the next section introduces the Rosarios, Carla, and Daniela, the ensemble returns to "normal" daily life activities.

Following these introductions, Usnavi introduces his cousin Sonny and tells of their lives working the bodega. The ensemble begins walking in a stop-time moonwalk. As they take one step forward, they drag that foot back to meet the other. After a quick pause, they repeat on the other foot so that they are walking in place in a stylized way.

As Usnavi steps out of the bodega to address the audience and introduce the partnership with his cousin Sonny, ensemble member Ricky Tripp makes his way to Usnavi and executes a series of pop and lock hip-hop dance moves. For the first few counts of this, the rest of the ensemble is continuing their individualized heightened-walk sequence in the background. Tripp becomes a focus alongside Usnavi; the two even interact when Tripp "buys" a lottery ticket from Usnavi. In the vocal score, a switch in music style is notated at this moment, shifting from "hip-hop, half-time feel" to "Dance-Hall Reggae."[45] By the lyrics "a few cold waters and / a lottery ticket," the entire ensemble joins in performing a few select movements that manifest hip-hop aesthetics.[46] Usnavi continues, "Just a part of the routine. / Everybody's got a job, everybody's got a dream."[47] The lyrics emphasize the individuality of the ensemble. As the individual ensemble bodies travel closer to and eventually enter the bodega on "One dollar, two dollars, one fifty, one sixty-nine," their steps grow larger and larger.[48]

At this moment, the stage directions in the libretto dictate, "People come through his store."[49] Reading the script and seeing the action propound the connection between reality and the heightened-everyday. During the following movement, Usnavi calls out types of purchases made by the customers. Fieldelman does a quick bounce toward the counter to complete her purchase. Lafarga squeezes into the store past Fiedelman doing a series of popping moves. Javier Muñoz walks in to buy a box of condoms—walking back out the door embarrassed.[50] Salgado browses the shelves doing a shoulder pop, then lifts Rodriguez over his head, pausing to see over someone. Graffiti Pete turns through the store to purchase a drink. And Hines and Tripp pop and lock to take coffee from Usnavi.

Blankenbuehler's interpretation of people coming through the bodega looks much different than what someone would imagine when merely reading the text. His abstraction of an everyday transaction between a community member and the bodega owner using hip-hop augments the piece's sociological subtext. Hip-hop's complicated lineage marks it, at its simplest, multicultural and the voice of the disenfranchised. Melissa Catillo-Garsow and Jason Nichols suggest, " … Hip Hop is often an early warning sign of social unrest, an expression of angst and economic or political dissatisfaction and a site for community building and sustainability."[51] By having every ensemble body take on hip-hop as the vocabulary at this moment, it unites the community in both the struggle and the hope for growth and betterment. In a personal interview, *Heights* first national tour ensemble member Morgan Marcell (Matayoshi), remarked:

> Hip-hop allows a lot of story to be told in a little space. It CAN [sic.] be more intricate than other styles, so your imagery tends to be specific. Andy incorporates that into his movement quality. *In the Heights* is a perfect example. You may not know the dancers are doing "double decker bus wreck" with their hands in the back of the bodega, but they are. It creates a vibe on stage that the audience subconsciously feels.[52]

Hip-hop allows people coming through Usnavi's store to become the community supporting the local bodega, eliciting a "shop small" mentality, fosters sustainability within the neighborhood. Incorporating such subtext through the individual ensemble bodies substantiates the milieu of staged Washington Heights.

After stopping at the bodega, the customers continue to the next part of their day. The stage becomes filled with bodies depicting a typical chaotic weekday morning in New York City. Another change of music style is notated in the vocal score, switching to "Salsa."[53] In accordance with this shift, Blankenbuehler choreographs a traveling step indicative of a basic salsa in a canon—half of the ensemble salsas while the other half stands still in second position, then they switch. This back and forth happens throughout the entire second chorus. Prior to this moment, only Fiedelman and Salgado have danced salsa. Growing the practice of salsa to include more bodies is crucial to the staged authenticity of *In the Heights*. While Latinx social dance is used very specifically in later numbers, as will be discussed, its slow inauguration here is calculated. The audience first encounters hip-hip as being the primary vocabulary of the piece. To reiterate, hip-hop is employed as the language of struggle and marginalization but also ambition and community. For *In the Heights,* this subtext is vital to the plot. But, the implementation of Latinx social dance as the mode by which the community moves and connects after they have woken up, had their coffee, and are ready to transition into the rest of their day, proposes a less labored, more intuitive component of the (staged) Washington Heights community. Latinx social dance symbolizes the traditions and values fundamental to their way of life.

Blankenbuehler implements another dialectic, this time between hip-hop and Latinx social dance that the ensemble body navigates throughout the production. Jonathan Burrows posits, "One of the greatest strengths of dance is this: if you put two people doing two different dances next to each other, we will almost always find a relationship between the two things we're seeing—we will even enjoy it."[54] While the chorus begins with the canon between salsa and stillness, it builds to dance between salsa and hip-hop. The push and pull between living peacefully and facing the weight of a neighborhood crumbling around them permeate the choreography.

Following two brief breakout scenes with Benny and Vanessa, respectively, Usnavi steps out of the bodega. The music pauses, switching to a bass beat, followed by seven counts of rest as he speaks—the vocal score labels this section "Hip-Hop."[55] This shift suggests a stop-time moment, introspective of Usnavi's thoughts. The ensemble begins moving seemingly in slow motion. On the first downbeat, Tripp and Graffiti Pete, center, drop to the ground into a low runner's lunge, right leg forward. Fiedelman is downstage right with her right leg forward, left leg back mirroring Tripp and Graffiti Pete but on a mid-level. Lafarga and Salgado are in a partner dance hold. Others are paused in the middle of reaching into their purse, walking, high-fiving, or completing a transaction. Usnavi sings, "Yeah, I'm a streetlight, / choking on the heat. / The world spins around / while I'm frozen to my seat."[56] Conversely, the ensemble shifts functions, becoming an extension of Usnavi's consciousness. They move abstractly and slowly closer to Usnavi. Drawing direct attention to the presentational nature of this new function, the first movement faces the audience. The ensemble bodies transform from individual characters living in staged Washington Heights to an extension of Usnavi's rendering of his personal history.

In a promotional video for *In the Heights,* Blankenbuehler, accompanied by a few of the ensemble members, annotates this dance break:

> In the opening number, there's a moment where the lead character Usnavi talks about seeing the neighborhood from the perspective of being in the middle of it; and it's all going around him. So, what we do is we hit this slow-motion circle where everybody is … going around him. And then when that comes back to life, he sings these lyrics about "my parents came from nothing" and just inherently those lyrics are saying that it's from nothing and it's going up.[57]

Usnavi sings, "So I'm switchin' up the beat. / 'cuz my parents came with nothing. / They got a little more. / And sure, we're poor."[58] As previously mentioned, the beat switches for this section from salsa, a sound and movement inherently connected to his Latinx heritage, to hip-hop. Because hip-hop is a sound and movement associated with socioeconomic struggles, the show seemingly chooses to activate it during such moments within the narrative. Here, this choice accompanies the challenges Usnavi's parents faced as immigrants. The ensemble faces front, steps forward onto their left leg, then steps their right heel forward to touch. With the right heel on the ground, the foot pivots slightly to accent "the beat." They rond de jambe, à terre their right leg backward.[59] The left leg follows, stepping straight back; both legs remain in a demi plié.[60] When the left leg steps, the elbows are up, parallel with the shoulders, and the hands make a dropping or throwing downward motion on the word "nothing." The ensemble bodies step the left leg forward again, following the downward throw of the arms. They cross their arms in an "X" over their lap and step the right leg to the side. The arms move from the "X" toward the hips, pulling the torso to the right. Describing this arm transition, Blankenbuehler elaborates, "This arm is electric right here. And then the word is 'got.' So as we step forward, it's like we're grasping opportunities. This step, I feel like, is a cornerstone thought in the show saying, 'Life in Washington Heights, life for a first-generation is really difficult.'"[61] Continuing to lean on his explanation, it is clear that as the ensemble rocks back and forth between forward movement and backward movement, they are laboring to succeed, to achieve that "American dream." Even though the ensemble is moving synchronously here and as a communal expression of Usnavi's words, the audience still sees them as individuals. Each ensemble body pliés at a different level and lunges at different distances. Each variation of the movement highlights their varied embodied experiences with this traditional immigrant narrative.

Usnavi slowly moves through the ensemble while they continue to reflect his consciousness. As his optimism grows, he sings, "But yo, / At least we got the store. / It's all about the legacy / They left with me, / It's destiny. / And one day I'll be on the beach / With Sonny writing checks / to me."[62] The multivalence of hip-hop allows its allusions to transition accordingly. Notably, Tripp does not execute the same choreography as the rest of the ensemble during this sequence. Instead, he is engaging in his own breakdance-based score around Usnavi, at one point even engaging in a handshake and following him on his cross-stage right. Tripp's hip-hop feels more improvised, free, hopeful. It is less rigid and structured than the other dance happening onstage. In resisting the synchronicity of the other ensemble members, Tripp's hip-hop establishes a juxtaposition between being afflicted by one's socioeconomic positionality and one's ability to transcend that disposition. As Usnavi optimistically sheds light on his feelings about his positionality within society, Tripp's hip-hop speaks to his ambition of eventually making enough money to keep his store afloat and visit this island of the Dominican Republic, where his parents were born.

After this section, the choreography for the remainder of the number flows between salsa, hip-hop, and peppers in other musical theatre-based movements. Such use of contrasting genres highlights dance's adaptability and intertextuality. Susan Leigh Foster suggests, "Dance's adaptability coordinates individual and social realms by focusing on dance's function and purpose in a given situation, giving it both a social and individual meaningfulness."[63] Reading the diverse assemblage of ensemble bodies as they perform varied hip-hops and salsas allows for the multiple narratives of heritage, community, strife, vitality, and aspiration to coalesce. On the final button of the number, "En Washington Heights," the company is evenly spread around the stage and strikes a pose according to their character or ensemble body.[64] As the audience applauses, they continue to absorb the unique characters of the staged Washington Heights community, who remain unmoving until the music picks back up and they continue with their day.

2.4 "Carnaval Del Barrio": Staging Latinx Nationality Through Social Dance

Building off of his use of staged authenticity and illuminating nuances of nation, race, class, and unity through choreography, Blankenbuehler actuates multiple Latinx social dance genres in "Carnaval Del Barrio" as celebratory tools of nostalgia and translocality. Juliet McMains summarizes Puerto Rican writer Mayra Santos-Febres's argument emphasizing that "salsa engendered a 'translocal' community because the common local experiences of oppression and rebellion described in salsa lyrics and echoed in the movement cut across national boundaries."[65] McMains posits, "Although this translocal community shares a common spoken language in Spanish, it might be better defined by the values and experiences encompassed by salsa: skill at improvisation, mixed origins, polymetered rhythms that coexist and fuse, economic deprivation in *el barrio*, and feet that constantly shift unpredictable patterns in response to the environment."[66] McMains's choice to italicize *el barrio* performatively elevates the Spanish term for neighborhood as a connective identity marker. Similarly, the increased use of the Spanish language throughout "Carnaval Del Barrio" connects these decedents or migrants from numerous Latin American countries. Blankenbuehler employs movement as an embodied communication of the translocal community of (staged) Washington Heights. He activates individualized choreographic scores that allow for the embracement of improvisation, mixed origins, and polyrhythm. Through this individualization, he once again draws attention to the diverse individual ensemble bodies of this community who are dealing with the after-effects of a power outage in *el barrio*.

As audiences of *In the Heights* witness the community of staged Washington Heights clean up following chaos that erupted in consequence of an electricity blackout, they observe residents fending for themselves as the ConEdison electric company tells them it will take twenty-four hours to fix. Transportation methods have been suspended, and they are stuck in the heat of the fourth of July. To calm everyone down and boost their spirits, Daniela begins to sing about her time in Puerto Rico as a young child. She reminisces about the joy of parranda's (Puerto Rican social events during Christmas time). Daniela calls for a spontaneous Carnaval to distract from the afflictions of the moment. The Piragüero Guy and Luis Salgado are among the first to join in her merriment. Salgado begins an accompanying beat by hitting the Piragüero Guy's cart. He is striking the front of the cart where a painted Puerto Rican flag is displayed. The Piragüero Guy starts a mambo upstage center. Mambo is a dance that originated in Cuba (sidestep left, right ball, change left, sidestep right, left ball, change right to the rhythm one and two, three and four). Sonny and Graffiti Pete watch him for a set, almost as if they are learning the step before they join him.

After some more encouragement, the stage directions indicate, "*The community gets into it.*"[67] The general salsa step rhythm is activated in the majority of the individual ensemble scores—step, step, step, pause. However, variations become visible. The subtle differences are located in the size of the step, the activation of the hips, and the way the pause is performed. For example, Lafarga kicks her foot out slightly, making a small circular motion during the pause before placing it back on the ground for the subsequent step, almost like a cumbia step. Cumbia is traditionally practiced in Colombia. Hines's step looks more like merengue; she chugs along as if they are marching. The merengue comes from the Dominican Republic.

The community joining in the impromptu celebration via these varied dance styles speaks to the significance of dance's purpose within each of these originating societies. John Charles Chasteen's *National Rhythms, African Roots: The Deep History of Latin American Popular Dance* contends that cultural dance practices—broadly—have generated connection and solidarity amongst groups. He specifically suggests, "Folk dance is frequently an aspect of ethnic identities, a stock element of nationalism. In Latin America few provinces or regions lack identifying dances, habitually staged on national holidays by school children. Latin America's national rhythms, then, are a high-energy, high-profile, high-stakes version of this phenomenon."[68] Much of *In the Heights* uses dance as a signifier of solidarity and connection. It is the emphasis on dance as a given element of nationalism in "Carnaval Del Barrio" that connects this staged translocal community through movement practices and philosophies as a response to their often-onerous environment. One frequently repeated chorus recites:

Lyrics	*Translation*
Alza La Bandera	Raise the Flag
La Bandera Dominicana	The Dominican Flag
Alza La Bandera	Raise the Flag
La Bandera Puertoriqueña	The Puerto Rican Flag
Alza La Bandera	Raise the Flag
La Bandera Mejicana	The Mexican Flag
Alza La Bandera	Raise the Flag
La Bandera Cubana[69]	The Cuban Flag

Many individual ensemble bodies wave these flags as they weave about the stage completing their varied Latinx social dance steps. The joyous waving of the flags alongside a myriad of dance styles promotes diverse identities while generating solidarity amongst the group. Hints of mambo, salsa, cumbia, merengue, and bomba can be seen throughout. As the rhythms of these movement styles of mixed origin can resist directly aligning with one another, the audience can perceive such moments as being improvised.

Upon analyzing the highly personalized choreographies, the question arises: how much of the number is actually improvised? The answer—very little. When placing two recordings of "Carnaval Del Barrio," performed by the Broadway cast, beside one another, the individual ensemble bodies undoubtedly have unique flourishes to their movements that vary between these recordings.[70] However, the overall movement score and traffic pattern for every individual are indeed repeated from performance to performance. Moreover, the cast in these videos differed somewhat as one features Lin-Manuel Miranda as Usnavi, and the other features Javier Muñoz, his understudy. The use of an understudy shifts the ensemble tracks slightly as swings are put in the place of anyone missing. In theory, this would affect how a track would look if it were truly improvised. Each individual ensemble body adds their own take onto the movement score—for example, the addition of arm movements, a hip sway, or even a quick turn—but, for the sake of replicability and consistency, the core of the choreography for each ensemble track remains intact.

Blankenbuehler structures brief sequences during the number that are very "musical theatre," synchronized dance. Consequently, when the individuals break away into their own score, the juxtaposition heightens the perception of improvisation. Following the first chorus of "Alza la bandera," Usnavi and Piragüero Guy sing together center as the ensemble dances around the edges of the stage space.[71] Each individual ensemble member is moving in their own style, but they occasionally meet in a synchronous arm gesture upward or turn. A few male ensemble members move inward toward Usnavi and Piragüero Guy. They place their hands on one another's shoulders to form a circle around them. The men take a few syncopated steps and then spin outward to partner with a female member. The pairs salsa with one another. While each pair has the same general pattern, the movement remains unique to the individuals. For example, Salgado and Lafarga, complete a few extra turns than the other couples. Rodriguez adds an arm flourish toward the end that others do not.

When Benny enters the scene, the synchronized moments stop and the individualized celebrations continue. The uniquity of ensemble bodies arguably becomes more intelligible as they seemingly dance to rejoice rather than to execute any sense of choreography. During the next chorus, the company begins two conga lines around the stage: the stage left conga line moves in a circle, the stage right conga line moves in a straight diagonal. This back and forth between perceived improvisation and synchronization in "Carnaval Del Barrio" promotes diversity, uniqueness, inclusivity, and solidarity. Additionally, it creates the perception of a staged translocal community. Jayna Brown argues, "Dance is a means for communication, forming new communities, remembering, and cultivating cultures ....Popular dance offers wonderful heterogeneity and contradiction. Forms can be immediately commercialized, yet they are incapable of being owned. They are by definition public and collective, yet they can also be intensely private, articulations of a bodily interority."[72] As the community of diverse ensemble bodies dance personalized notions of popular social styles within the frame of the Broadway production, they cultivate an understanding of culture that is presented to the audience. The dances communicate, remember, and offer a sense of heterogeneity while helping to unite those living in staged Washington Heights.

> For the final verse, everyone stops dancing as Usnavi sings:
> Maybe you're right, Sonny. Call in the Coroners!
> Maybe we're powerless, a corner full of foreigners.
> Maybe this neighborhood's changing forever
> Maybe tonight is our last night together, however!
> How do you wanna face it?
> Do you wanna waste it, when the end is so close you can taste it?
> You could cry with your head in the sand.
> I'm a-fly this flag that I got in my hand![73]

His provocation sparks a bolstering of energy within the choreography. Tripp and Graffiti Pete begin to integrate hip-hop dance movements. Lafarga and Salgado incorporate some advanced salsa. Henry hip-hops for a few counts, then salsas with Rodriguez. The dance continues to meet in brief moments of synchronicity while prioritizing the notion of improvisation. The doubled meaning in the word "powerless" as he alludes to the potential demise of *el barrio* heightens the stakes of needing community and optimism. The final few stage directions read, "*The community explodes into a final chorus … Neighbors exit as the carnaval continues onto the next block*."[74] Through their individual and synchronous dances, they maintain high-energy and pride toward the celebration of their different ethnic identities. Even as they face the high-stakes of gentrification, their dance generates an embodied connection that, at least at this moment, has the power to transcend any impending repression.

2.5 Conclusion: Adapting Environments

Reflecting on when he was first asked to interview for the role of *In the Heights* choreographer, Andy Blankenbuehler remembers,

> I really believed that I was not right for the show, but I wanted to give a really good audition … because I believed in the players involved … and so, I went in, and I have a great interview because all I did was quote Jerome Robbins … I couldn't present hip-hop or salsa cuz I didn't know anything about it.[75]

He explains how the music he was given to choreograph had rich moments of syncopation and lush lyrics that allowed him to use more percussive action to tell the story in a way that fit their tone, even though it was not hip-hop. Ultimately, he did not get the job. Another choreographer—who is unknown to the public—got the job, but when that did not work out, about a year later, he got a call from the team asking him to join them on the project. Reflecting on his work with *In the Heights,* Blankenbuehler remarked, "*In the Heights* was a life-altering experience."[76] In *Heights,* he was able to discover and practice what would become key Blankenbuehler-choreography vocabulary: stop-time moments, circular patterns, pauses, heightened pedestrian movement, hip-hop enhancement, and the active fourth position.

Blankenbuehler's prioritization of communication of ideas (narrative, metaphorical, subtextual, theoretical, or philosophical) over virtuosity and spectacle is arguably most tangible when he uses heightened pedestrian or pantomimic movement. Audiences witness the ensemble body yield an array of recognizable shapes that they can then attach to emotional states, character attributes, or narrative. Interpreting these postures and gestures through the individual ensemble body enacting them generates a complex sociological environment within the world of the production. The individual ensemble bodies portray individual characters living in (staged) Washington Heights and are positioned as necessary for comprehending the socioeconomic effects on their community. The staged authenticity of this world becomes established through the augmentation of the individual ensemble body moving in a uniquely personalized way. Particularly, when framed by Latinx social dance, the individual ensemble bodies read by the audience as a dramaturgically Latinx body become understood as presenting an unmediated encounter with a cultural product. Blankenbuehler's choreography adapts the milieu of the production into an embodied narrative (literal, supplemental, or nuanced) in service of manufacturing a lens through which these bodies and characters can transport the audience into experiencing heterogeneous, translocal community.

As Blankenbuehler's career progresses, his understanding regarding the potential for the ensemble to communicate with the audience beyond the text continues to develop and evolve. Moreover, his proficiency in the genre of hip-hop grows—even though he maintains that he does not *do* hip-hop, he does indeed *use* hip-hop movement aesthetics within his choreography. By adapting environments into a visceral, embodied arena, the audience receives multiple modes of communication by which they can absorb the plot and its associated metanarratives.

CHAPTER 3
"WE AIN'T NO CHEERLEADERS": CHEERLEADING BODIES, HIP-HOPPING BODIES, AND THE WORLD OF *BRING IT ON: THE MUSICAL*

In 2000, Jessica Bendinger brought the world the first *Bring It On* film. During the two decades following its inception, five additional filmed sequels and a Broadway musical would be developed. Bendinger originally pitched producers Max Wong and Caitlin Scanlon an idea called *Cheer Fever*, a documentary about national cheerleading championships. According to journalist Kase Wickman, Bendinger said, "I wanted to mix cheerleading and hip-hop, the two tastes that taste great together, it's like peanut butter and chocolate [...] It would be so funny to put them together because they are so antithetical to each other."[1] Her comment is seemingly ironic to anyone familiar with the sport in 2021 as the two concepts now go hand in hand.[2] Wong and Scanlon would help Bendinger turn her idea into a teen movie classic. Wong recalls:

> I hated cheerleaders. And you just realize that everyone in America has an opinion about cheerleaders. You love cheerleaders, you hate cheerleaders, you were a cheerleader, you want to f–k a cheerleader [...] we just really, really liked the fact that Jessica was talking about cultural appropriation. That hadn't been discussed in teen movies, and here's this sort of poppy cheerleading movie where she's actually talking about societal issues that are really engaging in a really important fashion.[3]

Wong's statement points out the potential for cheerleading to be an accessible subject for a large audience; from hating cheerleaders to sexualizing cheerleaders, people could connect on some level to the activity. Such a widespread association would allow Wong, Scanlon, and Bendinger to subvert cheerleading as a tool to discuss cultural appropriation and socioeconomic/sociopolitical disparities within the United States.

The *Bring It On* saga illuminates tensions inherent in the form of cheerleading in the United States related to race, class, gender, and sexualization. For example, the theme of an upper-middle-class, mostly white school competing against a working-class, school of color is at the forefront of nearly every iteration of *Bring It On,* including the musical. As Wong points out, the very form of cheerleading both affirms and challenges societal issues. Arguably the most perceptible issue the sport illuminates is the strict, gendered roles scripted onto the athletes, the uniforms, and the choreography. As the athletes conform to these strict gender roles, they simultaneously challenge assumptions of femininity as "dainty" and perform intense physical labor within their routines. Furthermore, there has been a long history of discord regarding race, class, and cheerleading. Popular culture consistently associates the sport with white, affluent teenagers. If cheerleading as a sport exposes such societal discrepancies, then how does cheerleading on Broadway challenge typical ideas of the chorus/ensemble?

In 2012, following an out-of-town tryout in Atlanta and a U.S. National Tour, *Bring It On: The Musical* would find its way to Broadway. Featuring music by Tom Kitt and Lin-Manuel Miranda, lyrics by Amanda Green and Miranda, and book by Jeff Whitty, the musical is inspired by the original 2000 film—though any *Bring It On* fan would tell you the plot actually aligns more with that of the third film installment *Bring It On: All or Nothing* starring Hayden Panettiere. It tells the story of a white cheerleader who must move schools, leaving behind her award-winning cheerleading team. Upon arriving at her new, inner-city school, she finds a diverse group of classmates but no cheerleading squad. Instead, they have a dance crew. In an attempt to maintain her status as a cheerleading champion, she convinces the dance crew to join her in developing their own cheerleading squad and compete against her former school. After a series of missteps, she learns the cinematic life lesson that being true to yourself and your friends is far more important than receiving a trophy.

In order to successfully pull off the task of staging the Varsity National Cheerleading Competition for this production, as well as legitimize the characters as cheerleaders, director-choreographer Andy Blankenbuehler cast precisely half of the ensemble/swings from a pool of collegiate and professional cheerleaders. Blankenbuehler described the casting process: "I wanted to surround myself with true authenticity. So, we made the decision early on to not teach actors to do cheerleading."[4] Jessica McDermott

(Colombo), a consultant for Varsity Spirit (one of the world's leading cheerleading associations) and judge for the Universal Cheerleading Association, was also brought onto the production team to ensure that all of the difficult and potentially dangerous cheerleading stunts and tumbling were choreographed and executed accurately and safely. McDermott attested, "Safety-wise when you are throwing people in the air, you need people who are trained to do that."[5] Cheerleading ensemble member Antwan Bethea reported:

> Andy Blankenbuehler and Jessica McDermott (Colombo) set out to recruit highly skilled collegiate and professional cheerleaders. Half of the ensemble were experienced cheerleaders, and the other half were skilled singers & dancers. In a nutshell, the cheerleaders taught the singers/dancers all the technical skills of cheer stunts and the cheer lingo. In turn, the ensemble members who were familiar with "stage life" taught the cheerleaders things like vocal exercises and stage etiquette. For example, as the cheerleaders were learning how to belt or the difference between downstage and upstage, we were teaching the dancers/singer the proper grips of an elevated stunt and how to absorb when catching a fall. In the performances, I think the goal was to have the two styles/backgrounds blend so well that it would appear everyone on stage was a cheerleader and a singer, and a dancer.[6]

Bethea's illustration of the rehearsal process points to Blankenbuehler's creation of a collaborative environment. Not dissimilar to *In the Heights,* he relied on others skilled in genres he was not to help enhance the execution of the choreography.

As Bethea suggests, with McDermott's guidance, Blankenbuehler successfully blends a group of dancing ensemble bodies and a group of cheerleading ensemble bodies that together make up the aggregate ensemble body of *Bring It On: The Musical.* Each of these bodies is skilled in their respective genre. Still, how Blankenbuehler has choreographed these bodies in cooperation with one another manufactures a cohesive lens through which the audience can view this particular world. Although some dancing ensemble bodies may play cheerleader characters, they may not have the specific skill of a trained cheerleader. For example, a cheerleading virtuoso can execute challenging stunts and gymnastics, while a dancer may not have such curated muscle capacity or tumbling ability. In fact, none of the principal characters are professionally trained cheerleaders.[7] Thus, a carefully crafted choreographic score is necessary to blend these components of the ensemble body to deflect from any disparities in cheerleading-based training amongst the entire cast, creating the illusion of an actual cheerleading squad.

This chapter analyzes the numbers "What I Was Born to Do" (Truman High School), "We Ain't No Cheerleaders" (Jackson High School), "Friday Night" (Jackson High School), "It's All Happening" (Jackson High School), "Legendary" (Truman High School), and "Cross the Line" (Jackson High School). By looking at the choreography in conversation with the practice of cheerleading historically, I argue that Blankenbuehler's work strategically choreographs the overarching ensemble body in order to promote a sharp juxtaposition between the majorly white, Truman High School and the predominantly non-white, Jackson High School socially, economically, and racially. Additionally, the dialogue between the forms of cheerleading and dance works to frame the cheerleading ensemble body and the dancing ensemble body in such a way that reveals and practices social and historical tensions of race, class, gender, and sexualization. Highlighting these tensions through the choreography transmits such narratives to an audience, even if they are not explicitly addressed within the text of the musical.

Blankenbuehler carefully blends cheerleading, dance, and heightened gesture to create a choreographic score that allows the audience to absorb what they are watching. For example, there may be a high-flying stunt in one location of the stage, followed by a slow dance movement in another location. Generating such fluidity between styles prevents the choreography from becoming ineffectual, for the audience is kept on the edge of their seat, waiting to see when the next high-flying stunt will happen. Keeping the audience energized in this way can help the choreography hold a strong position of importance to the narrative. In Jonathan Burrows's *A Choreographer's Handbook,* he suggests, "Virtuosity raises the stakes to a place where the audience knows something may go wrong. They enjoy watching this negotiation with disaster. Will the performer fall, or forget what they're doing, or will they get through it?"[8] The cheerleading ensemble body, in particular, enhances this negotiation with disaster due to their performance of high-risk maneuvers. Audiences enjoy watching skill; it keeps them invested in what is going to happen next.[9] Burrows adds, "However, if everything is virtuosic then there's nothing against which to read the virtuosity: it has to be in balance with other modes of engagement."[10] If the choreography were all cheerleading all the time, the juxtaposition between cheerleading and dance that communicates a narrative regarding sociocultural tensions would lose its potential to create meaning. As the audience leans in to witness such presentation of skill, they are also consuming what socially inscribed bodies are executing these movements, which in turn can call attention to or challenge the idea of who is "able" to perform what and how.

Blankenbuehler uses the dialogue between virtuosity and ensemble body to both illustrate and perform the relationships between race, class, gender, sexuality, cheerleading, and dance. Both of these styles frame the individual ensemble bodies to inform the overall message of the show. Using professional cheerleaders as cheerleading ensemble bodies and professional dancers as dancing ensemble bodies allows Blankenbuehler to accentuate further the layered differences between cheerleading and dance. For instance, the virtuosic cheerleading ensemble bodies are mostly white. When there are moments of high-flying stunts featuring white female bodies, audiences connect to those bodies as focal points, drawing attention to such an exhibition of whiteness within the form of cheerleading. whiteness becomes implicated as an obligatory component of cheerleading virtuosity. The non-white virtuosic cheerleading ensemble bodies, like Bethea, are obscured for the first half of the show to keep the focus on whiteness as a standard component of cheerleading. Conversely, by including a higher number of diverse bodies within the dance numbers of the entire production, non-whiteness becomes an ineluctable narrative element of dancing virtuosity, particularly hip-hop dancing virtuosity. Hip-hop's socioeconomic/sociopolitical relationship with minoritarian groups becomes elevated through these non-white virtuosic dancing ensemble bodies facilitating a strong juxtaposition between the forms.

Moreover, cheerleading and dance alike have historically become associated with femininity. Within each, there have been precise expectations regarding gendered roles and gendered aesthetics. For contemporary cheerleading, flyers in stunts are always female. Female cheerleaders wear skirts, while male cheerleaders wear pants. Additionally, female cheerleaders are often stereotyped as skinny, white, blonde girls, and male cheerleaders are often assumed to be gay or less manly. The number "It's All Happening" challenges these clichés and fosters acceptability of individuality through both the text and the ensemble bodies featured in the choreography. The all-female identifying hip-hop crew must recruit male bodies to create a cheerleading squad successfully. These male ensemble characters, specifically males of color, resist at first citing such stereotypes before giving in and participating. By the end of the production, the hip-hop dance crew becomes a champion-level cheerleading squad representing ensemble bodies of color and all genders, subverting the preconceived, predetermined notions regarding race, class, gender, sexuality, and virtuosity. The cheerleading virtuosos, specifically the few cheerleader virtuosos of color, become more visible for "It's All Happening" in order to supply the new squad with a higher level of cheerleading authority and validity. Blankenbuehler's choreographic score for the now syncretic hip-hop/cheerleading dance crew/squad challenges historical juxtapositions of the forms, promoting a newly inclusive and reparative arena.

3.1 "What I Was Born to Do"—Truman High School: Producing Whiteness Through Cheerleading

In *Bring It On: The Musical,* the (mostly white) suburban school praises its nationally ranked cheerleading team while casting judgment on the diverse inner-city school that does not have a cheerleading team. In order to convince students of the inner-city school to change their hip-hop crew to a cheerleading squad, Campbell (the white cheerleader transfer from the suburban school) lies to her new friends, saying, "each member of the winning squad gets a scholarship to the college of their choice."[11] The character Danielle, who is Black and the head of the hip-hop crew, agrees to make a squad because of this potential for financial gain and upward mobility. In *Bring It On: The Musical,* cheerleading becomes a tool to highlight and challenge such historically marginalizing systems within the United States.

However, the culture surrounding the form has certainly evolved to be rather dramatic. Who falls? Who wins? Who loses? Cheerleading competitions can become seemingly the most important thing in a young person's life. Winning nationals, for example, is what squads train for tirelessly. Blankenbuehler remembers this from his pre-production research, "I started attending a lot of cheerleading competitions, which was unreal. I remember the first competition I attended. I have never seen such raw emotion, both high and low—crying like the world was ending, screaming like you learned how to fly. It was an unbelievable education to me. It was frightening."[12] Therefore, in developing the show, he wanted to recreate such emotional stakes for these characters. He said the tension created within the plot "can be about cheerleading, but I have to firmly know that it is life and death for that person. And then the decision about whether I do something or not does not feel like 'Oh, I'm a blonde girl who is spoiled and has everything.' It doesn't feel unimportant because it truly is life or death."[13] Still, strong ideas of gendered prescriptions, class expectations, and racial divides within the sport of cheerleading are woven into the threads of *Bring It On: The Musical.*

The general story follows high school senior and cheerleading captain Campbell, as she is redistricted from Truman High School to Jackson High School. Strong juxtapositions between the two schools become evident through the script, lyrics, music, labels, movement styles, and bodies. Truman High School, the suburban, mostly-white school, has a cheerleading squad that is incredibly influential to its daily life. The audience is introduced to this celebrated group in the opening number, "What I Was Born to Do." Jackson High School, the inner-city, more diverse school, does not have a cheerleading squad; instead, they have a dance crew. The audience is introduced to this group five numbers later in "We Ain't No Cheerleaders."

When Campbell finds out she is being redistricted, her friends comment on how "scary" Jackson is and explicitly point out that they do not have a cheerleading squad. One of her friends, Kylar (who, like the others, is a white cheerleader), presents this piece of gossip during their conversation: "The legends of old say that five years ago the Jackson cheerleaders were a rough group of girls. Like Hells Angels, but cheerleaders. At the Cornucopia Dance, they started a school-wide riot and held a gaggle of cafeteria ladies in a three-day hostage standoff. And so the Jackson cheerleading program was canceled until the End of Days."[14] At this point in the production, the audience has yet to be introduced to Jackson High School. Though the audience is unaware of the racial demographic of Jackson at this time, these lines set up a perception of Jackson by those who go to Truman using racial stereotypes revolving around words such as "rough" and "riot." Calling attention to the idea that the school *had* cheerleading, but the sport was taken away because of the young women's supposed actions is a subtext that cheerleading has been reserved for a culturally sanctioned space of regimented suburbia versus the "undisciplined" inner-city. This rumor instills a socially dictated perception of *who* will be the students at Jackson.

When Campbell enters Jackson High School for the first time, the rumor simmers in the background as the diverse ensemble of students enters the space. Therefore, by the time the hip-hop crew sings their introduction, "We Ain't No Cheerleaders," the audience has already garnered preconceived notions of these characters and the history associated with their group. When analyzing "What I Was Born to Do" directly beside "We Ain't No Cheerleaders," the numbers highlight the antagonism between the forms.[15]

Members of the Truman High School cheerleading squad (and their apparently adoring fans) sing the song on the left. Members of the Jackson High School dance crew sing the song on the right.

These Truman girls are super-human girls
And there is nothing that they can't do
And beyond all the squads
They're semi-demi-gods
And when our powers combined
We do what we were born to do

"What I Was Born to Do"

Sing it wit me if ya feel me
We don't get down with no pom-poms
(Hell to the naw)
When we roll through with our crew
No one can do what we do, it's true
But we would still do it if no one was watching
And let's be real, who could blame them for watching?

"We Ain't No Cheerleaders"

These numbers, in lyrics and choreography, are an introduction to the distinct differences between a cheerleading squad and a dance crew, socially and aesthetically. "What I Was Born to Do" promotes athleticism, discipline, elitism, and whiteness. "We Ain't No Cheerleaders" suggests flexibility, informality, community, and a sense of Blackness and Brownness. The number provides an opportunity for the minoritarian groups to present themselves, countering preceding processes of othering. They both provide insight into the socioeconomic/sociopolitical environments surrounding their activity. Further analysis will showcase how Blankenbuehler choreographed the ensemble bodies within each of these numbers, among others, to illuminate the sociohistorical tensions between these forms.

Blankenbuehler has asserted that dance is a frame that informs what the audience should feel, look at, or understand in a moment. For *Bring It On: The Musical,* cheerleading is an additional element of this framing device. What cheerleading adds, in terms of pure visual spectacle, is a multitude of levels and dimensions not typical of any dance genre. Taking into consideration for a moment, the frame in photography typically brings the viewer into the picture. To be clear, this is not the wooden object you put the photograph inside; this is a presentation technique used in visual art mediums to place a subject in relation to other elements. It not only has the potential to make the picture more visually appealing, but the frame provides further details and information. The frame creates specific focal points through the relations it establishes. For example, cheerleading has the ability to draw the eye of the viewer more vertically than dance. It generates the possibility for a viewer to engage more actively as their eye has to travel a further distance to absorb all of the picture. Therefore, if the ensemble is the lens for the broader, more overarching messaging for the show, then the relational positioning of a body high in the air for a cheerleading stunt literally elevates their significance and ability to impact how the show is creating meaning.

Beginning with the opening number of *Bring It On: The Musical,* cheerleading frames the socioeconomic milieu of the production. Virtuosic cheerleading ensemble bodies are specifically featured throughout to introduce the audience to the form's inherent racial, class, and gender bias. On the surface, the opening number "What I Was Born to Do" introduces the audience to Campbell, her passions, and the Truman High School cheerleading squad. But underneath, through the individual ensemble bodies, it positions the form of cheerleading and its practitioners as elite and predominantly white. For anyone unfamiliar with the *Bring It On* films, they get their first taste of how these laboring athletic women are sexualized and how those very same women are typically white, middle to upper-middle class. In this opening number, Blankenbuehler postures the ensemble bodies to function not only as characters within Truman High School but as the socially dominant aesthetic by which audiences are to compare Jackson High School against later on in the show.

Lights come up on a young woman, Campbell, standing alone, occupying the strongest space onstage, slightly downstage of center, body facing the audience. She begins praying to a higher power that she be elected captain of the squad following tryouts that evening. Campbell expresses that she has worked her "whole life to lead Truman High to Nationals."[16] Then, she begins singing about the first time she discovered a vocation that would become a driving force in her life. Her importance is quickly established, but so too is the significance of the ensemble. The ensemble begins cheering, "Go! Go! Go, Campbell! Go!" crossing through the dimly lit space, and two co-ed partner cheerleading stunts (one base and one flyer) go up. As the male bases extend their arms, the flyers stand on their two legs with their arms extended into a "high-V." The pairs are positioned to Campbell's downstage diagonals, creating a frame around her while they slowly turn clockwise. These two stunts are very simple yet mouth-dropping to an audience member who is not frequently exposed to the art of cheerleading stunts.

In Jonathan Burrows's *A Choreographer's Handbook*, he states, "The first things the audience see when a performance begins form a contract. This contract teaches the audience how to read the performance, at the same time as the performance is unfolding. The contract is the key to understanding the continuity that holds and gives sense to the piece."[17] Because cheerleading aesthetics have rarely been included within musical theatre, bringing in actual cheerleading right from the top of the show lays a new foundation for this specific production. Including high-flying stunts in the first three minutes of the production forms this contract, immediately indicating that *Bring It On: The Musical* will be unambiguously staging the sport of cheerleading and all of its natural spectacle. Thinking back to the previous chapter's discussion regarding authenticity, the utilization of authentic cheerleading movements aids in the adaptation of the environment and generation of energy. Incorporating stunts at the top of the show also has the potential to precipitate energy and excitement for something new and different. The opening establishes a promise that the audience will continue to be engaged and energized for the duration of the production.

Blankenbuehler's decision to implement these stunts as the initial choreography piece in the show initiates the contract between the production and the audience. By showcasing virtuosic cheerleading ensemble bodies first, a high amount of energy is effectuated between the performers and the audience. In the first two minutes of the show, they watch the performers negotiate with disaster—will they fall?[18] The typical Broadway space—sans cheerleading—is adapted to allow for this high-spirited sport to be reciprocally adapted for the stage. Blankenbuehler's positioning of the stunts on the left and right thirds of the space, as well as in the foreground of the stage picture, allow the viewer's eye to see these (white) athletic ensemble bodies before being redirected to Campbell at the top of this triangle. These ensemble bodies are dressed in typical high school cheerleading uniforms—white sneakers, short skirts, and sleeveless tunics. And, because these ensemble bodies are professional cheerleaders, their labor appears effortless. Campbell's assertion that she made a vow to become a cheerleader like those in front of her, previously labeling them as "superhuman," is augmented by these trophy-like displays. Becoming a cheerleader was her first goal; winning nationals would become her second goal. At nationals, the cheerleaders win a big trophy. At this moment, the cheerleading ensemble bodies function as character, spectacle, and iconographic metaphors of trophies concurrently.

During the lyrics, "Slow motion down the hall as kids all stop and stare," Campbell remains downstage center as the Truman High School squad fills in the space around her. Just to her upstage right diagonal is another cheerleader that will become instrumental to the story, Skylar. She is sitting on a male's shoulder. The eye is then drawn upward over Skyler's left shoulder, directly behind/above Campbell, to a cheerleader in a pyramid stunt. This cheerleader is being manipulated by her two male bases so that her legs look as though she is walking (on air). To Campbell's left is her boyfriend Steven, and a few other cheerleaders are positioned at various levels within this group. They all move as if they are walking and waving in slow motion. All of the male bases are costumed in some version of red and white attire, noting that they are a part of the squad; though, they are not dressed in their performance uniforms like the female cheerleaders.

The above section begins the introduction to cheerleading as a gendered form. To begin, the costuming for the opening establishes the notion that cheerleading for the female squad members is their everyday life persona. By placing these characters in their full cheerleading uniform, it dictates this as their foundational identity. The male cheerleaders have hints of costuming that indicate they have a position on the squad; but, by blending uniform and everyday attire, they become distanced from their identity as a cheerleader. To affirm their gendered role in society and resist the feminization of the label "cheerleader," the men are doing all of the "heavy" liftings inferring that they have more laboring power. They lift the women who are tossing their hair, checking their make-up, and giving the *Princess Diaries* "thank you for being here today" wave.[19] These young women are stereotypically set up, at first, as being more delicate and concerned with their image. What is additionally vital to note about this featured group of cheerleaders is the members are mostly white.[20]

On the edges of the stage, forming a triangle around the featured cheerleaders, are other students from Truman High School. Dressed in everyday clothing, this group takes varied levels lower than those on the same plane as them in the featured center group. In other words, the cheerleader stunt in the back is at an extremely high level, and as a result, those ensemble members on the floor next to them are standing. Those on the same line as Campbell are at the lowest level, and they are kneeling. The differences in height between the cheerleader group and the student group keep the focus on the cheerleaders. They are glorified by the bodies lower than them. All of these students are facing into center stage and are positioned in dimly lit lighting. The bodies of these ensemble members also make up a more racially diverse demographic. The diverse student ensemble is set apart from the far less diverse group of cheerleaders setting up the ties between whiteness and the sport.

As the song continues, Campbell, Skylar, Kylar, and Steven exit the stage. The ensemble takes over singing the chorus: "These Truman girls are superhuman girls ... " The Truman High School students (non-cheerleaders) spread out amongst the stage. The racially diverse ensemble bodies are located much further upstage. An audience member watching this, especially from the orchestra section of the house, may not be focused on those bodies, as they are occupying the weakest spot on the stage. This suggested focus, then, directs the audience to understand the perceptively white ensemble bodies as holding a more dominant position within Truman. The downstage bodies move to stage left toward the cheerleaders as they reenter. The upstage bodies are unmasked; however, they plié their stage right leg so their bodies lean backward. Their focus is then directed to downstage right and upward, where the cheerleaders set up for a stunt that then files diagonally upstage, replacing the bodies that once occupied that space (now having repositioned themselves to upstage left). This stunt is called a "show and go," where the flyer is put straight up into a full with feet together and then taken back down to the ground in one fluid motion. By lowering their bodies and facing themselves in anticipation of the upcoming, high-flying spectacle, those non-cheerleading bodies are still kept out of focus. If these bodies are continually manipulated, so they are not the focus, why have them on stage at all? Simply put, to populate the space. Choreographing these bodies in such a way that they can be students of Truman without dismantling the crux of the story (suburbia vs. inner city) allows for the ensemble bodies portraying Truman cheerleaders to be more palpable.

One trope of the *Bring It On* saga is the "roll call cheer." "Roll call cheers" are used to introduce the individual cheerleaders by name to the crowd. For example, the iconic opening of the original *Bring It On* film is the roll call cheer for the Toros, "She's perky, she's fun! And now she's number one! K kick it, Torrance! T T T Torrance!"[21] *Bring It On: The Musical* has a similar moment in "What I Was Born to Do." It begins with Skylar, followed by Kylar, then the mascot Bridget. During each of these features, the ensemble is spread out around the individual speaking. The ensemble is positioned at lower levels or angled so that Skylar and Kylar are the focus.

Being angled toward someone is not, of course, the only way to give them focus. When Bridget scurries from upstage left to downstage right, the ensemble abruptly shields their faces from her. Each body onstage is positioned differently. Those bodies further downstage take an abstract position on the floor. Those further upstage take varied levels, contorting their bodies. The sharp contrast between facing and glorifying the previous two cheerleaders to awkwardly and outrightly blocking oneself from the mascot creates a unique antithesis to be deconstructed. The character of Bridget is written to be quirky, curvy, and unathletic. She takes on the popular trope of someone who was not attractive or popular enough to be a cheerleader, so she was given the seemingly lower-level position of mascot. The rejection of her existence portrayed by the bodily postures of the entire cast of characters onstage affirms the stereotype that female cheerleaders must be fetching, slender, and thus popular. Looking at Bridget through the lens of the ensemble bodies labels her as a type of other in this world. Such labeling will come to be important when Bridget is also redistricted but has a less stressful time assimilating to Jackson High School. As Bridget is desexualized at this moment, the window becomes wider for the female cheerleaders to be subject to just the opposite.

Even though there are plenty of male cheerleaders on the Truman High School squad singing this song, the sport is feminized and sexualized through the lyrics continually referring to the squad members as "girls." The final roll call is for Steven, the only time a male cheerleader is featured. Steven is the stereotypical "Ken Doll" type: athletic, tall, blonde hair, and blue eyes. When this moment happens, he objectifies his female counterparts in his lyrics: "What's up, my name is Steven I'm so (handsome it hurts) / Don't need an umbrella, I stand under miniskirts (What!) / Yeah, I'm a (boss), I don't care what the haters say / (How many dudes can say they pick up girls all day?)."[22] As these lyrics begin, a female ensemble cheerleader does a roundoff (a cartwheel where the feet come together in the middle) toward Steven. When she is upside down during this move, he bends down, and she flips over his downstage shoulder and pushes up into the hands of the male base standing behind Steven. The male base catches her foot, and she stands on one leg with the other in a heal-stretch. Steven stands underneath her. This action calls attention to the underneath of the female flyer's skirt, placing this space of the female body in direct conversation with the male bodies surrounding it. Steven moves to downstage center as the original partner stunt to his right and an additional partner stunt to his upstage left enter shoulder stands. The flyers tip toward stage right into the arms of two different bases, which then push them straight back up to where they were (almost like a Weeble Wobble)—once again, placing the male cheerleaders in a position of power. They are seen as the support system lifting the female cheerleaders; what goes unseen is the intense athletic labor of the core and other muscles being engaged by the female cheerleader.

Based on the production I watched, I believe it is important to note that the front group was perceivably white bodies.[23] However, in the back group, the base who catches the flyer then pushes her back up in the Weeble Wobble is a man of color. He is not in the focal point of the stunt, but he does labor to make the stunt work. His placement as a cheerleader on the Truman squad becomes an interesting pause point for investigation. The performer in question is Antwan Bethea. According to the Playbill for the production, he was a cheerleader for East Carolina University and a professional cheerleader for the North Carolina NBA team, the Charlotte Bobcats, making him one of the twelve professional cheerleader ensemble bodies in the cast.[24] Furthermore, out of the twelve professional cheerleader ensemble bodies, he is one of three bodies of color. In a personal interview with Bethea, he recounted:

> One reason I believe I was cast was because of my unique look; a young, black male with dreadlocks. Without a doubt, my appearance screams "Jackson High School," but in a pair of brown slacks, collared shirt, and my hair pulled back, I was a Truman prep. With help from the wardrobe and hair department, every ensemble member had a Truman side and a Jackson side. Don't get me wrong, in the Jackson scenes, I was definitely featured more than my stunt partner, Courtney, a petite, blonde white girl from Texas. Naturally, she was featured more than I was in the Truman scenes.[25]

Although his skills are necessary to help portray an award-winning cheerleading squad, to keep the apparent racial juxtaposition between Truman and Jackson clear, his body could not be in focus.

Immediately following the "roll call" section just discussed, there is a breakout scene where it is announced who on the squad is to be awarded the title of captain. Transitioning into this scene from the two stunts just discussed, the group downstage right crosses and joins the principal cheerleaders (Campbell, Skylar, Kylar, and Steven) downstage left. The main base and flyer from the upstage stunt also cross downstage right. Bethea, however, makes an exit upstage right and is not present in this focused moment. Bethea reflected, "I would ask myself, 'what motives and choices are made by a young, black kid in a preppy school?'"[26] One of these motivating factors was the very idea of not standing out and blending in when necessary. Bethea provided some critical insight into the relationship behind this idea of blending in and Blankenbuehler's creative process. He noted:

> I was fortunate enough to be the Cheer/Stunt Captain on the 2nd (Inter)National Tour, which gave me a different perspective of the production from an outsider's view. Watching a show more than once gives you the opportunity to discover something new happening on stage, something you may not have noticed before. Andy wanted the ensemble to always be acting in the moment but never taking any attention from the focal point, typically the principal actor on stage. He wanted there to always be cohesive movement, like a well-oiled machine, one moment flowing into the next. When I watched the show from the audience, it was like looking through a kaleidoscope: all the patterns, colors, and designs dancing around the focal point in the center. Of course, the lighting and wardrobe department played a role in that imagery, but the ensemble delivers the experience.[27]

Keeping cohesive movement in the ensemble while navigating a continually shifting focal point requires transition moments, such as the one described above. Transitions provide the audience with an opportunity to breathe and absorb what they just witnessed before the next moment begins. But, in these transitions, the narrative cannot stop; the piece's integrity must stay intact. So, even if this cohesive movement transitions from a stunt to walking to class (offstage), it plays an important role. Bethea's exit, accompanied by the exit of other diverse ensemble bodies, allows the focus to zero in on this specific group of (white) cheerleaders. Following this breakout scene, however, Bethea and others reenter. They do not just reenter to reenter. The next section requires the presence of cheerleader characters and thus cheerleading ensemble bodies. Those who exited for the breakout scene slowly come back into the space as if it is now cheerleading practice after school or sometime later at Cheer Camp. The action, as Bethea points out, is always motivated.

"What I Was Born to Do" attempts to highlight the mysticism of the female cheerleader, the outrageous expectation of perfection, superhuman, demi-gods. The cheerleaders build upon and counter this presumption of godliness by pointing out the work, the labor that goes into what they do. They have to train their bodies, fight for every stunt to stick, push every tumbling pass to be faster. The lyrics illuminate the notion of beauty with the mention of mani/pedis. An all too common stereotype projected upon women is they are too delicate to do work; they might break a nail. Here, there is the suggestion that although they may care about their looks, they still execute great physical exertion.

During this section, the spectacle ramps up. It is evident that the professional, virtuosic cheerleader bodies are now on the stage. As Campbell sings the lyrics discussed above, a series of dramatic tumbling passes and stunts begin around her. It is during this section that a sharp eye will notice the cheerleading ensemble body of Melody Mills. Previously in the number, Mills has blended in with the other Truman High School female cheerleaders. She has been consistently positioned on the ground in lower levels of elevation or upstage locations. Presumably, all of her moments leading up to this section have also been in softer lighting to not draw focus. Mills is a female body of color. The opening night Playbill cites that she "has danced and choreographed for the NBA, NFL and artists Jay-Z, Rihanna, Kayne West and Shakira."[28] It is not until this moment when the song switches from introducing the specific members of the Truman High cheerleading squad to highlighting the work performed by the cheerleaders that Mills is featured.

As Campbell counters toward downstage right to open the floor for this section, Mills and another female cheerleader complete synchronized roundoff back handspring, back-tucks from downstage right into the arms of male cheerleaders upstage left. Mills is in the group further downstage. Out of the male cheerleaders' arms, the two then tumble back to their starting positions, completing a roundoff into a roundoff, layout, step-out. A "layout, step-out" is when the person tumbling goes back into what seems like a backflip; however, the body is not tucked in; it is flat. The tumbler then separates their legs midair and lands on one foot, followed by the other, rather than landing with two feet together. The spectacle of these tumbling passes draws the audience's eye to those bodies rather than to Campbell, who is in a spotlight downstage right. Even though they are crossing to a weaker position on stage and are in a more dimly light space, this type of movement's impact is far more significant than the bodies themselves onstage. The virtuosity and the athleticism of the bodies supersede other elements of their individual dramaturgy.

As the sequence develops, both Mills and Bethea are active in the creation of awe-inspiring pyramids. Pyramids occur when more than one stunt becomes connected to make a cohesive tableau. Bethea is a base for the stage right section, while Mills is a flyer for the center section. Mills, however, is lower than the other two flyers, propping them up to be the focus. The stunt Mills is in eventually comes down, and she puts her back to the audience and points up to each of the fliers remaining in the air. These two flyers, perceptively white cheerleading ensemble bodies, are more brightly lit than Mills. The audience's full attention is on these two bodies. These stunts complete a twist down cradle. A twist down is when the bases slightly throw the flyer up out of their hands; she makes one full rotation with her body, then is caught in their arms in a cradle position.

Finally, the moment comes where Campbell, Broadway actress Taylor Louderman, is integrated into the world of cheerleading. Up until the end of the song, her feet have remained firmly on the ground. She is put into one of the simplest stunts in cheerleading, a half. A half is where the flyer stands on the hands of two bases, with the support of a back base, with her feet apart and level with the chests of the bases. On either side of her, professional cheerleaders complete twist up, show-and-goes. Taking one foot in the hands of the bases, the bodies of the flyers twist up to full extensions (above the bases' heads), then immediately back down. They back walkover out of these stunts. One of these flyers is Mills. But, the focal point is Campbell, who is in the middle, taking attention away from Mills's ensemble body.

Behind Campbell is the first basket toss of the production. A basket toss is where bases make a "basket" with their hands, using one hand to grab their own wrist and their other hand to grab the opposite base's wrist. The flyer is then put into this basket by the back base. From the basket, the flyer is launched into the air. She is able to complete several different skills while in the air before coming back down and being caught in a cradle position. In this instance, the flyer completes a toe touch. A basket toss can be jaw-dropping, especially to a viewer who has rarely seen them executed, if at all. The fast pace of each of these stunts is consistently pulling focus for an audience member.

When Campbell comes out of the stunt, she completes a simple pop-down dismount. A "pop-down" is when the flyer's feet are put together, and she is lowered straight to the floor. Arguably the simplest of dismounts, it removes any risk of injury for Louderman but still incorporates her into the world of cheerleading. Campbell's stationary position in the center stunt allows for all of these moments to be seen in relation to her. Though she is completing the first thing learned in Stunting101, she is supported by professionals performing thrilling stunts to distract the audience from the simplicity. André Lepecki suggests that curating an audience's perspective is crucial "to unify and harmonize the viewer's gaze with representational, theological, and discursive powers."[29] In art, photography, and architecture, a central vanishing point is defined as a point of convergence, often on the horizontal plane, where receding parallel lines meet and seem to disappear. By organizing the moments onstage in a triangle around Campbell, she seemingly becomes this single point that grounds the eye. The audience then operates in two ways: first, with an immobile eye focusing on this point; second, using peripheral sight through the visual pyramid surrounding the focal point. Lepecki contends that this creates a reduction of what is produced onstage:

> [W]hat is reduced in perspective is not only the tridimensionality of space, but the embodied nature of perception as the corporeal grounding of sensation surrenders itself to algorithms of visibility. What is lost then is the embodiment of vision by the means of an operation that subtracts from perception our stereoscopic, decentered, constantly moving eyes and replaces them with an artificially monocular monomaniacally fixed point of view.[30]

As the audience focuses on the action and the character of Campbell, what is surrendered is the acknowledgment of the corporeality of these performers. The kaleidoscope of action, as Bethea observed, moves the eyes of the spectator so that no one thing is focused on for too long, removing the possibility of in the moment, in-depth analysis.

In his interview with Lyn Cramer for *Creating Musical Theatre,* Blankenbuehler noted this:

> I view a lot of choreography as impressionist painting. So, when you see such a painting, your eye is forced to go to the focal point … Sometimes you don't want to know where to look because that mayhem makes the focus resonate. In general, you want to have a focal point. What's around the focal point tells the audience how to feel about the focal point, and that's what the artist says in an impressionist painting. That's what I view as texture. Focus is the narrative line ….If I've done my job well, I'm not looking at the other dancers. I'm only looking at the focal point … However, my brain is taking in the feeling around them, and that's what I call texture.[31]

Although Campbell is positioned as the focal point, the audience concurrently sees her and the texture of action surrounding her in their periphery. Her simplistic stunt choreography could call attention to her lack of cheerleading skills; however, the surround of virtuosic cheerleading ensemble bodies provides a lens that elevates the perception of her ability. If a still photograph were taken of this action, Campbell would be the focal point of the image. Attention could be directed toward her simplicity, but nevertheless she is doing a stunt alongside more intricate stunts. The ephemerality of the action keeps the eye of the viewer constantly moving. This allows Blankenbuehler to create the illusion that she is the fixed point of view but compels the audience to see her through the lens of the moving ensemble bodies.

Despite the movement controlling the stereoscopic experience and the number's texture, Blankenbuehler has still tended to which bodies he wants to aim the focus or the corresponding narrative line. In the next to last stunt in this number, two halves go up on either upstage corner and are angled toward downstage center. Mills is the flyer upstage right. In front of them, with their backs to the audience, two additional flyers step into their own stunts on one foot and are brought to a full extension keeping the weight on that singular foot. Bethea is a base for one of these stunts; his back is also to the audience. The flyers then step the open foot into the hands of the flyers in the two half stunts putting their weight onto that foot. They kick the foot that was previously in the male bases' hands into the air, then fall into a cradle. Mills and the other flyer in the half become lifting laborers alongside the male bases. Focus is on the higher-flying flyers, which are white bodies. The through-line that illuminates the sociohistorical connection between whiteness and cheerleading stays intact. However, the textured surround challenges this whiteness by including ensemble bodies of color.

Once the stunts are complete, the ensemble is spread out on stage, performing cheerleading-like dance movements, including jumps. For the final stage picture, the female cheerleaders complete a roundoff double back handspring toward upstage. Two of these cheerleaders enter into a final stunt, a full-extension liberty. A liberty is a one-legged stunt, where the free leg is bent, tucking the foot to the weight-bearing knee. All ensemble members make their way to the edges of the stage, outside of the line that signifies a competition cheerleading mat. The stage is clear, with the exception of these two stunts upstage, just off-center, and Campbell center stage. All bodies except Campbell and the two flyers are in dim lighting. Now still, unmoving, these three white cheerleading character bodies are the exclamation point on the number.

"What I Was Born to Do," on the surface, introduces the audience to Campbell, Truman High School, and the sport of cheerleading. But through an analysis of the specific choreographic scores of the ensemble, the number also introduces the audience to the nuances of race and class bias inherent in the form of cheerleading. This subtext is a key plot element for the entire production. While it is not necessarily discussed explicitly, the dramaturgy of the choreography and of the ensemble bodies functions as a supplemental narrative line that informs the audience how to feel about or understand the primary action.

3.2 "Yo, Hip-Hop Is Our National Pastime": Hip-Hop and the Crew

Before analyzing the Jackson High School numbers, it is essential to discuss a brief history of hip-hop as a signifier of both difference and community in *Bring It On: The Musical.* Throughout the *Bring It On* saga, hip-hop, specifically hip-hop dance, has been used as a way to introduce people of color and of minoritarian status as other. However, as the plot moves forward, hip-hop shifts functions to empower those once otherized people and become reflective of agency. The same is true for the musical. Hip-hop is layered with nuance; majoritarian (white) perspectives stigmatize it. Minoritarian groups embrace and activate hip-hop as a tool for unification and identity transmission. The creators of *Bring It On: The Musical* used hip-hop as it relates to music, dance, and identity as a key contrasting component to separate Truman and Jackson. Such a juxtaposition concludes in a reparative narrative that uplifts the marginalized characters and attempts to legitimize their practice of hip-hop in the majoritarian public sphere of the Varsity National Cheerleading Competition.[32]

According to Patrick Hinds of the *Broadway Backstory* podcast for TodayTix, "Knowing that the music for the show would need to have two distinctly different sounds for the music of Truman High School and the music of Jackson High School, Andy wanted to bring on two different music writers."[33] He first approached Tom Kit for the Truman High School music and then Lin-Manuel Miranda for the Jackson High School music. Miranda recalls being wooed by Blankenbuehler to work on the project, "I said, 'I don't know if I have a whole score in me.' He goes, 'I don't want you to write the whole score.' I was like, 'what?' And he goes, 'I would like you to split it with Tom Kitt and you guys kind of write the rival schools.'" Amanda

Green, who was added to the team as a lyricist, remembered, "So what it started out was, it wasn't a strict division of Truman and Jackson, of the two high schools, although it was roughly that, it was more of a division of the kinds of songs. Pop songs would be Tom and I, and the hip-hop songs would be Lin ... "[34] Despite Green signifying a less apportioned relationship between the two schools than initially intended in the end result, the general use of pop songs for Truman and hip-hop songs for Jackson created enough of a contrast that positioned the schools' respective soundscapes as identifiable characteristics.

Similarly, in *Bring It On: The Musical,* the hip-hop crew is framed by these U.S.-based phenomenologies that connect hip-hop music and "otherness". While not all of the hip-hop dancing bodies in the production are Black bodies, as Wright notes, it is not the location of Blackness in the body that otherizes them. The hip-hop crew is, at first, positioned as other due to its association with hip-hop as antithetical to majoritarian musical and social conventions. The hip-hop dancing bodies in *Bring It On: The Musical* become unequivocally opposite to the cheerleading bodies. In his piece "The Black Beat Made Visible: Hip Hop Dance and Body Power," Thomas DeFrantz argues,

> These listeners and dancers come, I think, to physically invest in the enactment of cool dissention; they learn the dances for obvious associations of physical power contained within the dancing body magnified by the crucible of race. If these dancers can empower impoverished black bodies of the inner city, surely they might offer dynamic celebration to young dancers in the vanilla suburbs.[35]

The hip-hop crew in *Bring It On: The Musical* is highly demonstrative of DeFrantz's statement. In 1977, the Rock Steady Crew became one of the first hip-hop dance crews formed in the Bronx. It was "an outlet for inner-city youth who were otherwise ignored by mainstream institutions, including the government and schools."[36] Jackson High School's hip-hop crew honors this history.

During the song "Friday Night," audiences are introduced to the importance of the inner-city Jackson High School hip-hop dance crew as an outlet for expression and fraternity. The title of this section, "Yo, hip-hop is our national pastime," is a line in the song sung by the character Cameron, played by Black American male actor Dominique Johnson.[37] In "Friday Night," audiences witness what the hip-hop crew looks like in action for the first time after observing the Truman High School cheerleading squad's performance. As previously indicated, the very label of "dance crew" is set up as a hip-hop variant to counter the cheerleading "squad."

When Campbell first meets Nautica, La Cienega, and Danielle, the lead members of the Jackson High School hip-hop dance crew, the interaction goes as follows:

Campbell Can I just say, your dancing, I thought your dancing was amazing?

Danielle Why, thank you. We work hard at it.

Campbell If you need someone else on your squad, I've got a ton of experience

Danielle Squad? We're a crew … a hip-hop crew.

Campbell Oh, sorry! My people call it a squad.[38]

Danielle walks away from Campbell in silence. Nautica and La Cienega vocally react and then call out Campbell's unknowing mistake. She naively meant "cheerleaders" as "her people," but it is obviously set up to seem as though she meant "white people." This scene precedes the number "We Ain't No Cheerleaders." What *is* the difference between a squad and a crew, cheerleading, and dance? Why is the subtext of this scene, as well as the lyrics of its correlating song, loaded with social, political, and economic issues? Does that subtext relate to the activity, the bodies performing the activity, or both? As a byproduct of the genre of hip-hop, hip-hop dance crews have been directly linked to people of color (specifically Black Americans). *Bring It On: The Musical* includes this connection as a clear plot point to counter the association of cheerleading and whiteness. Subsequently, the individual ensemble bodies who are choreographed as focal points in these numbers reflect the associated demographics.

3.3 "We Ain't No Cheerleaders" on a "Friday Night"—Jackson High School: Producing or Subverting Other Through Hip-Hop

"Do Your Own Thing" precedes "We Ain't No Cheerleaders" and moves the audience from the world of Truman High School to the diametrically opposed Jackson High School. "Do Your Own Thing" serves several purposes. First, it suggests Jackson has a rougher, less friendly atmosphere than Truman—as evident by the action of the live production and the stage directions in the libretto that read: "A metal detector onstage. Campbell arrives at school among a line of students passing through but she's the only one who sets it off."[39] Campbell's reaction to the alarm is, "Oh God, I didn't know—uh, hang on—" as she empties out her belongings. Campbell is met by a collective command "Move!" then two bars of music containing banging noises before another "Move!" from the Jackson High School students.[40] Second, the number establishes an entirely new set of vocabulary for the audience, hip-hop dance. And third, it sheds light on Campbell's less-than-unconscious bias toward both the students and the environment of the inner-city school. The use of hip-hop music, dance, and identification generate a new contract between the production and the audience. Therefore, by the time the audience reaches "We Ain't No Cheerleaders," the juxtaposition between the sociocultural milieu of the schools has already been established: upper-middle-class versus working-class, white bodies versus bodies of color, pop music versus hip-hop music, cheerleading versus hip-hop dance.

To visually signify the sociohistorical connection between hip-hop and demographics, Blankenbuehler creates a significant pivot in the ensemble bodies he prioritizes as focal points. At this moment in the show, the cheerleading ensemble bodies can take somewhat of a back seat, especially the white cheerleading ensemble bodies. The dancing ensemble bodies, a much more diverse population, are able to become a central focus. The ensemble body functions similarly to "What I Was Born to Do," promoting a narrative line that connects the historical associations of a form to the production through embodied practice.

In "What I Was Born to Do," Blankenbuehler commonly altered the stage positioning of groups of white bodies or bodies of color to call attention to the whiteness of the Truman High cheerleading squad. For the choreographic scores of Jackson High School, he is able to call attention to the diversity of the school by emphasizing individual bodies throughout the numbers so they can each be seen and read. There is minimal synchronized movement or flashy spectacle as there is in "What I Was Born to Do." These individual choreographic scores feature hip-hop-based dance movements. Blankenbuehler primarily features bodies of color throughout the Jackson High School numbers. Because the vocabulary at the top of the show set up the cheerleading, and by proxy whiteness, as the frame by which the audience understands the show, these hip-hop moving bodies of color are still positioned as antithetical to that idea. These characters become viewed as other, at least for the first twenty minutes or so of their stage time.

When Campbell enters the space through the metal detector center stage, the orchestrations are very percussive, almost as if it were an anxious heartbeat. The hip-hop-based dance movements through this section accompany the punctuated beats. Hip-hop is known for isolating body movements in such a percussive manner. Susan Leigh Foster states, "Specific features in the choreography of each genre, whether b-boying, popping, or roboting, manifested metaphors of strength and savy."[41] She continues highlighting popping, " … through its mastery of flow and explosion invoked the oppositions of powerlessness and power, enslaved and emancipated, inner bodily space and outer, threat of destruction and empowerment."[42] Her profound assertions become visceral when the audience witnesses Antwan Bethea, now featured downstage right at the top of the number "Do Your Own Thing." As Campbell makes her way around the stage, asking for help with navigating the new school, she moves to Bethea, who is performing an individualized hip-hop-based dance score. At this moment, everyone onstage is relatively still or engaging in quotidian-based movement (i.e., getting books out of one's locker), ensuring that this interaction will be the focal point. Bethea, dressed in black, baggy clothing, and long dreadlocks, dances toward her (centerstage). She walks backward, almost running away, as he "pops" at her. Bethea's hip-hop virtuosity and power position at this moment invoke a dismantling of norms for Campbell's character and the audience. The rumors that have been previously told to the audience are affirmed; Jackson High School will move and look differently to Truman. Consequently, Campbell will have less power at Jackson.

DeFrantz suggests that hip-hop dances "gain power from their subversive (black) stance outside the moral law of (white) America. The black body in America has long been legislated and controlled by political systems both legal and customary. In social dance, the black body achieves a freedom from traditional American strictures defining legitimate corporeality."[43] However, for a typical Broadway audience, the choreographed hip-hop maintains an indisputable connection to marginalized groups, informing how they read the bodies doing the movements. In "Do Your Own Thing," the hip-hop indeed functions as an othering tool. It is not yet free from the strictures; it is not yet a legitimate corporeality, for the juxtaposition between Truman and Jackson is still too palpable.

In the first moments of *Bring It On: The Musical,* the audience heard and witnessed the Truman cheerleading squad's pronouncement of self before preconceiving any assumptions about their group, the people in the group, and their practice. But, by the time the audience reaches the Jackson hip-hop crew's first number, they have already signed and accepted the "contract" for the Truman vocabulary; they have received information and judgments regarding Jackson. Nevertheless, I argue that it is with "We Ain't No Cheerleaders" that the use of hip-hop switches from an otherizing tool to an articulation of difference and uniquity. "We Ain't No Cheerleaders" is a moment for the audience to pause and hear the Jackson hip-hop crew identify themselves and their functions. The number attempts to demystify those conceptions through their lyrics and choreography. In theory, this number allows "hip-hop" to create difference and distinction without othering, becoming a method of empowerment and character development. However, the hip-hop crew dances little to no hip-hop in this number. Instead, the performing bodies of color, labeled as "hip-hop," are accompanied by familiar Broadway-style choreography challenging the expectations and stereotypes previously imposed upon the crew. This is the first time in the show that the audience is not confronted with an adventitious movement style.

Another one of Jonathan Burrows's choreography principles is "familiar movement." He claims, "Sometimes recognizable movement frees the audience from having to work out what they're seeing, enough that they notice more important things … Sometimes, however, recognizable movement becomes a subject so strong—for instance the subject 'contemporary dance,' or 'ballet'—that we don't notice anything else at all."[44] Blankenbuehler's choreographic score for the first thirty-five minutes of the show is relatively unlike anything Broadway audiences are used to seeing. Although he utilizes musical theatre dance throughout, the coalescence of cheerleading with musical theatre and hip-hop with musical theatre is unfamiliar to the majority of the audience. Therefore, they are asked to take in a great deal of information, working out what they are witnessing in the moment. Using primarily musical theatre dance for "We Ain't No Cheerleaders" offers the audience a moment to breathe and not have to process the movement, but rather process the ideas surrounding the movement. Blankenbuehler's use of musical theatre dance creates distance between the bodies of the hip-hop crew members and the implications concerning hip-hop as being rough and less congenial. Broadening the hip-hop crew's movement vocabulary unseats such misconceptions by reframing the dancing bodies as having the capacity to adapt to different environments or situations.

As suggested in the lyrics highlighted above, the number "We Ain't No Cheerleaders" is instantly juxtaposed to "What I Was Born to Do" in the first line. It proposes the idea that, even though there is an audience when the group performs, they dance for themselves rather than for the applause. When it is suggested that they are a squad (a term used to classify the group of white cheerleaders at Truman High School), they are quick to establish a new vocabulary, calling themselves a crew and insisting that they do not "rah-rah, sis boom bah." The notion of class is then brought up when the members of the dance crew call out the fact that they have to work for everything they have—suggesting that even their life outside of the dance crew is more of an uphill battle than the white cheerleader from Truman High School to whom they are singing. The characters performing this number are people of color connecting ideas of race and class. Both of these socially inscribed labels of identity are also potentially illuminated in the dialect suggested through the lyrics. So, what of the choreography and its relationship to the ensemble bodies?

A majority of the song is sung through as the characters walk around the stage. There are pockets of dance movements that never exceed an "eight-count" in length. Any movements enacted are done so by ensemble bodies of color. None of the white-ensemble bodies are onstage at this moment.[45] The dance movements are all relatively subtle: a few body rolls and gentle arm accents. Individuals within this small group have an opportunity to "show off" their dance skills as members of the hip-hop crew. As Danielle sings, "Now would a cheerleader do this?" an individual ensemble member executes a series of three or four movements, all of which add up to, at the most, "jazz-funk," not hip-hop.[46] For example, the first ensemble member windmills her arms from right to left, extends her right leg in a slow battement, and ends with a chaîné toward upstage.[47] Then, when Danielle sings, "Now would a cheerleader do that?" a second member executes a few undefined arm sways and a grand plié.[48] None of the movements in this number are particularly noteworthy. Still, in the moment, the audience hears that these bodies are a hip-hop crew while visually receiving and digesting movement they recognize.

Despite the relatively unexciting number, in comparison to the awe-inspiring cheerleading stunts of "What I Was Born to Do" and the thought-provoking hip-hop of "Do Your Own Thing," "We Ain't No Cheerleaders" produces a dissonance between hearing lyrics about hard work, skill, and nonconformance while witnessing graceful, mellow, and Euro-centered movement. Such dissonance subverts the hip-hop of "Do Your Own Thing" in order to reclaim the label and resituate the genre from the perspective of the crew rather than from the perspective of the ignorant squad. Even though the number did not actually produce much hip-hop, the audience was able to adjust their perceptions of Jackson High

School and the hip-hop crew, ultimately allowing for the return of hip-hop in "Friday Night." However, this time the bodies are not cast in a negative light; instead, they are seen as showcasing versatility, expressing ambition, and celebrating difference.

To transition into "Friday Night," the male ensemble bodies shift the physical scenery on stage, weaving in moments of hip-hop-based isolations. It is essential to point out that for this number, I will be using "male ensemble bodies" to mean "male scripted ensemble bodies." For this number only, a few of the professional female cheerleaders featured as flyers in stunts during the Truman High School numbers are hidden behind baggy clothing and hats, labeled as one of the "guys" in the scene, presumably to continue to the narrative of difference between Truman and Jackson without any hesitation. As the guys wait for the ladies of the crew to perform, several of the male ensemble members gesture as if they are straightening their "tie" with both hands accompanied by a slight head bobble. Others shrug their shoulders and "adjust" their "jackets" with the slight tug of a hand. They unite in a lunge forward onto one leg and thrust their hips forward and back on the lyrics, "We're waiting for the ladies / On Friday night."[49] Next, they square up to a partner locking in a handshake before breaking into individualized sequences. The scene builds as more and more male ensemble bodies enter the space and eventually all meet in a synchronous moment by the third "A' Get Your Hands Up!" as they rock in a deep second position, backs to the audience, between hands up overhead pointing stage left and hands down at the lap.[50]

Introducing the hip-hop crew through the lens of the enlivened male ensemble bodies sets up two key elements that will become important to understanding Jackson High's social dynamics: gender and sexuality. On a fundamental level, using language in the lyrics such as "ladies" and "girl" imprints the female gender onto the bodies of the hip-hop crew. Additionally, yelling "That's my girl in the middle of the crowd!" while enacting pelvic isolations conspicuously dictates a sexual connotation for the audience.[51] This overt use of gender labels in sexualizing the hip-hop crew is of particular note when considering prominent crew member La Cienega.

La Cienega is a female-identifying transgender character originally played by Gregory Haney. In an interview for *Broadway Backstory* book writer Jeff Whitty said this:

> The goal for me, from the very beginning was, I am going to put a trans character onstage, and then I am never going to talk about it

> the whole show. It is never going to be a discussion. There will never be that moment of after school special tears … just really, really make her absolutely the queen bee … La Cienega very often is the … one who is the voice of practicality … I object very strongly, saying that a trans character is *magical* … It's the equivalent of an archetype that people of color refer to the 'magical Negro' who is always coming in and sort of making white people's lives better. I didn't want to do that with a trans character either.[52]

Gregory Haney, himself, said this to *Broadway Backstory,* "I wanted her to be the powerful woman who walked in the room, and everybody had to look at her."[53] As hip-hop was used early in the show as a signifier of other, and La Cienega is one of the hip-hop crew's principal members, she initially takes on this label of other. Nonetheless, all of the characters in the show warmly accept La Cienega. Her identity has been well navigated far before the audience becomes involved in this moment of their lives. Seeing this moment through the male ensemble as they sexualize and fawn over the ladies of the crew assures the narrative of La Cienega's integration and embracement in their world is understood by the audience. Correspondingly, the hip-hop-based choreography score for all of the ensemble bodies (crew and non-crew, male and female scripted) during "Friday Night" now gestures toward more than racial acceptance, but also acceptance of gender identity—though there remains a distinct divide between male and female roles.

By choreographing only male scripted ensemble bodies in the crowd, a male gaze is produced, guiding the audience to read the female-identifying bodies in a sexualized way. Laura Mulvey's now-classic essay "Visual Pleasure and Narrative Cinema" coining the term "male gaze" has been appropriated to other disciplines such as dance. She writes, "In their traditional exhibitionist role women are simultaneously looked at and displayed, with their appearance coded for strong visual and erotic impact so that they can be said to connote *to-be-looked-at-ness.*"[54] It is obvious that if someone is performing, the objective is to be seen. Even so, this Friday night performance of the hip-hop dance crew is curated for the audience through how the male ensemble sees it. Mulvey elaborates, "As the spectator identifies with the main male protagonist … " (during the introduction of "Friday Night" the male ensemble is the main voice advocating for the watching of the ladies) " … he projects his look onto that of his like, his screen surrogate … " ("That's my girl") " … so that the power of the male protagonist as he controls events coincides with the active power of the erotic look ... " (pelvic-thrusting and pointing as the ladies enter the space) " ... both giving a satisfying sense of omnipotence."[55] She continues, "The male protagonist is free to command the stage, a stage of spatial illusion in which he articulates the look and creates the action."[56] The male ensemble set up the physical stage environment, dictating where the female bodies will go when they enter the space. They provided themselves with risers on which they can sit or stand and look down upon the girls from their position of power.

In a way, there is still a process of othering occurring during the choreography of "Friday Night," males othering the females. Juxtaposing the male/female ensemble bodies in this way establishes a narrative regarding an explicit gender dynamic within Jackson High School. Remember, in Truman High School, there were indeed male cheerleaders. While they, too, sexualized the female cheerleaders, they were on the squad together. There was a dampening of an us versus them mentality. Nevertheless, the incredibly specific gendered scripts within the form of cheerleading maintain a collocation. By establishing an assumed status quo of gender-based roles for the first half of the production, even if La Cienega is wholeheartedly accepted as female-identifying transgender student, when these rules become broken by the end of the show, the reparative nuance is received more strongly.

The crew, wearing tight leggings and shiny jackets, enters the space from the upstage left diagonal, an entrance Blankenbuehler asserts suggests "a child's perspective on life."[57] Choreographing their entrance from a location that is symbolic of naivety amplifies the power of the male bodies who hold more prominent stage positions. As they enter, they sing, "I know you came here just to see me tonight, / So what are you waiting for."[58] The crew performs a hip-hop-based dance sequence to an electronic music sound. Half of their sequence is choreographed with their backs to the audience. At one point, two ensemble males actually step between the crew dancers and the audience, taking a squat to watch the backs of the dancing ladies from a lower angle.

During the next section, Cameron sings: "Yo, hip-hop is our national pastime, / tick-tock, now it's 'shakin' that ass' time. / All a y'all are wishin' that ya lady was that fine—/ The little lady in the middle, yeah, that's mine!"[59] At this point, Danielle is on one of the risers, back to the audience, surrounded by the male ensemble and the crew. Twig steps in with lyrics that announce his lust for the character Bridget, who has switched places with Danielle. Twig's sexualization of Bridget is also remarkable here. At Truman High School, she was subjugated as the mascot. Her curvy figure and quirky personality caused her to be cast aside by the cheerleaders and marked undesirable. Now, at Jackson High School, she is being welcomed and championed by the hip-hop crew and its fans.

Another dance break erupts; this time, the girls are all in a line, fluidly moving their arms and rolling their bodies through various positions. Danielle steps out of the line to introduce Jackson High School's mascot, "Lucky McClover." Earlier in the show, Campbell reveals to Danielle that she felt lost without cheerleading until she learned about the crew. Danielle decides that for Campbell to join, she must prove her worth by performing in the Leprechaun suit "from the old days when Jackson was an Irish neighborhood."[60] Campbell enters the dance break wearing the Leprechaun suit. She begins dancing solo, and eventually, the crew circles around her and starts mirroring her dance moves. This staged improvised dance battle is reminiscent of early hip-hop dance crews:

> Dancing became a hobby that was practiced all night. Fierce competitions came to define these events; their leaders encouraged dance competitions between members of various crews and posses as acceptable means of establishing a group's reputation.
>
> Winning these competitions became another way of dueling between rival gangs. Rivalries between crews, as groups of dancers came to be known, were handled in "battles," [...] The battles became a foundational element of hip hop as the competitive element replaced gang violence with an emphasis on talent, expressiveness, and strategic moves as battle tactics.[61]

This staged battle allows for unique breakout moments for each member of the hip-hop dance crew and even some of the male ensemble members who attempt to jump in before being pushed out by crew members. Voyeurs on the periphery encourage dancers in the battle by pumping their fists and shouting, "Move!"[62] This "Move!" is an echo of the opening of "Do Your Own Thing!" However, like the hip-hop in "Do Your Own Thing," it was initially used as an aggressive distancing tool. Now, it is used as encouragement. The movements throughout the number are enthusiastically celebrated as Campbell becomes accepted into the group.

The music slows into a time-stop moment where Danielle vocally admires Campbell-the-Leprechaun's dancing. She sings, "Look at this little rich white girl turnin' it out, / Wow, I can't be mad at that."[63] During her lyrics, the rest of the hip-hop crew is lined up diagonally behind Campbell, mirroring her dance moves. As I have previously argued, this switch to synchronistic movement suggests acceptance and embracement.

When the music shifts back into "live" time, the girls all sing, "I know you came here just to see me tonight, / So what are you waiting for?"[64] At this moment, each hip-hop crew member is paired up with a different male ensemble member. Campbell and Danielle are paired. They all stand in pause. Remembering that pauses indicate significant moments, Blankenbuehler is signaling that much of the ensemble's objective was rooted in the sexualized exhibitions. Moreover, this pause allows the audience to see the gendered pairs in contrast to Campbell and Danielle, who had other objectives for the evening. Danielle wanted to see what Campbell had to offer. Campbell wanted to prove herself. During this battle, Campbell competed to be included by this group, using their movement genre—to the best of her ability anyway. In the dialogue following the number, Danielle expresses her surprise in and acceptance of Campbell. She remarks, "This crew is a family. So welcome to our family."[65]

3.4 "It's All Happening"—Jackson High School: Turning a "Crew" into a "Squad"

When Campbell becomes desperate to take down her nemesis Eva and her formerly beloved Truman High School cheerleading squad, she lies to Danielle and her peers at Jackson, convincing them to create a cheerleading squad, abandon their label as a hip-hop dance crew, and compete at the Varsity Nationals Competition. Reacting to Campbell's suggestion, Danielle immediately responds with, "You know what this reminds me of? Those movies, you know what I'm saying, where the white dude or white lady makes a trip to the scary 'inner city' and, you know, fixes dem colored folks right up!"[66] Campbell ironically assures her that is not the case. Desperate for a positive outcome, she lies to Danielle, saying the winner would get a twelve-part reality series on MTV, and each squad member would receive a scholarship to the college of their choice. Previously in the show, Campbell encounters Danielle working at a fast-food restaurant where she learns Danielle is saving up money for college. Capitalizing on Danielle's vulnerabilities, the lie works, and the crew begins recruiting boys to join their new squad. The number "It's All Happening" tracks the evolution of this journey, blending hip-hop and cheerleading along the way. Though the use of hip-hop dance is perhaps less explicit than it is in "Do Your Own Thing" or "Friday Night," the Blankenbuehlerized hip-hop does remain the prominent vocabulary. He further blends movement aesthetics to aid in the transition between hip-hop crew and cheerleading squad. Hip-hop continues to act as a frame of difference, but the heightened hybridity of pedestrian movement, hip-hop, musical theatre dance, and cheerleading begins to assimilate the embodied Jackson vocabulary into a more Truman-centered movement vocabulary.

Blankenbuehler's choreography for "It's All Happening" renegotiates ideas of who can be a cheerleader in terms of race, class, and gender. He gradually begins to integrate the ensemble bodies dismantling previous structures used to frame Jackson as non-cheerleader. The virtuosic cheerleading ensemble bodies of color, previously masked in the Truman numbers, start unveiling and activating their skill; they are no longer *just* ensemble bodies functioning as students of Jackson. The white virtuosic cheerleading ensemble bodies, previously masked in the Jackson numbers, are inserted to point to an acquiring of cheerleading as a Jackson vocabulary. Nevertheless, their moments are brief and far more reduced than their performance for Truman. To ensure that the audience's comprehension of Jackson High School's demographic remains intact, the dancing ensemble bodies of color still maintain prominence as the lens for the number over white ensemble bodies. To deconstruct the notion that belonging to a movement-based performance group at Jackson was reserved for female-identifying characters, the plot of the number and Blankenbuehler's corresponding choreography integrates male and female ensemble bodies. Commingling the varied categories of ensemble bodies further propels the reparative process.

The majority of the Act II opening number "It's All Happening" centers around recruitment for the new squad, specifically finding "the very best boys."[67] After all, they will be unable to win if they cannot perform exceedingly athletic stunts, and for that, they need "manpower." Danielle sings, "They gotta be strong and they gotta be fine."[68] The first quarter of the song follows Danielle, Nautica, La Cienega, Campbell, and Bridget assembling their new roster. All of the male ensemble members keep turning them down or avoiding them. Leading up to asking Twig, the ladies only employ quotidian movements—staying within realist conventions of interacting with people. The irony is not lost on the fact that Twig is the name given to the smallest male character who would unquestionably have a more difficult time acting as a base in a cheerleading stunt. Still, the ladies are desperate, and perhaps he could persuade some of his male friends to join. Two ensemble ladies walk downstage of Twig. Heightening their persuasive techniques, they turn their backs to the audience, place a hand on each of his shoulders, bend forward slightly, sway their hips, and then body roll toward him. La Cienega is behind Twig, mirroring the two female dancing ensemble bodies. Expressing his avidity for this proposition, and arguably for the enhanced sensuous attention he is receiving, Twig sings:

> What are y'all, scared?
> Ya think cheerin' is feminine?
> Then I'm a feminist swimmin'-in-women gentleman![69]

By highlighting the potential to be surrounded by skilled women on television captures the attention of other guys. Twig's perspective seemingly shuts down the preconceived notion that cheerleading is feminine due to its libidinous prospects, successfully enticing other males to join. Although his sentiments perpetuate the sexualization of the female body, he succeeds in disrupting the Jackson gender divide status quo.

As Twig sings, the male ensemble members onstage watch the female ensemble members walk away from him. They look at Twig on the beat after "feminine" then pivot their body toward him on the accented beat after "gentleman." A few male ensemble members jump toward Twig from stage right. Now in a clump stage right slightly behind Twig, they are opposite a group of female ensemble members who have gathered stage left. On the word "magnificent," (white) professional cheerleading ensemble member Courtney Corbeille is revealed through a quick twist up, show and go—she is lifted by two of the male members of this clump. Blankenbuehler surrounds Corbeille with diverse male ensemble bodies as she is brought back to the ground prompting the audience to understand her allure from their perspective. Then, Corbeille does a round-off, back handspring toward stage left and joins the group of female ensemble members. The guys watch her virtuosity with wonderment and desire.

For much of this number, the women are scripted as incentives for the males if they join the squad. By subverting the male's proclivity for objectification, the female ensemble bodies seemingly lure them by activating their performance skills, both cheerleading and dance. Since the nineteenth century, the desire for embodied virtuosity set high expectations for those engaging in any physical practice. Such expectations implemented a body that would be bound to such promise of skilled performance for spectators. Susan Leigh Foster argues, "If the physical demands of virtuosity leached from the body any connection to a signifying sociability, they did not desexualize it. Rather, the objectification of the body accomplished in these physical regimens rendered it a more neutral and compartmentalized receptacle for an abundance of sexual connotations."[70] The very form of cheerleading is a prime example of this relationship between the physical body, virtuosity, and sexualization. If the lyrics are not intelligible enough for the audience, it is abundantly clear through the ensemble blocking and choreography that this group of guys are interested in cheerleading solely because of the prospect of being surrounded by women.

Slowly, as more ensemble bodies saunter onto the stage, the lockers set center stage separate to reveal male ensemble members individually pop and locking to the music's beat, inferring that the ladies are starting to affect and reel in the men. Soon, four male ensemble members, spread out in different locations, are completing synchronous hip-hop isolations with Nautica. Following the isolations, almost everyone onstage begins to do a variation of the running man bounce groove, hopping back and forth between the feet as if running in place. This gentle build-up narrativizes their growing squad. However, the use of hip-hop-based movement throughout this number frames the ensemble bodies of Jackson as lacking in the fluency of cheerleading vocabulary, perpetuating their dissimilitude.

Cameron makes his way downstage center. A small group of four female company members walk past him, pause, and continue to upstage right. Then, a small group of male and female-identifying company members cross to him from stage right before pivoting and returning to the location from which they came. It is as if they were still trying to convince him to join, but he declined. Through these groups, the audience sees the increasing pressure being placed on Cameron. Finally, he is approached from upstage left by eight male ensemble members, led by Campbell. Using a "Wikipedia Article" that claims Michael Jordan was a cheerleader as a last-ditch effort, they send him into an existential dream about becoming a professional basketball player. The stage lights go dark as the company flees the stage leaving Cameron alone.

Musically, the rhythm shifts from a metronomically regular beat to a syncopated beat that emulates the sound of basketballs bouncing. The lights come up for the downstage space, leaving upstage dark. Male ensemble members line up behind Cameron and execute hip-hop-like dance movements that pantomimically signal playing basketball. The male hip-hopping ensemble bodies speak to Cameron's resistance. Accompanying his lyrics, the "Guy Backups" yell, "RRRRRAH! RRRRRAH! SIS BOOM!"[71] This echoes "We Ain't No Cheerleaders" and Danielle's line, " … don't you ever call us/ Rah rah, sis boom bah."[72] Cameron sings, " … pop & lock till we bop to the top … / (Ladies), Bring it on if ya love hip hop! / (And me), I'll grab ya when ya flip and drop!"[73] On the word "Top," he turns to face upstage and points to the air space above upstage center (still unlit). Simultaneously, (white) professional cheerleader Lauren Whitt is thrown into a twist basket toss, coming into the light where Cameron is pointing. The inclusion of a virtuosic cheerleading moment here signals Cameron's acceptance of joining the squad.

Accordingly, the music shifts back to the pop sound and co-ed pairings form around the stage. The company completes a few small arm-focused dance movements together, fostering a sense of unity between the once separate Jackson males and Jackson female-identifying students. During a moment of celebration, Michael Naone-Carter, who identifies as "a Hawaiian Polynesian performer and self-taught tumbler," completes a back tuck downstage left.[74] He is the first non-white performer to be featured executing a virtuosic cheerleading moment. Following a moment of pause between Danielle and Campbell, the company clumps together in a "V" formation reminiscent of a standard formation used in cheerleading competitions, with Danielle at the point. They all pledge their commitment to this new adventure in a canon of hand-raising.

Quickly, the company spreads back out across the stage, this time all taking individual spots around the space. Each member has a downlight spotting their body and space they occupy; no *body* is hidden from view. Danielle and Campbell sing, "We can leave behind the world we," and the company joins in singing "know."[75] On "know," the company jumps to second position with arms and palms spread at either side—an active presentation of Blankenbuehler's belief that second position is a stance for believing in something.[76] The diversity of bodies onstage, in terms of race and gender, synchronously energizing this moment illuminates the optimism toward change and possibility.

For the 2013 Tony Awards, the staging of this moment diverts from its original choreographic score. In this iteration, to accentuate Campbell and Danielle's point, Whitt and Corbeille are put up into half stunts upstage right and left, respectively. Although these white virtuosic cheerleading ensemble bodies are once again focal points of the stage picture, the stillness of the entire company potentially allows the audience to see everything on stage, rather than quickly receiving flashes of moments. However, it is still noteworthy that no virtuosic female cheerleading body of color is featured. Activating a higher level of cheerleading for the Tony Awards performance illuminates a desire to enchant audience members, many of whom belong to the white middle-to-upper class. Adding this element and suppressing the hip-hop changes the idealist view being expressed by the company. Now, even though the new Jackson High School squad says they can leave behind the world they know, a world that privileges white cheerleaders, the inherent whiteness of cheerleading is seemingly still inescapable. Even though Bethea and Naone-Carter are virtuosic cheerleading bodies of color and are indeed bases for these stunts, they are not explicitly positioned as focal points. For the Tony Awards, featuring one more virtuosic cheerleading stunt follows to place a spectacular exclamation point on the number.

For the original production choreography, the company's diversity is on full display as they complete a series of synchronous hip-hop-enhanced movements. No cheerleading movements have been included in this score. Before the final button of this number, each row of bodies steps uniquely dances toward the front of the stage before circling back upstage, allowing the next row to come forward. The featured virtuosic cheerleading bodies who were flyers for Truman are now both quickly introduced with a star-like lift—the flyers are laying on their sides with their body spread out like a star as two male ensemble members each lift them over their heads, making a half-turn toward upstage before bringing them back to the ground. Once again, this is a hint at cheerleading, but it is not a formal cheerleading move. Blankenbuehler does use the white virtuosic cheerleading bodies, Whitt and Corbeille, but the combination of a fast-paced move, costumes that cover their arms and legs, and the turning of their bodies so that their backs are to the audience distracts away from their whiteness as a performing convention. The number wraps up with everyone firmly on the ground, walking into a straight line along the edge of the stage apron, followed by a blackout.

Although "It's All Happening" resists employing formal virtuosic cheerleading, its subtle integration alongside quotidian blocking and Blankenbuehlerized hip-hop dance begins the process of re-situating Jackson High School's relationship to the form. The music switches to a more pop-centered sonic scape, but the choreographic score resists fully submitting to a Truman-style way of moving. Blankenbuehler's blending of movement styles preserves the Jackson High School embodied identity while also forwarding their cheerleading-novice positionality. Coalescing the ensemble bodies disrupts the strict divide between male and female performers at Jackson as well as ignites the potential for the success of cheerleading bodies of color within the narrative. Ultimately Campbell's naïve plan to deceive the students of Jackson crumbles. Be that as it may, in favor of a happy ending, the students forgive her and agree to compete at the Varsity Nationals Cheerleading Competition anyway. Prioritizing uniquity, diversity, and resistance to majoritarian scripts, the Jackson squad chooses to put their own spin on their cheerleading routine.

3.5 Welcome to Varsity Nationals: Cheerleading Versus Hip-Hop

The climax of *Bring It On: The Musical* is, of course, the Varsity National Cheerleading Competition. Antwan Bethea reflected on the accuracy of the staged competition in the production:

> As far as depicting the progression of a cheer season (Tryouts, Summer Camp, Regional Competition, then Nationals) and depicting the importance and the weight of those events to the cheer world, *Bring It On: The Musical* was fairly accurate. Even down to the attitudes and demeanors of specific personalities because of how important perfecting the routine is. It can be quite obsessive at times, but that's the nature of a competitor and a champion. Andy visited one of these national championship competitions to observe athletes behind the scenes and in action. He wanted to deliver that same drive and intensity of a squad who has been practicing week after week all season long, preparing for that very moment. He even used the same branding throughout the show to perfectly match the actual cheer world; Varsity Brands ® [sic].[77]

Bethea's rumination illuminates Blankenbuehler's desire to produce a sense of verisimilitude beyond the skills needed to actuate the cheerleading. His taking into account attitudes, demeanors, and specific personalities further perpetuates the significance of his meticulous choreography of virtuosic cheerleading ensemble bodies versus dancing ensemble bodies, white ensemble bodies versus non-white ensemble bodies, and male ensemble bodies versus female ensemble bodies.

In his efforts to stage the competition, undoubtedly with the assistance of Jessica McDermott (Colombo), Blankenbuehler utilizes the rules and regulations of the Varsity National Championship to guide the choreographic scores for both Truman High School and Jackson High School. However, for Jackson High School's routine, "Cross the Line," Blankenbuehler deconstructs such specificities of the form regarding competition regulations, aesthetics, movement vocabulary, race, and gender to support the show's underlying message of embracing uniquity and challenging majoritarian scripts. Many of the intricacies of how he broke the competition rules would go unnoticed to an untrained eye. Having said that, Blankenbuehler uses the Truman High School score as a guidepost for creating or even contrasting the Jackson High School score for an unknowledgeable viewer. By dramaturgically placing Truman High School first, the audience is guided to how a routine should look. As a result, when they see Jackson High School's routine, at the very least, it is noticeably dissimilar. In order to successfully stage a national cheerleading competition, Blankenbuehler must employ all of the virtuosic cheerleading ensemble bodies and carefully craft routines that give or take focus to those bodies accordingly.

When Truman High School performs their entire two-minute and fifteen-second routine titled "Legendary," more virtuosic bodies are needed to stage the squad than were used in "What I Was Born to Do." In the opening number, all of the ensemble bodies were spread out between cheerleader characters and student characters. The cheerleaders wore uniforms or parts of uniforms, and most of the ensemble who were written as cheerleaders for that scene were professional cheerleading ensemble bodies. Contrarily, the non-white professional cheerleaders were not written as cheerleaders, for it was necessary to conceal their virtuosic cheerleading ensemble body until Jackson gained those skills. For the competition, however, it is all hands on deck. All of the virtuosic cheerleading ensemble bodies are necessary to legitimize Truman High School as a champion-level squad. Other scripted cheerleaders onstage include two female dancing ensemble members and principal characters Eva, Skylar, Kylar, and Steven.

Clearly delineated uniforms mark the cheerleading ensemble bodies and principal characters as a cohesive unit: matching white athletic sneakers, skirts for the females, pants for the males, and modest tunics. The female cheerleaders are also wearing a matching long-sleeve bodysuit under their tunic. By completely matching, unique personal ensemble body characteristics become more muted. Perhaps the most obvious example of this is Antwan Bethea. As he noted in an interview, his dreadlocks make him stand out as "Jackson," but by pulling his hair back into a ponytail, he becomes "Truman."[78]

Categorically, "Legendary" follows the format and expectations of a typical high school competition routine. The music for the routine is completely pre-recorded and includes sound effects that punctuate specific movements, such as a toe-touch or a basket toss. The only time the performing bodies utter words is when they are doing the short cheer portion of the routine. It begins with the entire squad on the mat, inside the white line, with their heads down, at attention.

When the music starts, the Truman squad begins their first dance sequence. All of the dance in routine implements the highly codified cheerleading movement vocabulary.[79] Admittedly, it is all still Blankenbuehlerized cheerleading, and a few pirouettes and chaîné turns make their way into the dance as well. Nevertheless, these are movements that are repeated throughout and are indicative of the practice of cheerleading. For example, one of the opening movements is a squad toe-touch. Toe-touches traditionally begin with the arms in a "High V," and as the legs come into the air on either side (toes pointed), the arms cross and swing to the "T" position. The entire squad executing a toe-touch in this codified way helps to blend the non-professional cheerleaders with the virtuosic cheerleading ensemble bodies.

Blankenbuehler's positioning of ensemble bodies throughout the Truman cheerleading routine attempts to resolidify the lens juxtaposing Truman and Jackson by once again using the choreography in such a way that draws attention to whiteness. Beyond the conformity of the uniforms, Bethea and other non-white cheerleading bodies, while actively involved in all things virtuosic for this number, are obscured by several (white) bodies so that they remain out of focus. Moreover, Ann Cooper Albright argues:

> Because it carries the intriguing possibility of being both very abstract and very literal, dance can foreground a body's identity differently. Some contemporary choreography focuses the audience's attention on the highly kinetic physicality of dancing bodies, minimizing the cultural differences between dancers by highlighting their common physical technique and ability to complete the often strenuous movement tasks.[80]

Because of the common kinetic exertion by the virtuosic cheerleading bodies, their physical technique and ability take precedence, though Blankenbuehler still employs specific tactics to solidify the lens. Following the group toe-touch, several members of the squad fan out and begin a short cheer-dance sequence. At the same time, a stunt group throws a basket toss upstage center, and two male cheerleaders complete round-off, back layouts from the center to the downstage corners. In the cheer-dance sequence, Melody Mills, a female cheerleading body of color, is located downstage, closest to the audience on the mat. Typically, this would give her more power regarding stage position. However, her dance moves all take place on the floor. This means that everything higher than her actually draws focus; her body is seen in the periphery, but it is only supplemental. Bethea is one of the two tumblers. Arguably, this does mark him as a focal point, for he is one of three spectacle-based moments on stage that are different from the dancing cheerleaders. But, as soon as his tumbling pass begins, the eye is drawn vertically to Whitt, who is high in the air from her basket toss. Among the dancers are Steven and Eva, who are center, in front of the basket toss group, performing different dance moves. Whitt, Steven, and Eva are the focal points.

From here, the squad transitions to the next formation, where the two dancing ensemble members and four principals are spread out. The virtuosic cheerleaders complete a standing back tuck. Out of the back tuck, Mills steps forward and, mirrored by another cheerleader, executes a tumbling pass toward stage right. Again, this would draw focus if a group pyramid was not being performed further upstage. The verticality of the stunts, along with their spectacular displays of athleticism and skill, automatically takes over the eye of the viewer. Every awe-inspiring moment features a white virtuosic cheerleading ensemble body, or principal, as the cornerstone of a moment. Frequently, in the event an audience member is not paying attention, a cheerleader on the ground is pointing up to where a girl will be in the air, actively telling them where to look.

The entire "Legendary" routine follows the rules dictated for the Varsity National Cheerleading Competition—aside from a few tumbling passes having to begin outside of the white line simply because the stage space is smaller than what a real mat space would be.[81] None of their stunts are illegal; they stay within the time frame, they use cheer movements, their actual cheer is adequately performed, and their uniforms are picture-perfect. Although they follow the rules of sportsmanship and conduct on the mat, in true *Bring It On* fashion, drama arises in the holding area following their performance. As Eva and Campbell come face to face for the first time in opposing cheerleading uniforms, Eva goes off the rails in a rant, trying to prove how wonderful she is. She sings, "You're all a bunch of losers! / I'm here to represent! / I'm dazzling! Magnificent! / I am the one percent!"[82] At this point in her rant, she turns to the Jackson squad, who have gathered around to witness her tantrum, and says, "The fact remains: there is no way you can win. In real life—people like you can't."[83] Eva's unambiguous sentiments once again frame the inner-city Jackson High School, particularly the students of color, as other. As she storms off, everyone stands stunned.

Jackson High School is called to the mat, and Danielle tells the squad, "Today we're gonna show them who we are, and not by their rules but by ours."[84] Her provocation is two-fold. On the one hand, it signals a challenge of the rules of cheerleading. On the other hand, it summons a confrontation against majoritarian scripts and assumptions. Their routine "Cross the Line" does both. The Jackson High School squad members include virtuosic cheerleading ensemble bodies, now in different costumes, dancing ensemble bodies, and the principal characters Campbell, Danielle, Bridget, Nautica, La Cienega, Twig, and Cameron. They work together to subvert and upend the "rules" of cheerleading.

When the number begins, all of the Jackson squad members are located outside of the white line. As the lyrics to "Cross the Line" begin overhead, they slowly step over the white line onto the designated mat space. Their uniforms are hardly a representation of how cheerleading uniforms should look. Immediately breaking the rules, several of the female members are wearing crop tops exposing their midriff.[85] Although this is not explicitly a rule, some of the female members are in pants, going against normative displays of femininity in the sport. Another break from the traditional practice of male athletes being in pants, many of the male Jackson cheerleaders are wearing shorts. Breaking the rules, some are even wearing basketball sneakers, certainly not the traditional white cheer sneaker. The choice to costume the Jackson squad discernibly different from the Truman squad (and typical cheerleading squads in general) elevates the focus on their embodied performance as also being distinct. Even as they stand still along the periphery of the mat, the audience is being prepared to witness an unprecedented competition performance.

The first stunt to go up features Danielle in a full extension center stage as Bethea and another male ensemble member tumble across the front of the stage. The second stunt to go up features Mills, who until now has kept up a low profile regarding the display of her cheerleading virtuosity. A third stunt occurs downstage left; this time, they lift Twig—the first male to function as a flyer in the entire show. Each of these stunts challenges the aesthetics of white female cheerleading bodies that have been featured as the standard via the Truman High School scenes and choreographic score. The audience is encouraged to notice the divergence through the amplification of these bodies.

In "Cross the Line," there is far less tumbling and stunts than during "Legendary." While those moments certainly exist and are necessary to the number's objective, they complement the narrative of the routine rather than drive it. Priority is placed on the diverse company bodies and how they are navigating this typically unfamiliar space. In contrast to Cooper Albright's thought regarding certain choreography minimizing emphasis on difference, she suggests:

> Other dances foreground the social markings of identity on the body, using movement and text to comment on (often subvert) the cultural meanings of those bodily markers. Tracing the layers of kinesthetic, aural, spatial, as well as visual and symbolic meanings in dance can help us to understand the complex interconnectedness of personal experience and cultural representation so critical to contemporary cultural theory. Indeed, much contemporary dance makes visible the movement between these personal and social realities.[86]

Blankenbuehler activates his highly hybrid dance-genre used in "It's All Happening" to foreground the social markings of difference while still promoting a sense of conformity. Despite none of the movements in "Cross the Line" being from the codified cheerleading vocabulary, the first half of the Jackson routine does use a prerecorded pop song, indicative of a standard cheerleading routine. Halfway through, the squad sings, "Everyone's gonna stand up and say 'rewind that!'"[87] The music makes a record scratch noise, and Blankenbuehler implements a stop-time moment where the squad pauses and physically backtracks through the prior few motions. Now, the music switches to a more aggressive hip-hop beat featuring a mash-up of "Do Your Own Thing" and "Friday Night." Although Blankenbuehler's hip-hop is undoubtedly "hip-hop-lite," it still illuminates a complex cultural reality, especially when directly situated against Truman High School. While the label of "cheerleading squad" afforded the students of Jackson High School access to a space that they may not have had otherwise, uplifting more explicit, hip-hop-centered aesthetics further mobilized, even if symbolically, the embodied voices of those from a disenfranchised community.

Throughout the remainder of the number, the dancing ensemble (and principal) bodies sustain their hip-hop choreography even as virtuosic cheerleading ensemble bodies execute tumbling and stunts around them.

Hip-hop frames the dancing bodies so that they continue facilitating this complicated socioeconomic lens. Mills remains one of the featured flyers, bolstering her capacity to function as a tangible representation of the reparation process. One of her stunts, about halfway through, is actually an "illegal" stunt for high school level. High schools are not allowed to go above two and a half high. Meaning, a base can lift a flyer, but the flyer who is lifted cannot lift another flyer—that would be three high and is precisely what occurs. Incorporating this stunt wows the audience as it is perhaps the most intricate of the stunts they have witnessed thus far. Furthermore, it frames Mills's body as highly virtuosic, on par with the other white flyers. Mills's ensemble body functions to add nuance that women of color can also perform such arduous maneuvers.

Following the three-high stunt, the entire Jackson squad slowly walks to the front of the mat. As they sing, "We don't need first place, we know how bright we shine," one by one they step over the white line located along the front edge of the mat.[88] Crossing the white line, the metaphor for the entire number, is against the rules.[89] As the diverse bodies line the front of the stage singing in reflection of what the future holds, the audience also receives a moment to absorb the unique individuals that make up the squad. The non-virtuosic company bodies take a few steps backward to make room for the virtuosic cheerleading ensemble bodies to complete a standing back tuck. The ensemble executes a few cheerleading arm movements before putting Campbell, Mills, Whitt, and Corbeille up in a final group stunt. The remainder of the choreography subversively employs cheerleading movements using hip-hop flourishes to transition between each. Finally using the cheerleading motions, after breaking the rules so that it would be impossible to win, proves that these bodies can indeed *do* this activity, but on their own terms. They defied the majoritarian script in favor of coming together and promoting their individuality.

Backstage after their routine, the Jackson squad encounters members of the Truman squad. Truman member Kylar enthusiastically responds to their performance, "You guys … were like, a clarion call of inspiration for all assembled."[90] Blankenbuehler's contiguity of "Legendary" (Truman High School) and "Cross the Line" (Jackson High School) provided a visceral confrontation between suburbia and inner-city, white and non-white, majoritarian and minoritarian, and cheerleading and hip-hop. By setting the two in literal competition with one another, the audience was asked to consider the differentiation between the squads. The framing and positioning of the ensemble bodies in relation to one another and with regard to the genre they were performing transitioned the lens through which the audience was to view each routine. In the end, "Cross the Line" challenged how cheerleading routines looked, how cheerleaders dressed, and *who* could be a cheerleader. It generated an optimistically reparative metanarrative regarding the socioeconomic, sociocultural, and sociopolitical future of cheerleading.

3.6 Conclusion: Reparative Cheerleading

Bring It On: The Musical in text, music, and choreography attempts to confront and alter the institution of cheerleading. Blankenbuehler choreographs multivalent ensemble bodies to signal majoritarian assumptions concerning identity. Then, once the majoritarian script is established through the text, music, and/or choreography, he intentionally deconstructs that narrative by repositioning the ensemble bodies in a way that visibly marks the embodied effect of that shift. Hip-hop is originally framed as marking other—rough and frightening—onto the ensemble bodies of the diverse, inner-city Jackson High School students. Once Campbell meets these individuals, he activates a hybrid dance aesthetic that lessens the harsh preconceptions of the hip-hop crew before revitalizing the hip-hop and the ensemble bodies as expressive, ambitious, and unique. During the Truman High School moments, Blankenbuehler uses white virtuosic cheerleading ensemble bodies as focal points to carefully mask virtuosic cheerleading ensemble bodies of color in order to promote the audience's viewing of Truman through the lens of whiteness. In the final moments of the show, he subverts the form of cheerleading to give agency to the previously suppressed virtuosic cheerleading ensemble bodies of color and the other squad members of Jackson High School, elevating a rectifying narrative and subtext that cheerleading does not need to be bound to majoritarian presumptions. *Bring It On: The Musical* only ended up running on Broadway for 173 performances. Although it did not necessarily make waves in the larger real-life context of cheerleading, Blankenbuehler's conscientious and meticulous choreography of the ensemble bodies generated an opportunity for an audience to critically reflect on such sociological metanarratives beyond the campy presentation of this idiosyncratic Broadway production.

CHAPTER 4
WHO TELLS THE STORY?: DIALECTIC ACTIVATIONS OF THE ENSEMBLE BODY

Jeremy McCarter shares a fundamental moment of Blankenbuehler's choreography development in *Hamilton: The Revolution:*

> When the Battle of Yorktown sequence ended that day, the largely black and Latino cast (singing a song written by a Puerto Rican composer, wearing costumes selected by an African-American designer) climbed on top of boxes and chairs to celebrate having done the impossible. Andy Blankenbuehler would spend the next 16 months trying to recapture how exhilarating the moment felt. It took him until a week before opening night on Broadway to feel that he had succeeded.[1]

What began as an improvised, celebratory moment between the cast during a workshop presentation in 2014 would become arguably one of the most powerful moments of choreography in *Hamilton*. At the end of "Yorktown (The World Turned Upside Down)," the cast is spread equally across the set: standing on boxes, benches, chairs, the stage deck, the stairs, and the second-level balcony. They are all doing just that, standing. As the ensemble, made up of predominantly bodies of color, sings about winning their (the United States of America's) freedom, the audience sees this triumph in U.S. history through these diverse bodies. This forced perspective illuminates and challenges current civil rights and equality narratives while adding a sense of pride, hope, and optimism. For the four-minute and two-second number filled with athletic, aggressive, sensational dance, the final fifteen seconds of stillness become the exclamation point on a compelling and informational piece.

Leading up to this chapter, I have argued that Andy Blankenbuehler has used individualized choreographic scores to draw attention to, or away from, the ensemble body in order to shape the narrative, characters, and overall meaning for the audience. His choreography for *In the*

Heights and *Bring It On: The Musical* have primarily steered away from the synchronous (ballet, jazz, or tap) choreography that has been iconic for large Broadway musical productions. Blankenbuehler has created room for individual characters to live their own unique lives within the ensemble. These individual ensemble bodies generate a comprehensive world for a production while effectuating multiple communication lines (story, mood, emotion, etc.). However, several routes of Blankenbuehler's work coalesce in *Hamilton* when he prioritizes the collective ensemble body to promote a narrative of inclusivity and ubiquity. There are moments throughout the production where the individual ensemble body is perceptible and affective, but these individual ensemble bodies are predominantly converged to form a collective ensemble body. Rather than distinctive individuals on their own journey, living in the world of the play, and sometimes coming together to convey a common idea through their unique voices, the collective ensemble body is a unified entity functioning to communicate an element of the story, a principal character's psychology, unspoken aspect of the libretto, abstract idea, or metaphor. The collective ensemble body, on some level, activates the traditional, generalized group concept of chorus character. Nevertheless, for Blankenbuehler, the individual ensemble body is an element of the collective; depending on the choreography and staging, one or the other takes precedence.

Additionally, Blankenbuehler's hybrid dance style that includes heightened everyday movement, hip-hop, jazz, among other genres, is once again the vocabulary for embodied communication. But, the choreography score implements far more synchronization. While he has always declared that narrative should supersede virtuosity, his choreographic score for *Hamilton* takes this notion to an even higher level as he ceaselessly presents ideas first and dance steps second. He attests to the concept that the ensemble, as both performers and characters, knows how the story of Alexander Hamilton ends; therefore, their omniscient capacity provides them with the knowledge to comment on a moment in a more nuanced manner. Blankenbuehler establishes a dialectical relationship between individual and collective in *Hamilton* that allows the ensemble body to function outside of time, linking the past with the present, opening up the opportunity for an audience to connect to sociological metanarratives generated from the inherently layered production.

This chapter analyzes the functions and philosophies of the individual and collective ensemble body in the numbers "Alexander Hamilton," "Helpless," "Satisfied," and "Yorktown (The World Turned Upside Down)." To conduct my analysis, I rely primarily on the film of *Hamilton* released for Disney+ on July 3, 2020.[2] To combat film edits, consider casting changes, or repeatability of moments, I also consider the *Hamilton* performances at the 2016 Annual Tony Awards and the 2016 Grammy Awards that have been uploaded onto YouTube and Vimeo, respectively.[3]

4.1 "Together We Can Turn the Tide": Moving From and Between Individual and Collective Ensemble Body

In order to investigate *Hamilton*'s collective ensemble body, it is essential to remember the building blocks of the "ensemble body." Beyond being cast as "ensemble," the "ensemble body" is that which takes into account the performer's dramaturgical body as it functions concurrently with the character's body. For *Hamilton*, the ensemble body is most notably framed through Blankenbuehler's work, but also through the work of costume designer Paul Tazewell. Because the ensemble is primarily a collective unit and the notion of the unique individual is ancillary, the ensemble body becomes distinguishable in a way different from what we saw with *In the Heights* or *Bring It On: The Musical.* Instead of relying on individualized choreography scores and movement interpretations, discerning the visibility of the ensemble body within the collective begins with Tazewell's creations.

Bridging the gap between past and present, Tazewell chose to have "'Period from the neck down, modern from the neck up.' … [he] 'didn't want Chris [Jackson] to be in a powdered wig as Washington.' … [he] 'wanted to see him for who he was.'"[4] At the beginning of the show, and for the majority of the production, the collective ensemble is wearing parchment-colored trousers, a matching sleeveless top (that ranges from button-up vests to corsets to waistcoats) and black leather riding boots. Tazewell arguably walks a fine line between period and modern in the costume as a whole. For example, the female ensemble members are also wearing trousers. Although the trousers themselves are period, women wearing pants in the late eighteenth century is not. Similarly, the use of vests or corsets is period-appropriate, but the fact that they are the primary garment used as the top, thus exposing the individual ensemble body's arms, is not. Throughout the production, the ensemble members occasionally layer on other clothing articles to add dimension or identification to their characters, but this will be discussed in further analysis. Contrary to *Heights* and *Bring It On*, where the costumes were vastly different for each character allowing for increased individuality, *Hamilton* utilizes the more or less matching ensemble costume to connect them as a collective visually.

Notwithstanding their clothing conformity, everyone in the company has their hair styled to fit their unique, individual contemporary personalities. While Tazewell's use of period clothing garments grounds the production in its historical time, the modern use of those pieces, accompanied by contemporary hair stylings, keeps the performers' bodies in the present.[5] Incorporating the perceptible aspects of the individual ensemble body (skin color, hairstyle, body shape, etc.) as part of the costume allows them to be visually distinguishable from one another. Their dramaturgical bodies, specifically their physical identifiers, are utilized and embraced as unique markers blending performer and character, all the while relinquishing to conceptions of a shared, embodied voice.

Tazewell's costuming quickly establishes the ensemble's unique position as a constant reminder of two distinctive revolutions—past and present. *Hamilton*'s fundamental principle challenges the conventionally white historical narrative of the founding of the United States by telling the story of America, then, by America now.[6] The company, made up of predominantly bodies of color, thrusts the show's existential question "who lives, who dies, who tells your story?" into a visceral arena. Jeremy McCarter's introduction to *Hamilton: the Revolution* suggests,

> It tells the stories of two revolutions. There's the American Revolution of the eighteenth century, which flares to life in Lin's libretto … There's also the revolution of the show itself: a musical that changes the way that Broadway sounds, that alters who gets to tell the story of our founding fathers, that lets us glimpse the new, more diverse America rushing our way.[7]

To tell the story of the American Revolution, the collective ensemble body, wearing hints of eighteenth-century clothing, functions as slaves, merchants, soldiers, townsfolk, and cabinet members. However, revolutionizing theatrical practices, the noticeably diverse individual ensemble bodies challenge traditional musical chorus aesthetics and functions. They maintain visual, contemporary uniquity as their ensemble bodies resonate between the eighteenth-century US and the twenty-first-century US, individual and collective.

Beyond Tazwell's costume design, how does ensemble communicate the dialectics between past and present, individual and collective? How does

Blankenbuehler's negotiation between the individual ensemble bodies and a collective ensemble affect an audience's comprehension of the material? Blankenbuehler still choreographs individualized ensemble scores throughout *Hamilton*. Even so, he often places the individual ensemble body alongside or in sync with other individual ensemble bodies allowing for multiple lines of communication to exist at once but through a connected embodied voice. This relationship prioritizes the collective ensemble making it more powerful. Both the individual and collective ensemble bodies comment on the historical narrative of Alexander Hamilton's time while also alluding to the social systems of the present. Specifically, according to the very premise of the production, the individual ensemble body can challenge historical narratives that have systematically marginalized non-white bodies. However, the collective ensemble body becomes necessary to achieve such a larger conversation about a diverse society made up of Black, Brown, Latinx, Asian, and white bodies. The bodies onstage cooperatively produce the historical discourse of Alexander Hamilton's life. Concurrently, those bodies are produced by both historical and contemporary cultural discourses of difference.

For example, ensemble member Sasha Hutchings remembered first hearing about *Hamilton* and the idea that a person of color would portray Thomas Jefferson. In an interview for the podcast *The Ensemblist*, she said:

> I was like, "That doesn't work. He was a slave owner. He was like terrible." And then I saw it, and I was like, "Oh! Totally works!" Because it's like this thing that's making you face an ugly truth about how we got here—but in a way that kind of empowers you to feel like you can change it or that there's hope. It's a hopeful way of looking at: we're not our worst selves, we're not our best selves. We have to deal with all that as people. And that's one of the things in the show; there's always this sense of like, not yet. There's more work to be done. There's that moment in the show [Hamilton's] like, "We studied, and we fought, and we killed / For the notion of a nation we now get to build." ... We're still doing that.[8]

She continues reflecting on her experience as a woman of color participating in the ensemble of the show. Remarking on her doubled-ness, her duality of Sasha/ensemble member, Hutchings tells of how she has a responsibility to support the show in whatever way is necessary—sometimes that means being an extension of Burr's thought process, sometimes that is being a senator, or sometimes that is being herself.[9] She explained, "A lot of times I come on, and yeah, I do enter the show just as Sasha. I like to come on as honest as possible to set the tone of the show because the show requires so much honesty … Just be you … Honesty is more interesting than anything else."[10] As I will explain later, Hutchings's proclamation that she moves between characters, ideas, and herself throughout the show creates a multivalent individual ensemble body that is able to live in the 1780s and the 2010s simultaneously. In a similar fashion, her ensemble body is equally a part of the collective ensemble that undertakes an omniscient narrator/participant capacity.

It is important to note that not every ensemble member shares this same philosophy. Neil Haskell, for example, reported this to *The Ensemblist*, "I'm not up there playing Neil, but I am playing these characters in their set circumstances, but trying to be as real as possible and not trying to look like a dancer, not trying to look like an actor."[11] Haskell's reflection speaks directly to the idea that each ensemble member *owns* their ensemble body. They have the autonomy to make character choices within the show that serve specific moments based on their consciousness. For Haskell, he intellectually and creatively chooses to develop unique, realistic characters that are more separate from his dramaturgical person, but the very notion that his body is present in this space and has a sense of autonomy energizes his ensemble body. When their individual ensemble bodies then move synchronously alongside others, all dressed alike yet different, the choreography generates a unified embodied voice that can be seen—the collective ensemble body—even though the individual body can still be read.

4.2 "We Move as One": Synchronism and Hip-Hop

Hamilton's dualities between historical and contemporary have opened a space for a reflective dialogue within the production regarding society's development in the United States. Blankenbuehler's choreographic dualities of heightened everyday movement versus codified dance and asynchronous versus synchronous impact the ways in which the bodies onstage are read and understood. By fluidly engaging these dichotomies, the audience receives layers of information that encourage them to consider the relationship between past and present social convictions. While Blankenbuehler occasionally positions the individual ensemble body as a focal point for critical consideration, it is the collective ensemble body that becomes vital to understanding the resonances of past and present illuminating and elevating metanarratives regarding the position of people of color within the society of the USA today. Moreover, the use of hip-hop movement by the collective ensemble body signals to the audience how to view history through a contemporary lens—a lens that amplifies socially/historically disenfranchised bodies, voices, and lived experiences.

Critics of *Hamilton*, such as Harvard professor and historian Annette Gordon Reed have called out the production's avoidances of the topic of slavery concerning the founding fathers portrayed. In an article by Liz Mineo, Reed criticizes the light portrayal of Hamilton as an advocate for freedom and equality for all:

> "In the sense of the Ellis Island immigrant narrative, he was not an immigrant," she said. "He was not pro-immigrant, either." [...] "He was not an abolitionist," [Reed] added. "He bought and sold slaves for his in-laws, and opposing slavery was never at the forefront of his agenda." [...] The musical simplifies and sanitizes history, said Gordon-Reed. "The Hamilton on the stage is more palatable and attractive to modern audiences."[12]

Many others have similarly criticized the hypocrisy and supposed problematic nature of having bodies of color portray characters who were identifiably white and had a hand in continuing slavery in the USA However, critics such as Tracy Clayton have recognized the production's attempt to cross-examine how history is conveyed and disseminated. In a tweet following the release of the production on Disney+, she said, "im late w the hamilton criticism stuff & im clearly biased but.. i really like that this conversation is happening. hamilton the play and the movie were given to us in two different worlds & our willingness to interrogate things in this way feels like a clear sign of change."[13] The "two different worlds" Clayton alludes to are the 2015 world in which we first were introduced to *Hamilton* at The Public and the 2020 world in which access to the production via Disney+ revived its pervasiveness in society. She continued to acknowledge that the nuance in the show deserves attention, especially now.

In the lead up to the Disney+ release of *Hamilton*, on June 29, 2020, activist and academic Rachel Cargle created a post on Instagram captioned, "Lin-Manuel Miranda reached out to me and we worked together to find parallels between his lyrics and the current times to use as yet another tool to bring attention to realities of what is going on right here and right now."[14] Cargle compares the news headline "Parents Are Bringing Their Children to Black Lives Matter Plaza For a 'Once in a Lifetime Experience'"[15] with the lyrics "If we lay a strong enough foundation / We'll pass it on to you, we'll give the world to you, / and you'll blow us all away."[16] Another comparison she draws is the headline "Confederate Symbols Are Coming Down, Despite Trump's Ire"[17] with the lyric, "We'll never be free / until we end slavery!"[18] Cargle's curation enhances Clayton's suggestion that the show's nuance needs to be examined to grasp the relationship between past and present. But text analysis is not enough. Lin-Manuel Miranda ultimately intended for the story of Alexander Hamilton to be seen, and more importantly, to be seen in this way—through the bodies of people of color. While the principal characters are undoubtedly a driving force for this conversation, I argue it is the collective ensemble representing the (past and present) society affected by these founding fathers' decisions that engenders and bolsters the vital nuance to which Clayton alludes.

Miranda's use of hip-hop music creates dissonance between *Hamilton* and traditional Broadway practices as well as the perception of *Hamilton* as a historical retelling. It helps to open up a dialogic space where it is possible for people of color to portray these traditionally white founding fathers. Contrary to hip-hop's presence in *In the Heights,* it is not used as a cultural product of the people in the world of *Hamilton*. Moreover, counter to *Bring It On: The Musical,* hip-hop is not used as a tool for othering. Instead, it is used as a common, unifying language. As Miranda and McCarter posit, "[hip-hop] is, at the bottom, the music of ambition, the soundtrack of defiance, whether the force that must be defied is poverty, cops, racism, rival rappers, or all of the above."[19] Hip-hop—music, dance, and philosophy—allows for the entire company to work together to not only braid itself into the historical narrative of Alexander Hamilton but also the political environment of the United States post-2015. As argued above, the political environment of the United States during the year 2020 is also now a recognizable factor for comprehending the production.

It is perhaps obvious to say that hip-hop music calls for hip-hop dance. As many, including myself, have emphasized, Blankenbuehler's hybrid style of dance in his choreography does indeed include hip-hop. However, thus far, I have argued hip-hop dance prioritizes the individual and is directly tied to the body from which it is performed. How does the genre of hip-hop, then, function for a collective ensemble body? Susan Leigh Foster argues that the original call for hip-hop dance to be performed by crews or in groups established the form as a collective entity with the ability to "[braid] itself into a local geographical and political environs."[20] For *Hamilton,* Blankenbuehler uses hip-hop dance aesthetics to frame and unite the collective ensemble as a lens through which the audience is to view a production. It functions as an apparatus that further focuses on how the ensemble is to be understood in relation to sociopolitical environs at a given moment within the production or in concert with the real world in which the show is being produced. As Foster suggests in *Choreographing Empathy: Kinesthesia in Performance*, "If the choreography helps viewers to contemplate where they have come from and where they might be going, it serves not so much as a repository of knowledge but as an orienting tool for determining and affirming a system of beliefs."[21] Choreographing synchronously and collectively danced hip-hop orients a viewer in a more or less contemporary setting with a set of beliefs akin to defiance associated with the past/present *Hamilton* environ. Hip-hop dance's connection to "the music of ambition [and] the soundtrack of defiance" has equally made it a site for sociopolitical commentary.[22] When danced synchronously, its ties to counterculture and resistance to oppressive forces unite the collective ensemble fighting for past/present revolution(s).

Traditionally, large, synchronized Broadway dance numbers have been directly categorized as pure spectacle, entertainment for entertainment's sake moments. "Brotherhood of Man" (1961), "Turkey Lurkey Time" (1968), "One" (1975), "42nd Street" (1980), "Jellicle Ball" (1980), "Anything Goes" (1987), and "Blow High, Blow Low" (2014) are just a few examples of these show-stopping numbers featuring a large chorus of synchronized dance. Reflecting on *Hamilton*, Neil Haskell explains, "When you see an old classic show and the dancers are in the background doing like 'falap, ball, change, falap, ball, change, jazz hands.' Ya, know? They don't really look like people because they aren't being people. But, when you see a show that makes the dancers more pedestrian and makes them more relatable, that's kinda cool."[23] His articulation of the "pedestrian" presence in *Hamilton* is precisely what makes the moments of synchronicity prioritize the ideas and the narrative over virtuosity and showmanship. As Blankenbuehler resists typical musical theatre choreography in preference of a heightened gesture-based score, he humanizes the collective ensemble. When he activates hybrid pedestrian/hip-hop moments, the audience recognizes the human ensemble body taking on an additional mode of communication that is sonorous with a complicated history and sociocultural associations.

Discussing the complex layers of hip-hop, Carla Stalling Huntington posits:

> While hip hop dance initially had its texts labeled as rebellious, able to evoke a revolution in regards to socio-economic and racial

> oppression, it quickly became usurped into reinforcing capitalism, happening quickly with respect to rap music and somewhat more slowly for danced texts. Nevertheless, hip hop dance texts combined the force of emotional and mental understandings of centuries of oppression and articulated bodily phrasing meant to spin capitalism around on its head and shoulders, and popped the locks of power (at least momentarily) so that African Americans knew that they did not have to go along or all get along under the guise of Western power structures.[24]

Huntington points to the codification of hip-hop and its yielding to capitalism as a form for mass consumption; *Hamilton*, in many ways, is no exception. Nonetheless, her point is that the underpinnings of struggle and oppression are still present in the text of hip-hop movements. The hip-hopping individual ensemble body and collective ensemble body in *Hamilton* concretize such narratives of socioeconomic and racial oppression. Their embodied nuance constitutes a conversation regarding slavery and racial injustices in the United States society. The collective ensemble body, made up of diverse individual ensemble bodies, has the potential to reflect the societal presence and thought that moves between the past/present dichotomy. In the analysis below, I illustrate how, although dance can always be argued in terms of spectacle, these notions of emphasizing narrative, nuance, and communication shape the collective ensemble's function as an active force.

4.3 "Alexander Hamilton": Establishing the Omnipresent and Omniscient Ensemble

Lin-Manuel Miranda's inspiration for the musical, Ron Chernow's biography *Alexander Hamilton*, embeds Hamilton's life firmly in the slave culture of Nevis, St. Croix, and the Caribbean.[25] Chapter One, "The Castaways," gives pause, reflection, and perspective on those enslaved bodies. It may have been easy for a biographer to skip the details that do not readily apply to Alexander Hamilton. But, Chernow's 731-page biography paints an arguably thorough picture of the backdrop of Hamilton's childhood. "It is hard to grasp Hamilton's later politics without contemplating the raw cruelty that he witnessed as a boy and that later deprived him of the hopefulness so contagious in the American milieu," writes Chernow.[26] Andy Blankenbuehler transposes this crucial backdrop onto the stage through his choreography for "Alexander Hamilton." Like the biography, the focus throughout the production is on the character Alexander Hamilton, but the surrounding bodies inform *how* the audience sees him. Without reading Chernow's biography, the cruelty and hardships that shaped Hamilton live on stage through the ensemble's bodies and movements from the moment the show begins.

Throughout "Alexander Hamilton," Blankenbuehler's choreography incorporates hip-hop dance as a tool to accentuate and translate the underlying events of historical "real life" while implementing contemporary critical inquiry. Heightening reality through hip-hop and gesture allows him to communicate diversity, reflection, and agency due to hip-hop's resistance to normative social and theatrical practices. In prioritizing the collective ensemble body, he is able to unify different embodied voices and augment subtext and nuance. *Hamilton*'s complex language and music techniques challenge an audience—that has not listened to the soundtrack on repeat—to pay close attention or be left in the dust. If he were to rely on the individual ensemble body, he would be asking the audience to also absorb eleven additional (sub)texts as opposed to one. This request is valid at specific moments, but if it were to be the dominant philosophy, it would potentially be overwhelming, especially during the opening number. Blankenbuehler argues, "The real success of *Hamilton* is that it succeeds on a lot of emotional levels, but you can follow the story even if you miss 35% of the lyrics."[27] By leaning on the collective ensemble, the story and message can be received beyond the lyric as they traverse between peripheral affect and explicit storytellers. In "Alexander Hamilton," specifically, the collective ensemble is positioned to inaugurate the onion of information ahead and implement hip-hop as an embodied text as well as an aural text. The collective hip-hopping ensemble body narrates past/present social struggles while providing an optimistic sense of change and possibility.

As lights go up on Leslie Odom Jr.'s Aaron Burr entering the playing space stage right, the ensemble is positioned around the edges of the stage leaning on walls, posts, etc., snapping to the slow spoken word of the opening number. Anthony Ramos's John Laurens/Philip Hamilton, Daveed Diggs's Marquis de Lafayette/Thomas Jefferson, and Okieriete Onaodowan's Hercules Mulligan/James Madison then enter the space, dressed in fully parchment-colored attire as they play simultaneously both—and neither—character throughout this number. To elaborate, from the beginning to nearly the end of "Alexander Hamilton," all of the principal characters in the company act as omniscient narrators, privileged to relay the narrative of historical events but not quite characters within the story. For the sake of perspicacity, I will be using the names of the characters these performers will portray with the understanding that they are not yet fully personified. Furthermore, I will be implementing the specific character names as Miranda has scripted them in *Hamilton: The Revolution*.

Following Aaron Burr and John Laurens, Thomas Jefferson sings, "And every day while slaves were being slaughtered and carted / Away across the waves, he struggled and kept his guard up."[28] After this line in the book *Hamilton: The Revolution*, Miranda adds a footnote to reflect; "At the top of every musical, it's essential to establish the world. Hamilton's early life was marked by trauma and a firsthand view of the brutal practices of the slave trade."[29] Featured on stage are Burr, Laurens, and Jefferson; everyone else is either off stage or in the periphery. It is not until after James Madison sings, "Put a pencil to his temple, connected it to his brain, / And he wrote his first refrain, a testament to his pain," that the ensemble steps further into the playing space and becomes more prominently involved in the action.[30]

In *The Hamilcast* interview, Blankenbuehler said this about his omnipresent, omniscient ensemble:

> I believe, in my head, that this show is told in hindsight [...] the company knows how the show ends [...] and the story is so good that they forget that it's a story [...]That they have to start living it actively in the present tense ... as storytellers, they actually need to become mesmerized by their own story because it's such an impossible story and a real story that applies to all of us that they live it urgently in the present.[31]

Established as observers at the top of the show, while Hamilton's story continues to develop, the collective ensemble begins to take on the role of narrator and have an active role in the storytelling, similar to the principal characters. Their method of telling is literal, metaphorical, and abstract. Living outside of time, they help create a layered dialogue regarding past and present. To convey these ideas through dance, Blankenbuehler has developed a concept he calls "The Three Engines": the intellectual engine, the heart engine, and the gut engine. He posits the idea that stories can affect us in different places at different times, maybe even from more than one place simultaneously. Movement, then, transpires from these engines. By Burr's lyric, "Well the word got around, they said, / 'This kid is insane, man,'" the ensemble has moved further toward center.[32] Facing different directions, they slowly lean toward Burr, moving their hand to their ear as if they are listening. Then, they repeat a few shoulder shrugs. Blankenbuehler reflected on this moment, saying, "I am receiving word about this kid named Alexander Hamilton, but look how hard my body has to work to reach the word. So, I am hearing it in my chest and my gut at the same time, and I move with it."[33] Demonstrating the dance movements, he sings, "'Word got around, they said,' yes he's cool .... I get the word, and I am cool with it."[34]

Burr continues, "'Get your education, don't forget from whence / you came,'" the ensemble moves their hands behind their heads with their elbows wide and parallel to the ground.[35] Blankenbuehler notes, "I think the first step of every show is really important, and I always get conflicted about how to start. So, the very first step of *Hamilton* is very intentional to say that intellect and intellectual accomplishment is what our show is going to be about."[36] Technically, this movement is not the "first step" because it takes two eight-counts for the ensemble to transition to the location where this gesture begins. Nevertheless, once they are in place, this moment stimulates focus and inaugurates the concept of embodied communication for the production. The movement is initiated from the head, suggesting that this part of the story comes from the body's intellectual engine. However, it is notable that Blankenbuehler chose, here, not to do a movement one would typically associate with education or knowledge. Instead, he selected a move that resembles someone putting their hands behind their head before an arrest. Intentionally or not, the choice of implementing a socially coded gesture semiotically communicates the impression of surrender to the audience. As the unmistakably racially diverse ensemble bodies hold this gesture, an underlying narrative emerges.

Hamilton was born during the onset of the Black Lives Matter (2013) movement accompanied by the "hands up, don't shoot" slogan, which followed the deaths of Black Americans Trayvon Martin, Michael Brown, and Eric Garner. The physical expression of putting one's hands up in the air became central to the movement's choreopolitics. André Lepecki argues that the notion of choreopolitics "requires a redistribution and reinvention of bodies, affects, and senses through which one may learn how to move politically, how to invent, activate, seek, or experiment with a movement whose only sense (meaning and direction) is the experimental exercise of freedom."[37] Dance scholar Anusha Kedhar mused:

> By raising their hands in the air, the protesters remind us over and over and over again that all the bodily proof we need of Michael Brown's

> innocence is the position of his body when he died. The gesture reminds us that Michael Brown was shot while he was kneeling, with his head down and his arms up. It reminds us that the police violated the code not to shoot when a person's hands are up. It reminds us that the black body is never presumed innocent moving in white spaces. That space itself is white.
>
> The hands up don't shoot slogan implores the protester not only to stand in solidarity with Michael Brown by re-enacting his last movements, but also to *empathize* by embodying his final corporeal act of agency. As a collective gesture, it compels us to take note of and publicly acknowledge the bodily proof of Michael Brown's innocence.[38]

As the Black Lives Matter protests continued through 2020, the choreopolitics included hands raised in the air, kneeling with hands behind the head, and laying on the ground with hands clasped behind the back. The reclamation of these surrender gestures by protesters generates "movement vocabularies—embodied acts of resistance—connect[ing] protesters in ensemble movement akin to that of a company of dancers."[39]

As Blankenbuehler employs this choreopolitical gesture on the words, "get your education," we are reminded that many Black and Brown families living in the United States are forced to educate their children on the harsh realities of racial bias in our police system.[40] These bodies are disproportionately affected by extreme police action. The re-reading of *Hamilton* upon its release on Disney+ was in the wake of the Black Lives Matter movement's resurgence following the killing of George Floyd and Breonna Taylor, giving this moment the potential to become even more palpable as an embodied act of resistance.

If we diegetically connect this kinesthetic sign of surrender with the choreography, a subtext of past/present struggle and oppression emerges. After the pause with their hands behind their head, the ensemble pulses downward, suggesting that the story is affecting the body's gut engine on the downbeats of "forget from whence you came."[41] The hands behind the head become perhaps even more active than they were previously during the pause on "education." As Kedhar suggests, such an enaction can implore the possibility of remembrance and empathy regarding the constant denial of innocence. How does reading this movement sequence in this way affect the narrative and events occurring onstage? Remember, the ensemble represents the people surrounding Hamilton's life in the Caribbean: plantation owners, merchants, and slaves, as well as alluding to our contemporary society in the United States. Chernow's biography describes, "Violence was commonplace in Nevis, as in all the slave-ridden sugar islands. The eight thousand captive blacks easily dwarfed in number the one thousand whites [...] Hamilton would regularly have passed the slave-auction blocks at Market Shop and Crosses Alley and beheld barbarous whippings in the public square."[42] As the audience bears witness to the story affecting the ensemble bodies' gut engines, the historical remembrance of violence, trauma, and brutality to Black bodies lives alongside the contemporary injustices inflicting Black bodies in the United States. The past and the present coalesce.

While Burr is standing still in second position center stage singing the lyrics, Laurens, Jefferson, and Madison counter the ensemble's movement from the periphery inward and travel to the outer edges of the stage facing away from the audience. During this sequence's choreography, the three men also stand, unmoving, in second position with their arms resting at their sides. Although movement typically pulls focus for an audience, the contrast between the moving ensemble bodies and the stillness of the four characters who hold positions of power in the story also generates its own metaphorical line. These four men (historically white men) stand still and turn their backs to the harm inflicted upon people of color.

I must reiterate that the connections I make here may or may not have necessarily been intended by Blankenbuehler. But, it is the ensemble body's, in particular the individual ensemble body of color's, propensity to carry the potential for such a reading that is profound. Staying with this moment a little longer, one ensemble member in the collective stands out as executing slightly different movement at the end of this sequence. Following the pulse downward, the choreography ends in a second position plié with "bucket arms"—simply put, this gesture emulates the act of picking up a bucket, arms down toward the ground in fits as if they are grasping handles. All of the collective ensemble members have their heads down, looking at the ground as they reach their bucket arms, except Thayne Jasperson. Jasperson is one of the few white ensemble bodies onstage. At this moment, located just upstage right of Burr, he holds a stronger position in relation to an ensemble member that may be further upstage left, for example. As the only white male visible at this moment, the choice to not lower his head is immediately juxtaposed to all of those, in particular the bodies of color, who do. Such a slight differentiation impacts how his individual ensemble body is read in conversation with the rest of the collective ensemble body.

For Blankenbuehler, these "bucket arms" on the word "came" symbolize hard work and labor. He explained this image further at the talk with Words on Dance at Symphony Space:

> This action on the word "came" is don't forget from where you came. Like, hard work .... Pick yourself up by the bootstraps. This moment is believably showing the tension it takes to actually go through with life .... So, if I have to pick up a bucket, I don't think like a ballet dancer and pick up the bucket. I do whatever it takes to pick up the bucket.[43]

The move is low to the ground, signaling the struggle of coming from a place of poverty or oppression. In just a few quick seconds, the collective ensemble body signals social concepts and stratifications that sculpt the past and the present. The individual ensemble bodies with their heads down convey more exhaustion, more labor. The story is affecting them in the gut engine of the body. Jasperson, with his head up, is affected in the intellect engine of the body. While he can conceptually empathize with his cohort of ensemble bodies, but he has not had such an onerous past afflicting him.[44] Despite the assumed intention of synchronized choreography, the collective ensemble body, complete with heads down and up, still functions within sociohistorical boundaries. The individual ensemble body within the synchronous collective narrates the notion that no contemporary retelling of history can erase the harmful hierarchies that are embedded in the body. Not everyone has had the same struggle, and we as a country still have yet to reach a place of equitability and equality.

Next, the ensemble sweeps their left arm diagonally upward toward Alexander Hamilton's soon-to-be entrance location, center stage on the lyric, "The world's gonna know your name. What's your name, man?"[45] As Lin-Manuel Miranda's Hamilton sings, "Alexander Hamilton," the ensemble stands in second position, arms down by their sides, elbows slightly away from the body, hands in fists, and backs toward Hamilton.[46] For Words on Dance, Blankenbuehler demonstrated the dance of this section with dancers Eliza Ohman, Corey John Snide, and Ryan VanDenBoom. Following the demonstration, he remarked:

> Let's talk about Impressionism for just a second. What happens on that phrase is, you're going to look at Aaron Burr. So, he's dead center. And so he is telling you the next plot point .... So Burr's walking in center, you're gonna see him. But I want you to feel everybody else.

> So that you don't necessarily have to watch the dance; you just feel their impact to it. And so then when it's finally time to introduce Alexander Hamilton, everybody turns away. And, literally, it is just like I turned the colors on the stage so that you have no choice but to look at Alexander Hamilton.[47]

The periphery of collective ensemble bodies focuses the audience's attention. Furthermore, their affective capacity gives them the power to suggest *how* an audience reads the body or event to which they are encouraging such recognition.

In the following section, a series of pantomimic scenes take place. The collective ensemble body becomes crucial to prescribing and reading the focal points of these segments. As Eliza Hamilton enters the space, telling the tragic story of Alexander Hamilton's parents, ensemble member Sasha Hutchings steps in as a symbol of Rachel, Hamilton's mother.[48] Hutchings's individual ensemble body momentarily breaks from the collective ensemble choreography and voice, elevating her capacity for embodied communication beyond the collective. On the lyric, "Two years later, see Alex and his / mother bed-ridden," Hutchings is lifted into the air by two male ensemble members and slowly turned clockwise.[49] She is lying on her right side with her arms stretched upward toward her head and her legs separated, almost in a "star" position.

Now, according to Chernow:

> A persistent mythology in the Caribbean asserts that Rachel was partly black, making Alexander Hamilton a quadroon or an octoroon. In this obsessively race-conscious society, however, Rachel was invariably listed among the whites on local tax rolls. Her identification as someone of mixed race has no basis in verifiable fact. (See pages 734–35.) The folklore that Hamilton was mulatto probably arose from the incontestable truth that many, if not most, illegitimate children in the West Indies bore mixed blood. At the time of Rachel's birth, the four thousand slaves on Nevis outnumbered whites by a ratio of four to one, making inequitable carnal relations between black slaves and white masters a dreadful commonplace.[50]

Regardless of this myth's validity, *Hamilton*'s casting choices and presumably Blankenbuehler's choice to use Hutchings as Rachel allows a place for this myth to live within the musical's space. What does the position of Hutchings's ensemble body suggest in this moment? Moreover, what does the collective ensemble body, pausing with arms raised, propound in this moment?

First and foremost, Hutchings's individual ensemble body navigates the dualities between her and performer, as well as between her and the character of Rachel. She is perceived as Sasha Hutchings, but also, in this moment, as Rachel Hamilton. The casting of Hutchings, a Black woman, as Rachel actuates the metanarrative regarding the comprehension of bodies and identity across past/present renderings. Notwithstanding the production's predilection of casting people of color in roles historically understood to be white bodies, Hutchings is cast as a white character whose identity was smeared because she was rumored to be mixed race. In her book *Choreographing Difference*, Ann Cooper Albright posits:

> In a historical moment when the 'body' is considered to be a direct purveyor of identity and is thus the object of so much intellectual and physical scrutiny, a moment when academics and scientists, as well as artists and politicians, are struggling to understand the cultural differences between bodies, dance can provide a critical example of the dialectical relationship between cultures and the bodies that inhabit them.[51]

Therefore, to begin comprehending the relationship between Rachel's identity suppositions and Hutchings's ensemble body—and subsequently a more extensive discussion about bodies of color and past/present society conceptions—we can look to the choreography as a translation apparatus.

Logistically speaking, the use of elevation as a blocking or choreography tool undoubtedly creates a more dynamic and engaging stage picture. Placing a body higher in the air as others remain on the ground will naturally attract a viewer's eye. When the act of elevating a body is accompanied by lyrics discussing their ultimate death, a visual metaphor ignites, suggesting the ascension of their soul from Earth into the spiritual world beyond. But, who this body is in relation to the production/story is important.

At *Hamilton*'s original opening at The Public in 2015, Hutchings's ensemble body as Rachel most likely would have been viewed similar to that of the other company members who took on the roles of white characters. Taking on the role of a white woman whose family owned slaves illuminates conversations regarding agency, reclamation, and power. However, when *Hamilton* was released on Disney+ in July 2020, following the killing of Breonna Taylor, an additional conversation was unveiled. While Rachel ascends into the beyond,

Alexander Hamilton is seated on a chair in front of her. The collective ensemble surrounds them, standing in a mirrored position to which Hutchings is laying: legs apart, arms stretched out, and palms open.

As discussed in Chapter 1, at the Words on Dance talk, Blankenbuehler reflected, "Raising the arms over the head must mean something—in real life, we don't often reach our arms over our head."[52] So, if a character does indeed reach their arms overhead, "[w]hatever [they] are reaching for better be important."[53] In other words, he does not choreograph arms over the head lightly. When the ensemble reaches their arms overhead, the attention is thus directed upward to Hutchings, but as Blankenbuehler contends, the arms over the head signal more than just a change of visual focus. Raising the arms in the air once again brings with it the socially coded gesture of "hands up, don't shoot"—this time associating the gesture with the death of a woman of color. Watching as Hutchings is slowly turned in the air before being brought back to the ground, the collective ensemble focused on her body with their arms up is reminiscent of the protests surrounding the death of countless Black and Brown bodies at the hands of police.

Albright suggests that dance has the capacity to generate critical thought regarding cultural difference and the body as supplier of identity. At this moment, the dance creates a juxtaposition between the stillness of the diverse collective ensemble bodies watching the moving individual ensemble body of Sasha Hutchings. The collective represents society's ability to act (or not) when an individual, particularly a Black individual, is being affected. The duality of the past/present omnipresent ensemble with arms raised communicates protest for racial justice. While the collective ensemble lives in the slash between historical/contemporary society, their identity is constructed through the audiences' perception of them in each movement. Dance, even if that dance is stillness, provides a critical look at the dialectical relationships between body/society, body/character, and character/stages society. The collective ensemble body representing past/present stands still, proposing an opportunity for intellectual reflection regarding Hutchings/Rachel/Black female bodies.

Next, Christopher Jackson's George Washington moves the story to another monumental loss in Alexander Hamilton's life—the apparent suicide of his cousin Peter Lytton. Lytton was given custody of Alexander and his brother James after the death of their mother, Rachel. Chernow reports:

> Lytton had a black mistress, Ledja, who had given birth to a mulatto boy with the impressive name of Don Alvarez de Valesco. On July

> 16, 1769, just when the Hamilton boys must have imagined that fate couldn't dole out more horrors, Peter Lytton was found dead in his bed, soaked in a pool of blood. According to court records, he had committed suicide and either "stabbed or shot himself to death." For the Hamilton boys, the sequel was equally mortifying. Peter had drafted a will that provided for Ledja and their mulatto child but didn't bother to acknowledge Alexander or James with even a token bequest.[54]

The passing of Lytton left the Hamilton brothers with nothing and the need to fend for themselves. It would mark their choice to split ways, and Alexander would choose a job as a "clerk for the mercantile house of Beekman and Cruger," ultimately setting him on his path to the United States.[55]

In *Hamilton*, this moment paints a different picture, and the dissonance between these retellings is consequential. Chernow highlights the court's dictation that Lytton committed suicide by either stabbing or shooting himself. Blankenbuehler's choreography pantomimes a hanging. Following the staging of Rachel's death, the ensemble transitions into the next section by moving to the periphery, some gathering set pieces and props. Ensemble member Ephraim Sykes takes on the role of Peter Lytton.[56] Sykes walks to center stage and steps up onto the chair where Hamilton had previously been sitting. He has a tight light focused around him, and the surrounding stage is dimly lit. The majority of the collective ensemble is seemingly "unaware" of his actions. As he stands on the chair, he pantomimes wrapping a rope around his neck before raising onto his toes, reaching the arm "holding the rope" up into the air, and dropping back onto his heels, letting his head hang loose. Sykes removes himself from the chair by shifting his weight onto his left foot and slowly pivoting to stage left by swinging his right leg around, hinting that he is swinging from the noose. The horrifically visceral image of a Black man being hanged is perhaps more tangible than staging Lytton shooting himself. This action, similar to the arms raised overhead, is compounded with sociohistorical meaning.

Although the moment Sykes enacts Lytton's fictitious hanging is under six seconds long, it has the potential to perform as a representation of the unimaginable violence against Blacks in the United States. Amy Louise Wood's *Lynching and Spectacle: Witnessing Racial Violence in America, 1890–1940*, tells of the horrific acts of racial violence that escalated following the Civil War and Reconstruction. Wood specifically analyzes the prevalence of photography as a reproduction of this brutality, so much so that the images themselves gained a high level of cultural power. Photography's ability to capture a moment instilled a sense of authenticity and tangibility that allowed those not physically present to witness after the fact. The common association of lynching with hanging is arguably derived from the popularity of such photographs. Wood purports, "images of confident, restrained white men beside bodies of debased black men could validate the racist convictions of the white southerners who gazed on them not only because viewers assumed the visual accuracy of the surface image but because they believed that the photographs made manifest interior truths about the essence of racial character."[57] These photographs were not created as documentation of such atrocities but rather as souvenirs for white people who enjoyed attending lynchings as a casual, amusing activity. While *Hamilton* is not explicitly referencing such a specific antecedent, this moment manifests a stage picture reminiscent of these photographs for a Broadway audience. Through the negotiation between Sykes's individual ensemble body and the onlooking collective ensemble bodies, the audience can receive an impressionistic allusion to this historical nuance.

In these six seconds of *Hamilton*, the majority of the collective ensemble has their backs to Lytton as the act is occurring. However, hauntingly evocative of the intrigue of bearing witness to such an act of inhumanity, one white ensemble body is gazing at the image of this Black ensemble body pantomiming being hanged. At first, it could be argued that this was an in-the-moment choice by that particular performer; however, it appears to be a choice choreographed into this ensemble track. When viewing both Betsy Struxness and Hope Easterbrook in this track, both are just behind Hamilton, looking up at Lytton.[58] Reflecting on choreographic philosophies during his interview for *The Hamilcast*, Blankenbuehler posits, " … if you want to feel the idea, [they] can't face front. If you want to see the idea, they have to face front."[59] The collective ensemble facing away from Lytton pulls back on the intensity of *seeing* the idea of his suicide—and allegorical lynching. Could they be the generalized society of the United States turning their backs on yet another catastrophic death of a Black body? When Sykes drops his heels to the chair as if he has been hanged, Hamilton contracts slightly from the torso. Could their backs be turned so that focus is being brought to the effects of this event on Hamilton? Could the individual white ensemble body *seeing* the idea echo the "tremendous symbolic power" of the "public and visually sensational" event that hundreds if not thousands of white spectators observed? This moment is fleeting and up to individual interpretation but nevertheless adds to the nuanced narrative embedded within *Hamilton*.

As Washington continues and the company joins in, "'Alex, / You gotta fend for / yourself.'"[60] The collective ensemble is spread around the stage in second position, now directing their attention inward toward Hamilton. Blankenbuehler's philosophy of second position as one that communicated believing shifts from the focus on Lytton to Hamilton. As the "voice" tells Hamilton he has to believe in and fight for himself, the "voice" is confident, embodied by the ensemble's stance. On the word "voice," the ensemble brings their hands near their hips, and on "saying," the hands build to the stomach. This movement comes from the gut engine: the famous "my gut is telling me" sentiment. On "Alex," their hands make fists, and their arms cross in an "X" shape in front of their chests. Not only is "X" in the name Alex, but "X" is also often utilized to represent the defense when drawing up a football play, as a mark to mean faith or sincerity, a signature—especially in the Middle Ages for those who did not have reading or writing skills, or even "X marks the spot" on a map. Susan Leigh Foster argues,

> Choreography, whatever its meaning, can provide clues to this specific experience of the physical in the ways that it records or documents movement, and also in the ways that it sets forth principles upon which movement is to be learned and crafted. The notion of empathy then theorizes the potential of one body's kinesthetic organization to infer the experience of another.[61]

Whatever the reading of the embodied "X" by the omniscient ensemble, this movement is generated from their gut engine but ends at the heart engine. Each individual ensemble member could interpret the objective of this "X" differently: Alex, fight for yourself, believe in yourself, educate yourself; the world may not know your name yet, but they will, or even trust your heart, and it will lead you to your goal. All of these messages apply to Alexander Hamilton at this low point in his life.

Next, Hamilton becomes completely surrounded by an abundance of seemingly chaotic movement as Aaron Burr sings. In *Hamilton: the Revolution*, Miranda reveals, "We double the tempo here because Hamilton's found his way out: He's going to double down on his education, and make himself undeniable. The image in my head is Harry Potter finding out he's a wizard. Everything suddenly makes sense."[62] Using a combination of Blankenbuehlerized hip-hop and heightened gesture, the ensemble bodies break out into individual choreographic scores that occasionally meet in moments of synchronicity. The individual ensemble body gains recognition as it moves in and out of sync with the collective of ensemble bodies. The duality between individual and collective is discernible throughout this section.

Additionally, hip-hop movement becomes more tangible from this sequence onward, elevating the past/present paradigm. Although the individual ensemble bodies maintain a connection as a collective entity, the detachment of synchronous choreography allows for the collective ensemble body to institute more than one function. The individual bodies smoothly move through the functions, to transition, to reveal a character's psychology, to tell a piece of the story, and to present an idea abstractly. This moment of hyperactivity allows for the individual ensemble body to obtain a sense of validation and significance, but the unified voice of the collective remains. As a whole, the choreography creates another pantomimic, metaphoric sequence narrativizing Hamilton's path from the Caribbean to New York City.

Burr's lyrics tell the story of Hamilton's time as an apprentice and clerk for Beekman and Cruger—later Kortright and Cruger—"tradin' sugar cane and rum and all the things / he can't afford."[63] Hamilton is center stage behind a table reading, writing, and navigating business deals. All the while, ensemble members make frequent crosses, both miming the holding of or actually manipulating physical props such as papers or barrels. Their action points to the work involved with moving these goods. However, in the text, Miranda has left out a crucial commodity, of which the production's critics say is a misstep of *Hamilton*, slaves. Chernow paints the following picture of Hamilton's apprenticeship in St. Croix:

> On January 23, 1771, during Hamilton's tenure, his firm ran a notice atop the front page of the local bilingual paper, the *Royal Danish American Gazette:* "Just imported from the Windward Coast of Africa, and to be sold on Monday next, by Messrs. Kortright & Cruger, At said Cruger's yard, Three Hundred Prime SLAVES." … One can only imagine the inhumane scenes that Hamilton observed as he helped to inspect, house, groom, and price the slaves about to be auctioned.[64]

Chernow's description illuminates Alexander Hamilton's direct relationship with slavery before coming to the United States. Although Hamilton himself did not own slaves, he was not naïve to the institution. In an interview with Terry Gross for National Public Radio, Miranda noted that slavery is "a system in which every character in our show is complicit in some way or another … Hamilton—although he voiced anti-slavery beliefs—remained complicit in the system."[65] As previously stated, *Hamilton* is often denounced for not including or challenging the notion that these founding fathers did little by way of abolishing slavery, not to mention those such as George Washington, who indeed owned slaves. Despite the omission of the word "slaves" in these lyrics and much of the production, I argue that there is space within the ensemble's choreography throughout the show, but particularly in this section, to include slaves as a crucial part of the narrative.

Throughout the organized chaos of mimed or real objects moving around the stage accompanied by both pedestrian and dance movements, there are also ensemble members who are executing more codified dance alongside heightened everyday movement in order to communicate more nuanced ideas. For example, there is a repetition of stacking one's fists on top of each other against any rhythm in the score, as if they are trying to climb or pull a rope. With the legs in a demi plié, there is a weight to the dance of this sequence, suggesting a more labored experience. Additionally, the syncopation and irregular rhythmic patterns of the hip-hop movements also propose a feeling of hard work or struggle. Reading the individual laboring bodies, whether dancing or manipulating "props," within the collective ensemble provides the opportunity for the audience to interpret these bodies as a part of the society of St. Croix, including those who were enslaved. Burr indicatively postulates sugar cane as the primary example of goods being traded. For the Caribbean Islands, sugar plantations were the driving force behind the economy. Those plantations operated using slaves as their primary source of labor. Burr's allusion to these plantations sets up the possibility for the pantomiming, laboring ensemble to exemplify such slave-based-labor.

The Black moving ensemble bodies contain the capacity to multiply signify, especially when the backdrop is an eighteenth-century plantation economy and the vocabulary is hip-hop. Jayna Brown contends, "Different sites of dance production, the where and the when, inform the meaning of the movements, but I argue emphatically that black movement is always multiply signifying. This means that the same dance phrase can be read differently by different people, depending on the place and the time."[66] However, although the white ensemble bodies may be enacting the same dance phrases, these bodies are going to be read differently within this setting. The collective ensemble body may represent the society of St. Croix at this moment, but the individual ensemble bodies are multiply signifying historically racialized ideas of class and labor. Depending on which body an audience member is focused on at a given time, they may be receiving different information. Still, the overall world is generated, allowing the multitude of possibilities to exist even if they are in the periphery.

After the landscape of St. Croix is painted, Blankenbuehler continues to use pantomimic gestures to complement the lyrics. He navigates a delicate balancing act between when to give the audience subtext through the movement and when to support the text being spoken. Such a negotiation allows the audience to have time to draw their own conclusions about an idea while also not having to work too hard to enjoy and understand the production's dense text. When Burr says, "Scammin; for every / book he can get his / hands on," he hands Hamilton, who crosses to him downstage, a red book.[67] At this time, much of the ensemble is in a second position, demi plié, spread across the stage. Blankenbuehler has choreographed a repetitive movement of the arms that replicates the turning of pages in a book. On the second-level balcony, the principal characters perform a similarly repetitive movement that suggests pulling books off a shelf. No matter where the audience is looking, the idea of reading books will be communicated. A similar tactic is used for the following line, "Plannin' for the future."[68] Once again, returning to the notion of which engine the story is affecting, most of the company completes a movement that directs the attention to the head, suggesting the simple idea of thinking and planning.

Throughout the number "Alexander Hamilton," we have seen that both the collective ensemble and individual ensemble body is continuously in a state of flux from historical character, to metaphorical idea, to representation of society, to narrator, etc. Neil Haskell reflected, "We transform a lot as the ensemble. Sometimes we're playing the lead character's reactions and emotions and different experiences, and then all of a sudden we'll *shwoo* and transfer into being a townsperson with our own ideas and thoughts and problems."[69] Following the pantomime complementing Burr's lyrics, the ensemble transitions once again into their omniscient observer role. Hamilton hands his red book to ensemble member Ariana DeBose, making eye contact with her before she backs up slightly to join the rest of the collective ensemble on the now bare stage (the table has been removed). As the lyrics, "In New York you can be a / new man," are repeated several times by the company, Hamilton responds each time with "Just you wait."[70] A few ensemble members remove ropes that have been hanging from above, tied to a mooring hook downstage left. DeBose turns and hands the red book off to Angelica Schuyler, and the rest of the ensemble watches as principal characters such as Eliza Hamilton, Angelica Schuyler, and John Laurens/ Philip Hamilton ready Alexander Hamilton: putting on his brown jacket, giving him books, and handing him his bag respectively. The company forms parallel groupings, making an aisle diagonally from downstage right to the stairs upstage left. On Hamilton's final "Just you wait," they all lunge in the direction that he will be walking, angling themselves so that their focus is on him and he becomes the highest character onstage. All of the focus is placed on Hamilton and his potential to affect the world upon his impending arrival in the United States.

As Hamilton is presumably on the ship crossing the Atlantic, while he walks upstage across the second-level balcony, the entire company is now looking out at the audience. The company moves to a straight line along the apron of the stage while foreshadowing Hamilton's fatal flaws, "You could never back down. / You never learned to take your time!" But perhaps more important than these lyrics is their stillness.[71] The lights are much brighter than they were at the beginning of the number, and the audience is now able to take a breath and truly absorb the diversity of the bodies in the cast—ensemble and principals. Jonathan Burrows argues, "Stillness and silence are as strong as any other material, and without them your audience will become exhausted … Pause as material can be very powerful."[72]

Following the pause in movement, the company simultaneously turns their heads to the right, once again putting Hamilton back in focus. Before Hamilton descends the stairs, the ensemble breaks out across the stage and performs individual scores that contain, once again, layered meaning. For the narrative of this final stretch of the song, Hamilton's "ship is in the harbor now."[73] The collective ensemble acts as the crew, preparing the mooring lines for the ship to dock—some of the ensemble is manipulating actual ropes, some of them are pantomiming the existence of ropes. Those using real ropes convey the story of the ship docking. The pedestrian nature of this choreography prioritizes the communication of this portion of the story over any sense of virtuosity or showmanship. But, for those without the actual ropes, their score breathes between pantomimic, heightened everyday movement, and codified dance to communicate more metaphoric or abstract lines of thought. By the end of the line, "Oh, Alexander Hamilton … " the ensemble not navigating ropes and set pieces pauses in fourth position.[74] Blankenbuehler asserts that the fourth position is active. The synchronicity of this position, combined with the omniscience of those engaging the position, elevates its potential meaning. Hamilton is about to take action in the United States. The ensemble bodies commencing their action in this production. And, the ensemble characters are going to begin their work to bring the ship to dock.

The company completes a drag turn, followed by hip-hop dance-based movement reminiscent of pulling ropes. Each ensemble member has a slightly different version of where their arms are in relation to the rope—pulling it and then tying or untying it to/from the mooring hook. They then gather any "leftover rope" and take it to where it needs to go, but they do this in an exquisitely stylized fashion. Contiguously, the individual ensemble bodies then simply walk around the space, not to any particular beat. They are interrupted by Burr singing, "see if you / can spot him."[75] The collective ensemble synchronously takes a quick stutter and uses a hand to move their head as if to look for him. On "Another immigrant, / comin' up from the bottom," they scoop their hands down to the ground and back up and move into slightly more up-tempo hip-hop style choreography.[76] Narratively, their actions here personify the characters of slaves or lower-class shipyard workers, but quickly they return to a more ambiguous position as omniscient narrators. Through the lyrics "America forgot him," the collective ensemble steps toward the audience mimes putting on a backpack, nodding to the idea that school children in the United States do not learn about Alexander Hamilton and the contributions he made to the establishment of the country.[77] They then pivot, turning their backs to the audience. The lights dim on the main stage deck, and attention is then directed to the lead characters in spotlights on the second-level balcony.

Lyrically, there is a fundamental shift that occurs with this final section. The number speaks either about Alexander Hamilton in third person or to Alexander Hamilton in second person. On Mulligan/Madison and Lafayette/Jefferson's "We fought / with him," first-person perspective is used for the remainder of the song.[78] The characters Mulligan/Madison, Lafayette/Jefferson, Philp/Laurens, Eliza Hamilton, Angelica Schuyler (Church), Maria Reynolds, and Aaron Burr are speaking in first person. Blankenbuehler's assertion that the story is told in hindsight is evident by the fact that the entire number uses past-tense to introduce the audience to the narrative. However, the Mulligan/Madison, Lafayette/Jefferson line initiates a pivot in function for these company members as they begin to transition from omniscient narrators to principal characters within the story. The ensemble has a less obvious adjustment. Following Burr's, "I'm the damn fool that / shot him," the ensemble takes one step to pivot their bodies ninety-degrees, with their torsos facing the wings and their heads looking over their shoulders at Burr, who is center stage.[79] Then, the entire company (sans Alexander Hamilton) faces front and sings, "There's a million things I / haven't done … "[80] There is a multitude of ways the "I" in this line can be read. First, the notion that the company, specifically the collective ensemble, is often positioned as Alexander Hamilton's consciousness suggests that they could be speaking on his behalf. Second, the collective ensemble and Burr are slowly walking toward the audience during this line, giving them more focus than the principal characters located around the second-level balcony. Intentionally moving the collective ensemble with Burr at this moment connects them as omniscient narrators. Still, their "I" is multifaceted. The "I" could simply refer to their character positioned within the narrative of the show. Or, and perhaps more interestingly, the "I" could be their individual ensemble body living both inside and outside of the production. As the audience looks at the menagerie of individual ensemble bodies on stage, the notion that those contemporary bodies have a million things left to do in this world is equally efficacious.

The final line, sung by all, including Alexander Hamilton, is "Alexander Hamilton." Following this line, there is a button in the music, a final beat, in which Burr looks at Hamilton, Hamilton looks diagonally up and out, and the rest of the company bows their head toward the floor. Blankenbuehler divulged, "As Americans, we owe a lot of people, a lot of people sacrificed and used their hearts and souls and brains to make this country. And so, the end of the opening number is not a bow to Alexander Hamilton; it is a bow to the ideals that make us our country."[81] The bow as a punctuation to the opening number, synthesized in this way, further supports the fluidity between the dialectics of past/present and collective/individual.

Furthermore, the dichotomy between imagination/reality is also operative within the bow. Randy Martin argues in his book *Critical Moves: Dance Studies in Theory and Politics*, "Dance both appears in the conjuncture of imaginary and performative spaces and puts the constitutive features of a composite body on display. For dance is both a bodily practice that figures an imagined world and a momentary materialization through performance of social principles that otherwise remain implicit."[82] His idea of the composite body is one "mediated across a conflicted space of the imaginary (literally the representational domain where images appear) and the performative (the practical means through which imaginary forms are enacted)."[83] In the imaginary/performative space of *Hamilton*'s Revolution-era America, dance, even if it is encompassed within a hybrid genre that includes pedestrian movement, connects embodied social principles of

Figure 5 *Hamilton* rehearsal notes. Photo courtesy of Andy Blankenbuehler.

today with the imaginary narrative of the past. The bow given by the collective ensemble body is mediated between these spaces of past/present, imaginary/performative. It is a bow to the United States's history, the United States's present, and the United States's future—a future that is hopefully made better through the telling of this story in this way.

4.4 "Helpless" / "Satisfied": Subverting Patriarchal Practices

The numbers "Helpless" and "Satisfied" featuring Eliza and Angelica Schuyler, respectively, unveil the love triangle between Alexander Hamilton and the two elder Schuyler sisters. During "Helpless," the ensemble takes on the roles of party guests at the winter soldiers' ball. Conversely, during "Satisfied," when the number essentially repeats from Angelica's perspective, the ensemble doubly plays echoes of the party guests while also providing omniscient, retrospective commentary. They become two of only a few numbers where the female ensemble members are noticeably female characters. Throughout each, the ensemble maintains its collective ensemble body identity, but it becomes divided along gender lines; analysis can observe a male collective ensemble body, a female collective ensemble body, and an overall collective ensemble body. Accompanying this articulation of gendered ensemble bodies, Blankenbuehler choreographs a hip-hop-enhanced, social ballroom-based dance score that dialectically follows and challenges typical patriarchal conventions.[84] The choreography of the overall collective ensemble complicates past/present gender relationships creating a subtext that gives agency and power to the collective female ensemble body.

In an article published through *HowlRound.com* titled, "Why *Hamilton* is Not the Revolution You Think it Is," James McMaster asks a popular question, "Given all of the cross-racial casting, why was gender-bent casting beyond the musical's imagination?"[85] His article continues to challenge why the production neglected to make more "revolutionary" moves regarding feminism. Undoubtedly, McMaster's piece sparked a great debate in the comments section below. As a response to this article, Liz Whittaker Chapman responded:

> I recently read an article that praised Hamilton for the way in which it presents its female characters … They're allowed to be complex and real and they defy the tropes that women are usually given in musical theatre. It's true the show doesn't pass the Bechdel test. But it seems unfair to criticize the women for having lives that revolve around Hamilton IN A SHOW CALLED HAMILTON. This particular story doesn't focus on the women. It focuses on Alexander Hamilton. It doesn't claim to do anything else. There simply isn't enough time or room in this particular narrative for the women to be given the same stage time. That's okay. They're still given complexity. Furthermore, the ensemble IS gender-blind casting.[86]

Chapman's assertation that the ensemble "IS gender-blind casting" missteps slightly in that the ensemble is very decisively made up of six male and five female ensemble tracks. But, her point is that the ensemble *functions*, for the most part, outside of gender prescriptions; thus, it is in that regard different and even revolutionary regarding feminism and traditional musical theatre practices. Semantics of this debate aside, I argue that what these critiques suggest is "missing" from the show is actually present within the ensemble, more specifically within the choreography of the ensemble body—collective and individual.

For all intents and purposes, every piece of musical theatre that scripts a social ballroom dance sequence employs socially dictated expressions of patriarchy. The 1997 Official Syllabus of the College Ballroom Dance Association, *Ballroom Dance: American Style* by Shirley Rushing and Patrick McMillan instructs, "It is the responsibility of the man to initiate and complete a movement pattern. His knowledge of a variety of movement patterns makes dancing more interesting just as one's knowledge of different subject matter makes conversations more interesting."[87] Grand numbers such as *My Fair Lady's* "Embassy Waltz" (1956), *Cinderella's* "Ten Minutes Ago"/ "Waltz for a Ball" (1957), *The Sound of Music's* "Ländler" (1959), and even more modern productions such as *Anastasia's* "Once Upon a December" (2017) use the traditional practice of the male chorus member as the lead figure, while the female chorus member is turned, dipped, and lifted. Blankenbuehler leans on such patriarchal male/female coupling as well as the basic practices of turning, dipping, and lifting the female body. Janet Wolff's piece "Reinstating Corporeality: Feminism and Body Politics" argues:

> Body politics need not depend on an uncritical, ahistorical notion of the (female) body. Beginning from the lived experience of women in their currently constituted bodily identities—identities which are *real* at the same time as being socially inscribed and discursively produced—feminist artists and cultural workers can engage in the challenging and exhilarating task of simultaneously affirming those identities, questioning their origins and ideological functions, and working toward a nonpatriarchal expression of gender and the body.[88]

Blankenbuehler's use of ideologically gendered social ballroom practices aid in affirming the identity of the characters within this historical moment in the 1780s alongside Paul Tazewell's costuming.

Tazewell's use of trousers as the base costume for the collective ensemble resists "period-appropriate" practices regarding gender. Simply put, women in the late eighteenth century would wear a large skirt or dress, certainly not pants. Although the use of a corset for the female ensemble top versus the vest for the male ensemble top does still hint at a construction of gender, for the majority of the production, the ensemble presents and functions rather androgynously. For this scene, Tazewell adds parchment-colored, petticoat skirts to the bottom of the female ensemble costumes, small parchment-colored bows to their corset shoulder straps, as well as high heels and Continental Army jackets to the top of the male ensemble costumes.[89] Additionally, the female ensemble body maintains the exposure of her arms. When juxtaposed to Angelica, Eliza, and Peggy Schuyler's more eighteenth-century appropriate costumes, silk taffeta dresses with long sleeves, the collective female ensemble body becomes emblematic of the promise of freedom, sexuality, and autonomy for women in U.S. society. In "Helpless," the overall collective ensemble is closer to the *character in the story* side of the function scale than the *narrator of the story* side of the function scale. Though, when the number becomes duplicated in "Satisfied," we will see the feminist work that challenges the traditional female role within social ballroom dance, shifting the collective female ensemble body's function to omniscient commentator.

It is during "Helpless" that the audience learns of Alexander Hamilton's rapidly developing relationship with Elizabeth Schuyler. When discussing this moment in *Hamilton: the Revolution*, Jeremy McCarter points out, "The musical theatre canon offers many ways to depict this courtship: sweeping waltzes, soaring ballads, the conventions of stage romance. Lin had a better idea. Having grown up on hip-hop and R&B, he saw that the story of Alexander and Eliza's relationship is hip-hop and R&B's *wheelhouse*."[90] Once again, Miranda's tendency toward hip-hop opened a window for Blankenbuehler to layer in a hybrid movement style that calls on the overall collective ensemble body as an instrument for social commentary. Within the social ballroom dance score, Blankenbuehler uses hip-hop and twenty-first-century social dance practices to provide a contemporary dialogue of feminine sexuality and bodily agency.

The short number "A Winter's Ball" sets up the narrative of Alexander and Eliza's courtship as Burr, Hamilton, Laurens, and the ensemble men take over the stage. As Burr begins, a call and response is created with 'all men' replying "Ladies" to his declamations. On the first "Ladies!" female ensemble member Carleigh Bettiol enters downstage right holding a wine glass. This is the first time the audience sees the new additions to the female ensemble costume (skirt, bows, and heels). She walks diagonally to upstage left, acknowledging the men seemingly trying to flirt with her, and exits. Bettiol began her path from the strongest position onstage, suggesting to the audience that the idea of "Ladies!" will be an essential concept for the foreseeable future. The choice to have her move upstage guides the audience's view to the point of her exit, where Angelica Schuyler then enters—despite the collective male ensemble moving and singing. Angelica, unmoving, maintains the focus onstage. The power given to these women through the staging echoes a subtle detail in Chernow's biography on which Miranda seems to have latched for inspiration:

> Sleighing parties full of pretty young women succeeded in crossing snowdrifts to attend receptions. Hamilton subscribed to 'dancing assemblies'—fancy-dress balls attended by chief officers—held at a nearby storehouse ....In this anomalous setting, the women courted these revolutionaries in powdered hair and high heels.[91]

Chernow's articulation that it was the women engaging in the act of courting men, rather than the traditional practice of men instigating the courting, gives a bit of insight into the power dynamics within the winter soldiers' ball. As will be shown through the choreography, the women have agency; they are beyond props to be manipulated by male actors.

Burr continues to narrate, crossing along the apron downstage, "A winter's ball / And the Schuyler sisters are the envy of all."[92] Hamilton, eager to climb the social ladder from a once penniless orphan to a respected statesman, meets Angelica centerstage. While the audience is not yet privy to their conversation, the suspense of this seemingly secretive interaction will be resolved in due time.

As the company transitions into "Helpless," the stage deck turntable is activated, helping to swirl the rest of the overall collective ensemble onto the stage. As Eliza begins to sing, she is accompanied by "Female Ensemble, Angelica, Peggy," rhythmically singing "Hey" on the upbeat.[93] This pert, "Hey," suggests that these women are making the first move toward the men as they choose their partners for dancing. Four male/female ensemble couples commence on the rim of the turntable. Eliza, Angelica, and Peggy Schuyler are center. By the lyric "Helpless," the choreography of the four couples synchronizes and begins to frame Eliza.

For the majority of the overall collective ensemble's choreography, the couples avoid "closed position."[94] Instead, they use a cuddle position, parallel position, promenade position, or sweetheart position.[95] In short, each of these requires the partners to stand next to one another in some fashion rather than to face one another. This avoidance of a closed position is indicative of eighteenth and nineteenth-century social ballroom dance practices. The closed position was once thought to be utterly scandalous. Jane Desmond reports:

> … dance manuals included drawings showing "proper" and "improper" ways to embrace while dancing, specifically the position of the head, arms, and upper body, and the required distance that should be maintained between male and female torsos. In manuals directed toward the middle and upper classes, bodies that pressed close, spines that relaxed, and clutching arms were all denigrated as signs of lower-class dance style.[96]

She continues by highlighting the idea that the closed position was once considered to be sexually dangerous as it was thought to cause women to "take leave of their senses."[97] If the closed position did indeed cause women to relinquish themselves to their male partner, avoiding the closed position in this choreography prevents any suggestion of losing one's autonomy.

Additionally, Baroque minuets such as the fleuret or the allemande were used as courting tools. Carol Téten describes, "The social dances reflected a mating ritual which gives an eloquent picture of the social mores of the era ….There was a constant interplay between maintaining polite distance and fulfilling the pull of sexual attraction."[98] Although Blankenbuehler certainly curates a piece of choreography that is historically inaccurate, he plays with this push and pull between 1780s decorum and 2010s decorum in the dance sphere. As Chernow articulates, these soldiers' balls were themselves anomalous. During *The Hamilcast* podcast, Blankenbuehler reflects, "I wanted the atmosphere to feel like, 'Who is the hottest person to catch?' … I had no interest in a gavotte. I had no interest in a social dance of the period. But, like, how do we take the social dance of a period idea and make it hip?"[99] The atmosphere that Blankenbuehler creates fosters the anomaly of the soldiers' balls, allowing the women to step out of the social mores of the era. But, for an audience ignorant of that nuance, it also allows the collective female ensemble body to freely court the male collective ensemble body, hinting at a contemporary norm of permissiveness and independence.

Peppering in social ballroom movements such as arch turns, parallel pivots, hesitations, spirals, balances, walkarounds, cuddles, and twinkles,

Blankenbuehler creates the idea of a social ballroom dance. Because each couple remains in a designated location, at least for the first section of the dance, it could be labeled a "spot dance."[100] The audience sees the female/male couples, recognizes these more formal movements, and understands it to be a social ballroom dance. However, the majority of the movement throughout is hip-hop isolations and groves such as pop-locks, bounces, snakes, lunges, and even grinding. When Eliza and the women sing "Grind to the rhythm as we / wine and dine," the male ensemble bodies are in front of their female counterparts; both are facing the same direction.[101] The "polite distance" of social ballroom dances of the era is broken as the men grind on the women.

In her article "Grinding on the Dance Floor: Gendered Scripts and Sexualized Dancing at College Parties," Shelly Ronen articulates that grinding generally involves "a woman rubbing her buttocks into a man's groin and her back against his torso in a repetitive motion to the beat of the music."[102] Although Ronen maintains that the male partner is predominantly in control of the action within this danced interaction, she suggests, "The line for women's agency was drawn at initiation, as they could only be powerful by submitting or withholding their bodies from initiating men."[103] Ronen labels grinding as a "significant means of sexual signaling," which directly speaks to the use of social dance as a mating ritual across time. Continuing she notes, "Once approached, therefore, women would choose compliance or cessation."[104] During the winter soldiers' ball, the women initiate the courting and choose their dancing partner. They, then, hold the dominant position, typically reserved for the male partner during standard grinding practices. Contrary to Ronen's observation, the female partners do not completely relinquish or submit to the male immediately following the initiation challenging the philosophy that the woman either has to comply with the male or cease their interaction. The choreographic score swiftly maneuvers between patriarchal social ballroom dance conventions and the collective female ensemble, maintaining a sense of agency and control.

It is through the use of hip-hop that the collective female ensemble bodies can exude power in a world in which they might otherwise have had none. Original Broadway *Hamilton* ensemble member Betsy Struxness elaborates:

> I think the rise of hip-hop on Broadway is allowing the women to finally show the community what we're worth. There are very few times on Broadway when women aren't being either sexy, dainty, or

> cute as dancers. Hip-hop needs strength, aggression, and athleticism. There is nothing weak about hip-hop … It can seem very pedestrian and ridiculously intricate within the same breath. Very few genres offer the same.[105]

To Struxness's point, staging a synchronous mating ritual through hip-hop, controlled by the collective female ensemble body, is relatively the opposite of Eliza's choreography. As the collective ensemble body, male and female, carnivalizes patriarchal social dance practices, they elevate the audience's understanding of Eliza's character as being purer and more refined. Her stillness in a sea of salacious dancing, her sleeves surrounded by exposed women's arms, her coy approach to Alexander following the fast-paced coupling of the others at the party all frame Eliza as being unique. Chernow cites Alexander Hamilton saying this about Eliza: "'Her good sense is destitute of that happy mixture of vanity and ostentation which would make it conspicuous to the whole tribe of fools and foplings … She has good nature, affability, and vivacity unembellished with that charming frivolousness which is justly deemed one of the principal accomplishments of a *belle*.'"[106] Contrasting the collective female ensemble body with Eliza in this way reminds the audience that they exist both inside and outside of time. By casting a contemporary feminist perspective on their historically scripted characters, they can be read as having the prerogative to choose what social mores they abide by or not. Within the show, they are given the capacity to oscillate between and around traditional gender roles while Eliza is rooted firmly to plot and is bound, more or less, to traditional gender roles.

The following section of "Helpless" tells of the introduction of Eliza to Hamilton by Angelica. As these conversations begin to take place downstage, behind the principal characters, the ensemble couples transition from moving with their partner to moving as a group—emulating the large group social dances of the eighteenth century. The overall collective ensemble begins moving in a counter-clockwise direction to the upstage right space forming a diagonal line structured from the downstage right corner upwards toward the left.[107] The collective female ensemble is facing toward the audience, and the collective male ensemble is facing away from the audience. The women fan their right arm up and over into the right hand of their male partner. Then, the male partner lifts the connected hands prompting a loop turn, moving their female partner under their arm, switching places.[108] The couples now face front in a cuddle position and complete a full turn together in either direction. Blankenbuehler explains the events during the dialogue between Hamilton, Angelica, and Eliza:

> ... there's a dance that's happening stage right that's like you see in many a movie where [...] the hands are up, and there's that couple going under the arm and, like, that's as close as we get to anything period-appropriate in the entire show. And, I also wanted to use that there cuz [sic] I knew I wanted to use it as the recognizable framing device when it repeats—cuz [sic] it's so specific—and then intentionally break it the second time when Angelica breaks for "Satisfied." ... [T]ake something that you recognize so that when it repeats and breaks, you notice the break. You have to make it obvious.[109]

Choreographing a more patriarchal, period-appropriate moment during Eliza's "Helpless" once again speaks to her naïve, abide by expected social conventions personality. Therefore, when Blankenbuehler subverts this moment during Angelica's "Satisfied," the collective female ensemble body gains more power. Likewise, the audience comes to understand Angelica to be more mature, wise, and pushing against the gendered conventions of the time in the historical moment.

The remainder of "Helpless" stages Eliza and Alexander's courtship through their wedding. "Satisfied" begins as Angelica's toast to Eliza and Alexander at their wedding but quickly *rewinds* to "A Winter's Ball" as she remembers the first moment she met Alexander. The company of bodies onstage abstractly moves through a series of lighting effects and returns to the staging that begins with Bettiol's entrance downstage right as the men sing, "Ladies!" in their diagonal formation. Blankenbuehler narrates this moment for *The Hamilcast*, "That shade of the men there, like every man, just wants to score ... when the audience sees it repeat, they start to see 'Oh Hamilton, that's Hamilton. Hamilton wants that.'"[110] The staging becomes understood to have doubled meaning as "Helpless" is duplicated but seen through Angelica's perspective rather than Eliza's.

After the company sings "This is not a game ... " in "Satisfied," the staging has returned to Hamilton and Angelica's first encounter, but this time the audience hears their conversation.[111] It is arguably at this moment that Blankenbuehler's metaphorical use of diagonals begins to take shape. Blankenbuehler discloses:

> In symbolism, in painting, a diagonal that goes from—like an ingenue's entrance—so she's upstage left, and she's facing downstage right, it's

> a child's perspective on life. And if you are facing the other way, it's a mature adult's perspective on life … and so that's why an ingenue in a show enters from up left and rushes down right. It's cuz she's hopeful; she wants the right things. And so, when somebody's cynical, they're facing downstage left.[112]

After Angelica makes her ingenue entrance upstage left, Hamilton executes a counter cross assuming the downright diagonal looking at Angelica with hope and youthful longing. Angelica remains relatively center until she sings, "And I realize … "[113] Halfway through the line, the company vocally joins her. At this moment, she turns slightly to face the downright, idealistic angle. The overall collective ensemble has now returned to the upstage right space in their diagonal line that featured the eighteenth-century social ballroom dance style choreography in "Helpless." They command the mature adult's perspective angle to punctuate the internal conflict Angelica is encountering.

As Blankenbuehler pointed out, the social ballroom sequence becomes a recognizable moment in time for the audience; but as it is repeated, the choreography is directly broken in order to communicate Angelica's subtext. The collective female ensemble is facing toward the audience, and the collective male ensemble is facing away from the audience. The women fan their right arm up and over toward the right hand of their male partner. Then, the male partner ducks under the arm of their female partner as the female partner steps forward past them, switching places. The collective male ensemble stands straight with their left arm behind their back. The right arm is bent upward, holding the gesture to count "Number one!"[114] Rather than turning back to face their male partner as they did in "Helpless," the collective female ensemble lunges toward Angelica onto their left leg. The collective female ensemble's deviation from the social ballroom dance sequence here, adding a contemporary spin, allows them to become an abstract, retrospective extension of Angelica's consciousness. Their right arm goes straight back into a diagonal with their left arm bent, hand to toward their heart, palms are open in "blades." The collective female ensemble gaze is toward Angelica—from the upstage right to the downstage left diagonal, the cynical angle. Their body posture mirrors the diagonal on which they are looking, suggesting to the audience that Angelica's consciousness knows she will have to be mature and responsible about her situation, even if it is not what her heart wants.

Correspondingly, the role of the overall collective ensemble during this number is now noticeably different. Rather than being characters at the winter soldiers' ball, within the story of "Helpless," they are now omniscient narrators and commentators on the complicated social and personal dynamic of the elder Schuyler sister. Not only are they singing with Angelica, but their movements now complement *her* as opposed to the setting of the ball. The overall collective ensemble is no longer engaging in more traditional social ballroom dance practices that were present in the first iteration of this scene. Instead, their movements have taken on a more metaphorical subtext quality. As she sings, "My father has no sons, so I', the one / Who has to social climb for one," the overall collective ensemble is now facing away from her, right arm behind their backs, left arm slowly pointing up toward the sky.[115] Miranda points out, " … Philip Schulyer really had *loads* of sons. I conveniently forgot that while I was writing this in service of a larger point: Angelica is a world-class intellect that does not allow her to flex it."[116] The overall collective ensemble's back is to her, pointing to such exclusion.

When Angelica introduces Hamilton to Eliza, she faces the downstage left corner, the angle of a mature adult. During the introduction between Hamilton and Eliza, the overall collective ensemble replicates the recognizable social dance movement in the upstage right diagonal from which they deviated on "Number one!" The women fan their right arm up and over into the right hand of their male partner. Then, the male partner lifts the connected hands prompting a loop turn, moving their female partner under their arm, switching places.[117] The couples now face front in a cuddle position and complete a full turn together. As the scene momentarily steps back into real-time, as opposed to Angelica's retrospective narration, the overall collective ensemble resumes the social ballroom dance choreography as it was in "Helpless." Not only does this help to establish the shift in time, but it also complements Angelica's mature decision to introduce him to her sister because of her responsibility as the older sibling to marry up in the world. She is choosing to maintain the status quo.

On "Number two!" the male dips the female partner out of the cuddle position toward Angelica before releasing the hold. The collective female ensemble bodies turn to face upstage right with their arms up in the air, heads slightly lowered. A gestural image of surrender is evoked through the collective female ensemble. Angelica must surrender her feelings for Alexander; she must surrender her intelligence and independence to take her place as wife to an upper-class businessman.[118] The collective male ensemble separates from the collective female ensemble and moves to stage left. The collective female ensemble is left alone, surrendering, and independent. Recreating a stage picture reminiscent of the end of "Right Hand Man," the collective male ensemble forms a single-file line, as if they are in a military formation, positioning Hamilton in the middle of the line. They manipulate their heads with their left hand to direct their focus toward Angelica, who is just off of center. When Angelica suggests that marrying a Schuyler sister would elevate his status, the male ensemble members separate in either direction revealing Hamilton, and they reform the line behind him. His status is metaphorically elevated to the front of the line. The collective male ensemble then takes various levels to turn Hamilton to his left to face Eliza. This puppeteering, physically done by the male ensemble but intellectually done by Angelica, highlights the push and pull between gendered dynamics of control and power. Although Angelica possessed the ability to quietly elevate Hamilton's social status by introducing him to her sister (inciting their marriage), the male body or male person still maintained a heightened position within colonial American society.

Amid the dialogue between Eliza, Alexander, and Angelica, the overall collective ensemble has reinstated the social dance sequence one more time. They quickly move through the scenes regarding Eliza and Alexander's courtship before pausing one last time in Angelica's thoughts. Blankenbuehler reflects:

> And so, at the end of "Satisfied," the diagonal, like you meet Hamilton on the correct diagonal, all of those things happen on the correct diagonal. And then, when Angelica's offering her toast, it's on the mature diagonal. And then, at the end of "Satisfied," when she's saying he could be mine, she's facing him on the idealistic angle and then chooses to switch the angle, and so she chooses the angle, so Eliza rotates downstage, Hamilton goes upstage, Angelica turns to face the other way and says, "at least I have his eyes in my life," and then she restores the original toast on the angle that says, 'im going to face life like a mature adult, knowing how things really work.
>
> [...]
>
> She's like I could've been idealistic and in love and have hope in my life, but that's not the way it works. She shifts the entire number to face the other way ... Hamilton's down right, and then they both switch places, and she turns her focus to the left, and at the very last second ... Eliza turns her head to the right ....so Angelica is looking the cynical angle [and] Eliza [is looking] the idealistic angle.[119]

The dynamic of the angles Blankenbuehler articulates here also resonates within the ensemble. During this second entendre of Angelica's toast, the entire company faces the downstage left diagonal toward Alexander and Eliza. The omniscient ensemble possesses more knowledge than in the first iteration. They have shifted from being naïve and in the moment with Eliza to being learned, mature, and supporting Angelica.

During "Helpless" and "Satisfied," the overall collective ensemble body subverts both eighteenth-century gendered social practices, but also gendered practices of dance within musical theatre. The collective female ensemble body negotiates the past/present duality as they move between permitting patriarchal conventions and challenging them. Through Blankenbuehler's choreography and inclusion of hip-hop movements, the female ensemble body can be seen as autonomously initiating, encouraging, and practicing sexuality. They affirm the identity of feminine characters within the plot while also challenging ideological forces that would have typically structured them within patriarchal scripts—particularly during the Revolutionary War. Blankenbuehler still works within selected patriarchal practices such as the male/female coupling and hits at social ballroom dance choreography of the time. However, by choreographing "Satisfied" to directly subvert these ideas, the collective female ensemble body signals the promise that gendered philosophies will indeed shift. Because "Helpless" and "Satisfied" split the collective ensemble along gendered lines, a divergence from the majority of the production, when the collective ensemble coalesces, their unified embodied voice supports a twenty-first-century feminist sociological metanarrative of equality and freedom from patriarchal conventions.

4.5 "Yorktown (The World Turned Upside Down)": Communicating Revolution

Long-time collaborator and original *Hamilton* swing ensemble member Morgan Marcell mused, "I like being a soldier. It's pretty badass that men and women are given the same choreography. It's only sort of gender-specific in the ball, actually."[120] Continuing to reflect upon her time working with Blankenbuehler, Marcell divulged:

> I know many choreographers that address issues such as class, gender, race, sexuality through movement. But that is such a vast list of civil rights issues we face in the current climate, that I think it is hard not

> to address one of them. I do think using dance as a narrative tool, however, is Andy's strength, so it makes his views on those issues subtle yet effective. The RIGHT [sic.] in our civil rights, humanity, is woven into the backbone of the piece like a constant thread you never see, but feel. For instance, in *Hamilton's* "Yorktown," female dancers play soldiers, customarily men for that time. As an audience member, you're focused on the battle at hand, but you leave the theater noticing that females carried as much weight as the males, both physically and in their storytelling. The actual number isn't about equality for women, but it's a thread in the blanket.[121]

Following "Satisfied" and leading up to "Yorktown (The World Turned Upside Down)," the female ensemble bodies have resumed their more gender-neutral position within the collective ensemble. They returned to their riding boots and pants immediately following "Satisfied," and one by one began to acquire the Continental Army jacket. Tazwell also adds a matching parchment-colored waistcoat to the collective ensemble costume. These additional clothing elements visually orient the collective ensemble further into the past historical narrative of *Hamilton*. Throughout "Yorktown (The World Turned Upside Down)," the collective ensemble seamlessly transitions between soldiers and embodied illustration of Hamilton's consciousness. As Marcell suggests, the visibility of the contemporary association augmenting the ensemble body is still present and woven into the piece, but it is not as explicit as it was in "Alexander Hamilton" or "Helpless"/ "Satisfied." Reunifying the collective ensemble body for the battle marks a vital shift or advancement in the historical narrative, and consequently, the production narrative once again uplifts the optimistic outlook of revolution—the American Revolution and the theatrical revolution.

Remembering the 2014 workshop presentation of *Hamilton*, McCarter illuminates:

> The biggest jolt came toward the end of Act One, when the actors came onstage wearing blue coats with red trim and brass buttons: unmistakably the uniforms of George Washington's Continental Army. That day, for the first time, 150 audience members had the mind-altering experience of watching black and Latino actors, young men and women from communities that have seen their freedom infringed for hundreds of years, win freedom for us all.[122]

Regimented by their uniforms, the collective ensemble bodies portray the soldiers fighting for the freedom of the United States—male, female, Black, white, Brown, et al. This pivotal battle in the war for independence marks a transition in the country's history, in Alexander Hamilton's life, and the production. At the top of "Yorktown (The World Turned Upside Down)," Lafayette and Hamilton's illustrious "Immigrants: We get the job done" reemphasizes the importance of this story told in this way (by people of color).[123] In the event that the audience has become complacent to the significance of the bodies on stage in the hour leading up to the number, the quintessential principle behind the production is revived. Although the collective ensemble bodies are written character-wise to represent more of the past narrative than the liminal past/present omniscient observer/commentator that they have portrayed for the majority of the production, through Blankenbuehler's heightened gesture and hip-hop (and arguably their hairstyles), the individual ensemble bodies within the collective can still be discerned keeping the past/present dichotomy operational.

To energize and intensify the vitality of the Battle of Yorktown within the narrative, Blankenbuehler moves from choreographed pedestrian movement to a more aggressive hip-hop score complemented by the use of guns as a crucial prop. He fluidly moves the collective ensemble in and out of narrator, principal character's consciousness, metaphor, and character(s) within the story to elevate their significance. Additionally, he strategically utilizes moments of stillness to amplify viewing and reading the *bodies* onstage. Susan Leigh Foster suggests that sometimes choreography can be "envisioned as providing an arena in which to encounter and potentially transcend the histories of oppression, colonization, or enslavement that form part of the corporeal legacies of potential collaborators so as to celebrate a common humanity."[124] Blankenbuehler's amplified hip-hop dance aesthetic creates an opportunity for the choreography to transcend the white founding father narrative and unite an optimistic contemporary community in an embodied celebration of optimism.

After Lafayette and Hamilton part ways, the collective ensemble inches into a semi-circle around Hamilton—who has moved center stage. They reprise lyrics from the number "My Shot," but the choreography is different. Repeating the words, "I am not throwin' away my shot!" seven of the collective ensemble bodies take a deep step every two counts to enter the space.[125] It is as if they are quietly sneaking through the woods. Beginning with Sasha Hutchings downstage right, they initiate a canon of lunges, moving their hands to their chests with elbows up, parallel to the ground. Each ensemble body moves to the syncopated rhythm within, "Hey yo, I'm just like my country, I'm young, / scrappy and hungry."[126] Hamilton slowly turns counter-clockwise to follow their movements. The audience is able to absorb each individual ensemble body taking and holding their step in this sequence. Not only is it a unified voice of the troops and Hamilton readying for battle, but it is individual voices reminding themselves what they are fighting for.

When George Washington enters the space, they all meet in a salute and pulse as if they are marching. On the lyric "'Til the world turned upside down!" the salute shifts into an abstract gesture where the fist grinds against the head.[127] Each individual ensemble body interprets this movement differently. For example, Thayne Jasperson rests the back of his hand on the forehead, the palm opens, and the fingers one by one twist the hand in a circle. For Seth Stewart, the salute ever so slightly remains, crossing the bladed hand across the front of the face. For Ephriam Sykes, the palm opens outward from the salute, closes into a fist, and the elbow moves the arm in front of the face. These subtle differences allow the individual ensemble body to remain present and have agency within the collective ensemble—particularly in a number where their unique bodies have become more masked by the jackets.

In a video interview for the *Wall Street Journal*, Blankenbuehler, with the help of associate Stephanie Klemons, explains the movement accompanying Hamilton's monologue, beginning with "I imagine death so much it feels / more like a memory."[128] Through this sequence, the collective ensemble functions as an embodied interpretation of Hamilton's consciousness. Blankenbuehler begins:

> So throughout the show, there's many times where Hamilton sort of goes into his own head, speaks about his fears, speaks about his desires, his needs. There's a monologue that says "I imagine death," and he does it several times in the show. And in my head, what I wanted to capture was, like, the pause of time and do a filmic close up to almost, like, see what's in the back of his head. So, as they're marching into the Battle of Yorktown, his first time in total command of his battalion, what we see is his group of marching troops sort of freeze, and they bring to life this lyric that he says.[129]

He continues: "So, right away, a thing that is very important is that we stop-time so that the audience knows this gesture is very stylized."[130] In a formation behind Hamilton, five members of the collective ensemble, active but controlled, move forward into a lunge on their left leg allowing the arms to follow as if they are walking in slow motion. On the word "memory," they move their right hand with an open palm behind their head, and their left hand comes up to point to their forehead. They nod up on "this is" and back to center on "where it." On "gets me," the left hand is brought down below the chin, open palm, chin resting between the thumb and the pointer finger. Blankenbuehler adds, "This position right here is important to me. It's this sense of pride that says, 'I believe in something so much you can put a knife to my neck and I'm not gonna change how I feel.'"[131] Acknowledging the open palm of the right arm, still located behind the head, as the notion of a "memory," he adds, " … from memory up in the back of my head, we have this very vicious, violent position where now he's not afraid of facing death."[132] For the phrase, "On my feet, / The enemy ahead of me," the step activates a metaphor for marching, and an arm movement forward emulates looking down the barrel of a gun.[133]

During this Hamilton consciousness section, the collective ensemble body provides a contemporary, embodied, and metaphorical introspection to Hamilton's thoughts through the Blankenbuehlerized pedestrian and hip-hop gestures. They move in and out of fourth position anticipating the action of battle that is about to happen. Continuing through the movements of this section, the following breakdown Blankenbuehler gives is about the lyric "at least I have a friend / with me."[134]

He discloses:

> I have two kids, and one of my favorite things to do is spend the end of my day, like right before the kids' bedtime, watching the Yankees. So that time I have with my son is really, really important. This lyric is "at least I have a friend/ with me." And so this is sort of channeling that idea. So from here [left hand up as if it is a pitcher with a baseball glove, right hand with the ball in the glove preparing for a pitch], I take the baseball behind my back into my glove [now the body is in profile with the left leg in a passé]. Instead of the pitch, it goes all the way to point to my rifle, which gets held up over my head. So it's equating that sense of, "that weapon is gonna save me." And that idea is as important as my best friend by my side.[135]

Behind the group of five are four additional ensemble members in a horizontal line. They are also executing the choreography articulated above.

However, they are doing so with a gun in their hand. When the group of five moves the baseball from the glove to point overhead to the rifle on the lyric "Weapon in my hand," the group of four lifts the rifle up in the air with both hands so that it is parallel to the ground.[136] The use of the prop here makes the gesture of pointing up overhead at a "gun" undeniably clear. While they predominantly are functioning as a tangible representation of Hamilton's consciousness, the collective ensemble body also elevates a sense of humanity for the group of soldiers that will follow his unprecedented plan of attack.

From the rifle gesture, the collective ensemble hints toward Hamilton's growing confidence and power as they bend their arms upwards to form a move that resembles flexing one's biceps on "a command."[137] Blankenbuehler elaborates, "[I]t's like the rank, my epaulets, the uniform, but also this musculature of being totally in charge."[138] They, then, turn inward to face one another behind Hamilton as he sings about Eliza and their unborn child. Blankenbuehler continues,

> I always heard a heartbeat. So, it goes, "*boom, boom*," And so, that's sort of reflected in the music; but for me, what I needed the cast to do was *feel* that heartbeat. So right away, we have a roll [backward of the shoulders], and it goes to a contraction [of the torso, with corresponding arm motion] that starts to point to my head as if all I'm thinking about is what's in my [heart].[139]

The collective ensemble then turns to face upstage—continuing the *feeling* of this moment rather than the *seeing* of this moment. Their right arm extends from their head, diagonally upward as if pulling a thought out of one's mind. Once the arm is completely stretched, the wrist flicks downward, dropping the thought to the ground. Blankenbuehler suggests that this moment says, "the thing that's in the back of my head is ruling me."[140] Concurrently, Eliza is conveniently walking across the second-level balcony, helping to further the notion that Hamilton's thoughts and feelings for Eliza and his unborn child are reigning over his consciousness.

As the thought is dropped to the ground, the stop-time moment starts to fade; Hamilton and the soldiers reenter a space of real-time. The collective ensemble body of soldiers regains their own identity apart from Hamilton. Blankenbuehler's choreography transitions from heightened gesture to a more amplified, active hip-hop reminding the audience to view this collective ensemble of soldiers through their contemporary ensemble bodies. The past/present dialectic resurges as the collective ensemble body made up of diverse individual ensemble bodies cooperatively tells the story of the Battle of Yorktown using the embodied vocabulary of contemporary ambition, defiance, and revolution. Continuing with his demonstration Blankenbuehler illuminates, "When we were working on this … it was about saying how can we find a hip-hop step that feels like march?"[141] Blankenbuehler's step decidedly keeps the hands in open blades rather than clenched fists. If the clenched fist suggests tension or distress in this step, the hand's opening eases such association. Moreover, as the step turns to the front and the open hands reach forward, there is an air of hope for the future. Similarly, regarding the feet, the step does progress, freeing the body from the repeated torment. The collective ensemble body begins their march but actively resists its monotony in favor of change—change in the historical way of fighting a war, change in the contemporary way of narrativizing history.

"Marching" forward to the apron of the stage, the collective ensemble of soldiers enters their rank-and-file line to hear their orders. Chernow reports:

> After nightfall on October 14, the allies fired several consecutive shells in the air that brilliantly illuminated the sky. Hamilton and his men then rose from their trenches and raced with fixed bayonets toward redoubt ten, springing across a quarter-mile of landscape pocked and rutted from exploding shells. For the sake of silence, surprise, and soldierly pride, they had unloaded their guns to take the position with bayonets alone.[142]

This illustration comes alive through the collective ensemble for the remainder of the number. When Hamilton sings, "Take the bullets out your gun!" they raise their arms overhead into fifth position with their hands in fists facing the sky.[143] Paused in this position, the audience is given the opportunity to observe the line of individual ensemble bodies united along the front of the stage and receives them as a battalion of soldiers listening to their leader give them an unprecedented command. Concurrently, the past/present collective ensemble of diverse bodies being asked to fight in an unconventional manner promotes a nuance that reminds the audience of the anomalous nature of their retelling and the need for such a contemporary change in sociopolitical philosophy. Maintaining the clenched fists, moving them down to the hips on "What?" signals a communal moment of tension before they release in optimism and disperse.

When Hercules Mulligan first enters the scene from upstage center, he is noticeably surrounded by a collective of male ensemble bodies. They initiate an intensified hip-hop choreography sequence that features movements similar to krumping. Guy Trebay's article for the *New York Times* titled "The Clowning, Rump-Shaking: How a dance called krumping took over an inner-city neighborhood" defines krumping as "equal parts break dance, pantomimed battle and demonic possession."[144] *The Oxford Dictionary of Dance (2 ed)* defines krumping as:

> a style of hip-hop that originated in California, drawing on elements of clowning (face painting, comic expressiveness), popping, and African dance. It is characterized by inventive, free style movement, often focusing on the chest and arms, and often involving some physical contact between the dancers suggestive of a ritual battle. It has become more aggressive in tone than its clowning origins.[145]

Blankenbuehler seizes on the aggressive, battle nature of this subgenre of hip-hop dance to both escalate to and engage in combat. At first, the use of the collective male ensemble connects this action with a sense of masculinity. Their movements emanate from the pelvis up the torso through bellicose arm gestures.

However, the men drop to the floor and slide outward as the collective female ensemble similarly krumps their way to the center of the stage. Momentarily separating the collective ensemble by gender reminds the audience that in this retelling, not only are they a racially diverse group of people telling the story of the founding fathers through a unified voice, but they are also varied in gender and linked through movement. When the dance break begins, the overall collective ensemble synchronously krumps and break-dances. Blankenbuehler deliberately sets up a juxtaposition just to break it, promoting the idea that the women fight just as aggressively and skillfully as the men. As Marcell explained, the number is not about equality for women, but it is a thread within the choreography that feeds into the past/present duality of *Hamilton*.

Reminiscing about the section of the dance break where the collective ensemble obtains and manipulates their weapons, Blankenbuehler disclosed:

> They have become so good at their craft and the imitating of the British that they could spin on a dime and focus on a dime and kill anything that's in front of them. So, the turn is showing, like, how

> exceptional they have gotten at their skill. Where when you met them in "Right Hand Man," they couldn't even load their gun. And now they are better than the best thing that the Red Coats could do. And the Red Coats aren't kicking and bayonetting and guerilla warfaring. So, they're sloppy Americans doing dirty ass stuff, and at the same time, doing the best thing that the Red Coats could do.[146]

The collective ensemble body vehemently twirls their guns as if they belong to an exhibition drill team. They initiate a pencil turn, freezing in a shooting stance on the penultimate button of the dance break.[147] After about five counts of stillness, they spin on a dime to switch their angle before slowly laying down their gun and gently pushing it away from them. They begin to transition out of the climax of the battle, seemingly walking back to their camp or back home. Laurens observes, "Black and white soldiers wonder / alike if this really means freedom."[148] The collective ensemble pauses in their tracks, looking diagonally upward. George Washington responds, "Not yet."[149] On the downbeat following, the collective ensemble bodies collapse into a second position, grand plié with their torsos folded over toward the ground. Their hands go to their knees; one knee drops to the ground. The individual ensemble bodies—male, female, Black, white, Brown, et al.—convey exhaustion and anguish. They just fought for the very premise of freedom and equality, but justice is still out of reach. The past/present dialogue is palpable.

Melancholically, the company walks around the stage. Their past/present bodies are exhausted from the never-ending fight for freedom and equality. Successively they bring on pieces of furniture, stylistically lifting them overhead and upside down. Soon, the entire company is either standing on furniture, the stairs, or the second-level balcony facing front. Blankenbuehler emphasizes, "When community ideas become bigger, more people face front."[150] In spite of not fully emancipating all bodies residing in the United States during the American Revolution, there is an air of optimism as these diverse, contemporary individual bodies—ensemble and principal—stand in stillness, *showing* that despite this setback, they are free. Nevertheless, this doubleness points to the notion that there is still so much more fighting to do to reach ubiquitous equitability. The stillness of the company allows this dialectic to resonate as the audience bears witness to "black and Latino actors, young men and women from communities that have seen their freedom infringed for hundreds of years, win freedom for us all."[151]

Overall, "Yorktown (The World Turned Upside Down)" advocates a dual narrative regarding the fight for past/present freedoms. Although the collective ensemble's costume and assumed role as soldiers situates them more so in the past, through the comprehension of their diverse individual ensemble bodies within the collective, the audience can perceive them as still being connected to the present. Blankenbuehler's gradual increase from heightened gesture to an amplified hip-hop choreography score stimulates an elevated sense of humanity for these ambiguous soldiers but aggrandizes the contemporary subtext of the number. Although the "Yorktown (The World Turned Upside Down)" could undoubtedly function as an act finale, the number's dramaturgical position as being the fifth number from the end of Act I allows the narrative, subtext, and nuances of the number to continue resonating through "What Comes Next," "Dear Theodosia," "Tomorrow There'll Be More of Us," and "Non-Stop." For the remainder of *Hamilton,* Blankenbuehler continues to impose and promote the past/present duality through the omniscient and omnipresent collective ensemble body and individual ensemble body, encouraging the reception of sociological metanarratives.

4.6 Conclusion: The World Is Wide Enough

Hamilton's position as a cultural phenomenon, now extending beyond the Broadway stage and into the living rooms of those with access to a subscription to Disney+, creates an urgency in interrogating the possibilities of its effects on audiences and the industry. In the six years since it opened at The Public, critics, enthusiasts, academics, and scholars alike have written and analyzed Miranda's text and style. However, like much of musical theatre history, the significance of the ensemble has been left out of the vast majority of these conversations. The production has taken to new heights of subverting traditional musical theatre practices in order to comment on and critique larger questions regarding sociocultural/socioeconomic/sociopolitical institutions and practices—particularly within the United States. Susan Leigh Foster writes, "If the choreography helps viewers to contemplate where they have come from and where they might be going, it serves not so much as a repository of knowledge but as an orienting tool for determining and affirming a system of beliefs."[152] Blankenbuehler's choreography ubiquitously positions the individual and collective ensemble as a way to help viewers contemplate the journey and future of society in the United States.

PART 3
CONTINUED PRACTICE

CHAPTER 5
BLANKENBUEHLER BEYOND MIRANDA

In the Heights, *Bring It On: The Musical*, and *Hamilton* have these things in common: Andy Blankenbuehler, Lin-Manuel Miranda, hip-hop, and a dynamic ensemble.[1] These commonalities beg the question, would the ensemble body, or the ensemble as the lens, be possible without one or more of these ingredients? There is no question that Miranda has written space for the ensemble to function as a fundamental component in each of his pieces.[2] Hip-hop has allowed for a dismantling of hierarchical structures regarding dance aesthetics and functions. In an interview for *Playbill*, he emphasized:

> I believe in the power of a Broadway ensemble; that is my core mission. That's why I started choreographing when I did because I thought dance could be more integral and the ensemble could be more integral. And so, I use the ensemble in a way that always pushes through the principal, always pushes through the narrative. And so, the narrative of the principal's storyline is buffered up by the way we hold them in the show.[3]

Blankenbuehler has developed a philosophy and technique regarding the ensemble—and as, I argue, consequently the ensemble body—in his work on these musicals that he has carried with him elsewhere, beyond Miranda and beyond hip-hop.

While his Broadway directorial debut was with *Bring It On*, since *Hamilton*, Blankenbuehler has taken up the director-choreographer role more frequently. The most notable post-*Hamilton* project was the 2017 production of *Bandstand*, for which he won his third Tony Award for Best Choreography. Despite that project being his last major Broadway gig, Blankenbuehler has been anything but lacking when it comes to passion projects and productions in the queue. In the fall of 2022, he opened a new work, titled *Only Gold*, at the Manhattan Class Company (MCC). In August 2024, Blankenbuehler created a stunning interpretation of the famed musical *Nine* for the Kennedy Center, with hopes of a Broadway transfer. He has also been collaborating on a new musical titled *Bone Music*, created a ballet with Jacob's Pillow titled *Never Alone*, and has expressed early work on the newly anticipated Lin-Manuel Miranda musical, *Warriors*.

Certainly, a director-choreographer comes with a whole new world of responsibilities, creative ownership, and challenges.

> I have found myself in the trickiest place my entire career because my choreography is already directorially minded and so it takes a really secure director to partner with and secure writers and takes me—which I have not always been great at—being able to really slowly articulate my thoughts in a way that doesn't infringe on other people's responsibilities. I haven't done that well in my career, and my career, in some ways, has paid that price, in other ways it hasn't paid the price because my career, my work is directorially minded and when it has worked, it has worked. But, what I found now is that it kind of works its best when I am the director and choreographer. The problem is, I eliminate collaborators so sometimes I get too close to the forest, and I don't see the forest through the trees. I can spend too much time on detail work—which is what happened to *Only Gold*.
>
> Oftentimes, the director can see things from further away because they don't have to be in that room chiseling out the six hours of dance rehearsal and are able to have a bigger perspective on things. I still notice things about *In the Heights* or about *Hamilton* that are so brilliant, and I wonder what the conversation was between Tommy and Paul Tazwell or Tommy and 'so and so.' I have reaped the benefits of being set up to do a good job and, it's easier to have a singular vision when you're doing both, but I've noticed in the past few years that it requires more work on the front end …
>
> *Nine* was a perfect example of that. I had an associate team who was willing to spend hours with me way far in advance and they could really understand where I was coming from so before I got totally stressed out in the eleventh hour they were going to understand my thinking already. It's tricky because I would like to just be a choreographer … I just want to be in the room with smart people. So, I'm willing to do their version of the show, and if they're directing it should be their version of the show. But, it's hard when you have an idea that you think is good to not try to keep pushing your idea … emotionally it might be easier right now for me to be the director and choreographer

> just on a day to day emotional level, but I know I'm robbing myself of the opportunity to continue to deepen my skills and my humanity by having other people in the conversation. And, that's hard. I frankly feel the same way about movement and script because I want to write, but I don't want to wear too many hats, and I'm also removing the ability for somebody who's much smarter than me to be in the room helping the show. *Hamilton's* so good because Lin is brilliant, and *Hamilton's* choreography is good because Lin is brilliant …
>
> I think as a choreographer, I do come from story. I'm going to have opinions about things like underscore and how the song, how the heightened number comes out of the scene … that traditionally wasn't always the role of the choreographer, and so it's baked into the DNA of our industry, where that choreography is not necessarily seen as the same kind of collaboration. I know a lot of people who bring on the entire design team before they bring in the choreographer, so it's difficult to figure out ways to communicate about things that are in your lane …
>
> Then, the idea of how long it takes to make dance come to life is a really difficult thing. I think in a lot of theatre history that time wasn't given and there are a lot of times that the director really does run the room and gives only a little time for dance. That dance, then, becomes about jazz squares. It's too simplistic. In great praise to Tommy, Lin, and Alex, they gave me a lot of time. They let me take the time it needed to make "My Shot" or whatever it is. That is a big commitment. They offered me a lot by giving me that allowance.[4]

One night at dinner, Blankenbuehler ruminated on the conundrums facing the current Broadway industry. New projects are challenging to get off the ground for a myriad of reasons. Aside from securing financial backing and a theatre space, the most significant questions on his mind were: what stories need to be told now? Does the world need this story? And is he the one who should be telling that story? He wants shows to be good, and he wants them to mean something to an audience. Blankenbuehler has also encountered the challenges of new productions that are not written with choreography in mind, where dance is not a necessary vocabulary to tell those stories. So, to confront these difficulties, he has been collaborating with writers to make new projects or revitalizing existing productions that speak to his interests and affinity for seeing storytelling through the body and through an ensemble. Moreover, he has been confronting the challenges of outside perspectives—reviewers and audiences alike—who can have difficulty in understanding dance as an integrative and integral vocabulary for storytelling.

5.1 Bandstand

Perhaps the most notable production Blankenbuehler has taken on post-*Hamilton* was *Bandstand* (2017). Set in the late 1940s, post-World War II, *Bandstand* tells the story of a young veteran who pursues his career as a musician. The story navigates the challenges of love, loss, and post-traumatic stress. A prominent component of the production is the swing band. Music by Richard Oberacker, with book and lyrics by Oberacker and Robert Taylor, hip-hop is unquestionably absent from this production. What is not absent, however, is a dynamic ensemble and a hybrid-dance genre choreography score that places emphasis on ideas over virtuosity.

Blankenbuehler developed and fine-tuned his choreography style during *In the Heights*, *Bring It On: The Musical*, and *Hamilton*, but it was alive and well in *Bandstand*. Even though he was able to bring his beloved 50s and 60s jazz dance genre to the forefront of the dance vocabulary, the ensemble and thus the ensemble body still function in similar ways. Blankenbuehler emphasizes, "We must tell stories about people, and we must tell honest stories about people … We must be believable. We must tell the truth … We need realism and the ability to heighten realism."[5] His emphasis on the ensemble as the fundamental link between the audience and the narrative is not lost when he shifts from Miranda's hip-hop centered pieces to a more traditional musical theatre music and movement score.

In *Bandstand* Blankenbuehler uses the ensemble (bodies) to convey and cope with alcoholism, mental illness, and post-traumatic stress. His favorite moment in the show is what he calls "the piano push" and it happened by complete accident. During their rehearsal process the piano was originally set to come onstage using an automated device; when that device was cut, he needed to find a way to get the piano to center stage. The stage directions for this moment, now written into the libretto, read: "SERVICEMEN *surround* [Donny's] *piano, seeming to push him forward in his composition as he spins out a melody that is gradually overtaken by the sound of the full orchestra in his imagination.*"[6] As the character Donny—who is gravely suffering from survivor's guilt—sits down at the piano to compose a melody to the words of a poem his late-best friend's widow wrote, the figment of soldiers surround

Figure 6 *Hamilton* team sets up in London. Photo courtesy of Stephanie Klemons.

him. They slowly labor to push him and the piano to center stage while he plays. When he begins to make progress with his composition the soldier maintaining the lowest, most hunched over posture suddenly sprints off the stage. One by one others break off taking on their own, individual styles of energetically separating from the piano, either exiting or running around the stage as Donny, at least momentarily, imagines the release of his emotional pain. Commenting on this moment, Blankenbuehler discloses:

> Choreography has to be honest. Like, in *Bandstand* you quickly learn if this person's a believable vet they're not doing a grand jeté ... what soldiers do is they sprint. They run. And so, to see these wounded ghosts actually go back to where they were before it all happened with that sense of speed, it just was an uplifting moment in the theatre that was really, really visceral. And there's no dance step ... about any of it.[7]

Throughout *Bandstand* there are many similar moments that use the ensemble (bodies) to suggest profound connotations.

In contrast is the number "Nobody" which opens the second act of the production. Audiences observe the leading characters of the swing band individually prepare for a performance where they will raise money to travel to New York and participate in a swing band competition. In the surround, individual male ensemble bodies face upstage and move through various Fosse-style poses or moves that add a touch of angst and anticipation into the scene. However, following the initial moments of preparation for the lead characters, the overall collective ensemble enters and moves through a series of dance sequences. The ensemble transitions between individual movement scores as well as small and large group movement scores. They activate the 1950s and 1960s jazz of which Blankenbuehler was more accustomed prior to *In the Heights*. Acknowledging the use of more codified dance Blankenbuehler suggests, "the only reason [the servicemen] are doing a pirouette is if they are excited about something ... [demonstrates jazz pirouette followed by a few finger snaps] and the band is playing, the pirouette informs how I feel about the band."[8] The confidence of the lead characters increases as they closely approach their performance; as Blankenbuehler suggests, this air of confidence is given to the audience through the enthusiasm emanating from the ensemble. There is no question that the dance functions in a variety of ways to serve the number; but, what about the ensemble themselves?

Certainly, in *Bandstand* the notion of "ensemble" is established as Blankenbuehler choreographs individual scores throughout and elevates individual voices within the collective. However, what of the ensemble *body*? Although the ensemble *body* can be seen in moments like "the piano push," it is arguably less present or even absent for the majority of "Nobody." When "Nobody" switches from narrating preparation to showing performance the stage directions read[9]: "*We see their various vignettes ultimately coalesce onto the stage of the Pavilion Nightclub.* DANCING COUPLES *take to the dance floor and mingle at tables in front of the* BAND *as they blast an instrumental break.*" Correspondingly, the dance and ensemble, in part, transition to function as social and atmospheric elements. Nevertheless, the number is exceedingly presentational and spectacle driven supporting the swing band's need for virtuosic swing and jazz dancers. Blankenbuehler does choreograph a few solo moments; but for the most part, the choreography is synchronized. In contrast to *Hamilton*, this synchronicity is uniform, there is little to no wavering in interpretation of a dance movement. Aside from a divide along patriarchal gender lines, there is relatively no distinction between ensemble members. So, how does it affect our understanding of Blankenbuehler's work and the possibilities of the ensemble (body)?

All in all, the ensemble continues to serve a myriad of functions as articulated throughout this project. For "Nobody," the audience receives the vital information from the athletically and synchronistically dancing ensemble that the swing band is celebrated and spectacular. But, the more dance is codified, uniformed, and distanced from heightened gesture, the more the ensemble seemingly becomes invariable. While the genre of hip-hop, or even Blankenbuehlerized hip-hop, indisputably brings with it a sense of uniquity, it does not seem to be the defining factor regarding the ensemble body's fruition. Rather, the use of stylized, pedestrian movement—at least lightly up to interpretation by the individuals in the ensemble—suggests an elevated sense of humanity allowing for the enhanced visibility of the ensemble body. Even though the ensemble *body* is not as ubiquitous in *Bandstand* as it was in the productions associated with Lin-Manuel Miranda, Blankenbuehler continues to ensure the ensemble serves as a lens through which the audience views the piece and the dance serves as a framing device for the ensemble. *Bandstand's* position in Blankebuehler's story marks a key shift from choreographer to director-choreographer, and propels him into a new world to stretch his muscles and see the breadth of possibility that lies within his choreographic methodologies.

5.2 Only Gold

A staccato piano music box melody begins as a black and white film begins to play. Couples appear, and romance is in full bloom as the day dawns. As the light accordion chimes in, the narrative takes shape through the building of simple gestures, heightened ways of walking, into more stylized dance. Elegant lifts begin, and synchronized angled movements are featured throughout the ensemble. A radio-style voice-over begins: "The city of lights shakes off its sleep from the darkness of the Great War. With an insatiable appetite and a rage to live, decadence flourishes. And Paris, once again, reigns as a center of modernity, creativity, and passion. Even the center of the entire world is not prepared for the arrival of the Maharaja of Patiala." The music shifts to British pop artist Kate Nash's 2010 song "Paris" from her album *My Best Friend Is You.*[10] Graceful arms, sharp angles, and head accents take over the bodies of the community as they pair up, observe, and become whisked away through the scene. Nash's song fades as the voice-over resumes:

> A simple story of love, one man, his three wives, ego, Expectation. Temptation. Perfection. Abandoned. Extravagance. Fearlessness. Innocence. And did I mention gold? Six huge trunks of gold and priceless jewels with an impossible challenge. In 90 days, can the finest artisans in Paris create a treasure equal to the perfection of love?

Nash's strong syncopated beats take over as her lyric, "You'll never listen to me" overlays a myriad of relationships before the company ends in a final attitude talk down stage and the video fades. Blankenbuehler's four minute and twenty second pitch video for *Only Gold* highlights a work that had been in progress for nearly a decade before opening at the off-Broadway MCC theatre on November 7, 2022.

Music and lyrics by Kate Nash, book by Andy Blankenbuehler and Ted Malawer, *Only Gold* us about "A royal family's arrival in Paris sets a flurry of activity into motion, forcing nobility and townsfolk alike to examine the choices they've made. As loyalties and loves are tested, will they find the courage to follow their hearts? Paris will never be the same."[11] Playbill's simple synopsis of this new production alone illuminates Blankenbuehler's presence as a writer on this show. The town, Paris, made up of an exquisite ensemble is a central focus of the story. Paris is set up to be the protagonist. Unfortunately, this passion project feel short in the eyes of the reviewers. One such article is Jesse Green's *New York Times* piece, "In 'Only Gold,' Each Move Is Worth 1,000 Words," which praises Blankenbuehler's choreography, but doubles down on script and lyrical struggles:

> "Paris. 1928. A time when rules were ready to be broken." A show that starts that way should come with a content warning: These cliches may

> hurt your teeth. The upside of "Only Gold," … is that it is so pretty to look at, and so musically dreamy, you can mostly tune out the words. Nash's are hard to decipher anyway; because rhyme and scansion aren't her thing, the ear gets no help … Tiresomely, each of these characters has a lesson to learn. And when the watchmaker's fame as a royal provisioner drives a wedge between him and his frustrated wife (Hannah Cruz), even they must learn something—I'm not sure what, but it involves a piano …
>
> [A]ll the dancing is thrilling; perhaps it's the magic in the cobblestones. And if it comes as no surprise that Blankenbuehler, the choreographer of "Hamilton," can assemble eye-catching sequences into long narrative arcs, it's nice to see him working with a full cast of dancers, not just an ensemble … But in "Only Gold," the simplistic story and trite dialogue drag the dancing down. Perhaps the authors spent too much time listening to their hearts and not enough to organs higher and lower.[12]

Sometime later, in an article for *Dance Magazine* senior advising editor Sylviane Gold, who has written about Blankenbuehler throughout his career for the publication, followed up with him regarding the successes and failures of *Only Gold.* For her article he reflected:

> In some ways the reviews surprised me, and in someways they didn't. I know there are tremendous moments—moments I'm extraordinarily proud of. At the same time, I'm aware of how the audience is reacting. So I knew that there were still a lot of things that we had to work on—I was game for that […] Even though a lot said really nice things, they still pointed up the problems more than the pros. So (pause) … that was just a little hard. […] Trying to figure out the way a story grasps an audience is difficult […] I'm really good at it as a choreographer. But when I'm looking at a wider swath, a much wider picture, then it's a complicated thing. I guess that's the trouble you get into when you wear a lot of hats.[13]

Blankenbuehler revealed that in a lot of ways this production was a therapy project for him, affording him the opportunity to exercise his impulses, try new things, problem solve, while working on huge productions such as the famed *Hamilton* and *Bandstand.* You can see moments in both shows throughout *Only Gold*—so much so, that the show has become in a lot of ways a catalogue of Blankenbuehler movement vocabulary and style. A thorough study of *Only Gold* would be a master class in Blankenbuehler dance and methodology.

One move that has become synonymous with Blankenbuehler's choreography is when a character is experiencing an internal struggle, cognitively processing a moment, or developing an idea—storytelling that happens inside a character as opposed to through dialogue—he signals this tension by having the ensemble bring both hands up and to the sides of the head, without touching it, activating tension in the hands. We see moments of this throughout "Yorktown" in *Hamilton*. For *Only Gold*, one clear moment of this is during the number "Work" when the jeweler is given a task to create the most magical necklace fit for a queen. As the ensemble men begin to spread around the stage Henri (played by Ryan Vandenboom) wanders/wonders around the stage attempting to conjure a vision for the necklace. As he pushes a gold trunk upstage, the ensemble brings their hands up to their temples, elbows in, and slowly push their right hand out as if laser-beam focusing in on a specific idea.

On the lyrics "feel the heat, heat, heat" five of the ensemble men make a "V" shape opening toward down stage, sitting on wooden stools while Henri enters the center.[14] They accent each word as their hand gestures toward their head and their bodies face stage left. For Blankenbuehler, this left angle is one of cynicism and doubt. Though, Vandenboom's body remains on the downstage right angle, the angle of optimism and hope. As the ensemble gesture turns to a pantomimic telling of examining a jewel stone—holding a jeweler's loupe—he turns to face the left saying, "ignore limits, ignore reason."[15] After they examine the stone, they flick their right hand down toward the ground—similar to the "scrappy" step discussed earlier in this book that was inspired by a painter in Boston. While Henri coaches his team of jewelers, the audience receives a layered narrative. They are given the pantomime of jewelers working tirelessly to come up with an idea—but more importantly, they are giving an intimate look as to what is happening inside of Henri's head. He is experiencing hope for his future, love for his creativity, pressure to live up to his father's legacy, and a high-stakes client.

In 2017, Dance Lab New York shared a video of Andy Blankenbuehler discussing how he uses the company to workshop ideas and develop choreography. Throughout this video, you can hear the sounds of Nash's music and see bits of dance that will become choreography for *Only Gold*.

> The securing of dancers and the figuring out how to do your own prep is a vicious learning curve, which I'm still not on top of. I mean, I've

> choreographed seven Broadway shows now, and I'm always flailing. I'm always trying to find a studio at the last second and finding dancers at the last second … I had an image when I was working on *Hamilton* where I needed my choreographed brain to be like a jar of water, and I could imagine sand in it, and if you shake it, you couldn't see through the water.
>
> I needed to keep that water clear. What I realize is I have to do a very large amount of my own work first. Also, is not to have your real cast around, because your real cast, you want them to bring the final product to, and their final personalities to. Before you get to that last minute, you want to exhaust every possibility.

As he speaks, you can see dancers playing with the contemplation, internal struggle dance essence among others that would make their way to the final iterations of the show years later. Blankenbuehler's methodology centers around such exploration, such experimentation. But can too much exploration become a problem for a show? Reflecting on such a question, Blankenbuehler muses about how he considers movement for a work that is very much still in progress in a myriad of ways:

> I've done a class combination to a song for that moment already, and the choreography won't apply to that scene. But in working on that combination, I'm able to understand the scene better. And so, it's kind of as if an actor's preparing for an audition, it's the same kind of thing. I'm preparing to understand how to do that scene when I eventually do that scene. And that can't happen until the story is in a place of being solid enough.
>
> That was like a big *Only Gold* problem. I kept doing that exercise to scenes that weren't going to see the light of day. The scene itself wasn't going to work, but I wanted to be making the show. So, I kept choreographing to things that were unfinished. And since the choreography was interesting, I would convince myself the moment could work when really the moment wasn't going to work. Even though the moment could be really cool, it doesn't add to the bigger picture.[16]

Only Gold ultimately closed on November 27, 2022. Despite not meeting the expectations and dreams of the creators, it did win the 2023 Chita Rivera Award for Outstanding Choreography in an Off-Broadway Show, the 2023

Lucille Lortel Award for Outstanding Choreography, among a few other nominations within the Drama Desk and Outer Critics Circle Awards. In his interview with Gold, Blankenbuehler surmised:

> There's a line in the show about how you define success [...] So I'm like, "Okay, Andy how do you define success?" You wrote a show that was produced, and people said, "These are some of the best dances I've ever seen." And I look at them with such *pride*. That should all be success. Unfortunately, I'm also the maker of the show, so figuring out how to define success is a big deal. For me, success isn't: You run the show for four weeks and it goes into people's hearts and minds and dies. It's gone—that's not success to me. Success to me is it keeps going.[17]

5.3 Nine

"Review: Women Show Their Might in a Mesmerizing Revival of *Nine*," by Keith Loria for *Theatre Mania* reports, "Though it would be easy to pay deserving compliments to all the magnificent actresses who grace the stage—more than a dozen—I'll simply add that the beautiful voices and magnetism of the ensemble shines through in every scene, thanks in great part to Blankenbuehler's mesmerizing choreography."[18] The title of this review and Loria's simple observation is precisely what Blankenbuehler's interpretation of the 1982 Broadway musical *Nine* intended. Music and lyrics by Maury Yeston and book by Arthur Kopit, the Tony Award winning musical—based on the film *8½* by Federico Fellini—follows infamous Italian film director, Guido Contini and his flailing need to write a script for a film he is days away from shooting. Caught between his wife Luisa, his mistress Carla, his film star muse Claudia, his producer Liliane la Fleur, and past visions of other women in his life—the standard directorial choice for this production is to place Guido as the protagonist, at the central focus point. This interpretation hypersexualizes the women surrounding him as objects of his desire, of his downfall, of his ruin. Blankenbuehler flips this narrative over using his ensemble as the lens methodology and adds a much needed, feminist revision.

Blankenbuehler's *Nine* opened at The Kennedy Center in Washington, D.C. on August 2, 2024, for a limited run in the Eisenhower Theatre. Approaching revivals can always be a tricky adventure. How much liberty can you take with the original source material? How much should you take? Why does the world need this story again now? Blankenbuehler is no stranger to revivals, but approaching *Nine* his perspective has shifted:

> Before, I wanted to be a chameleon. I thought I was a chameleon. I am very versatile choreographically. But I looked at somebody's career like Robbins and he did *Fiddler*, *West Side Story*, *Bells Are Ringing*. He did all kinds of shows. The Charleston that he did is unbelievable. And so, I grew up thinking that's what I would want to do. If it's Charleston, I want to do a Charleston. But now I realize, yeah, I love the speakeasy. I love that Charleston music, but I don't need to do it like the Charleston. I can do my own version of it …
>
> But for many years, I thought my answer was just to do the traditional version of it really well … In terms of revivals, I know I need to do something that fits my style and fits my entry point to a show. I also want it to feel contemporary in the way it resonates story-wise. It has to be pliable so that the movement, the staging, can be impressionistic. When I look at material now, I feel like it needs to be able to have a reinterpretation. But the bones of it have to be able to

Figure 7 Andy workshopping. Photo courtesy of Andy Blankenbuehler.

> support a reinterpretation. In a lot of revivals, the bones can't support an aggressive retelling. *Nine* can. *Nine,* in content and in material, can support a really aggressive entry point to the show.[19]

Take One. "Ti Voglio Bene/Be Italian," originally choreographed by Thommie Walsh with direction by Tommy Tune, featured a chorus of women dressed in gaudy white costumes. The number began with a still Fosse-esk tableau before revealing Saraghina (played by Kathi Moss), a sex worker monologuing to a group of young boys about how to love, dressed in all black. The chorus of women line up in a "V" opened to downstage with Saraghina and the boys sitting center. A dance break then takes form as Saraghina engages in a sexualized, seated choreography, carefully guiding a tambourine to accent various parts of her body. One by one, the boys reveal a tambourine and begin to echo her. The chorus of women remain standing in position, singing a series of "las" toward the boys, cheering them on as their tambourine choreography becomes more robust. The number concludes with the chorus closing in tighter around Saraghina and the boys, clapping until the button.[20]

Take Two. "Ti Voglio Bene/Be Italian," directed and choreographed by Andy Blankenbuehler, features an ensemble of women dressed in all black. The number begins with the women spread around the stage—some are on a second-level deck, some are sitting around the pit orchestra which is prominently featured across upstage, while Luisa and Guido's mother are downstage right deep in conversation. Young Guido is hiding behind the chaise lounge. On the first snare slap of the song Carla (who was previously in conversation with adult Guido—played by Steven Pasquale—about the two of them getting a divorce so they may marry) turns upstage and throws her arms up in a sharp accent, before exiting. At this same moment, Luisa and Guido's mother reposition to lean on a pillar stage right, and a sprinkling of other ensemble members also hit a varied set of accents with their arms and legs. Adult Guido stands center, facing the downstage right angle, as Saraghina (played by Lesli Margherita) beings singing and young Guido comes out from behind the chaise. They both sit (young Guido on the chaise, adult Guido on the floor) while he is reflecting on an influential moment from his past. Saraghina sings:

> "Ti voglio bene" you will say
> It means "I want you every day"
> "Ti voglio bene" (Ti voglio bene)[21]

Saraghina's message for Guido is a fundamental part of his backstory, of the way he would go on to live his life. As this verse unfolds, ensemble of women begin to creep in around the stage, closing in on the Guidos. While still very much activating a sexualized aesthetic, the ensemble's power elevates the severity of this moment for the Guidos. Even a line set of lights is lowered further into view to increase the pressure. A spotlight hits the Guidos as the ensemble seated behind him uncross and recross their legs, allowing the outside rim of the spotlight to call them into view. Maintaining the original essence of the tambourines, the ensemble begins to dance around the Guidos. Thomas Floyd's review in *The Washington Post* reported:

> There is no more striking implementation of Blankenbuehler's concept than "Be Italian," the ode to heated promiscuity sung by the prostitute Saraghina (Lesli Margherita) to a 9-year-old Guido (Charlie Firlik) in the adult auteur's memory. As Margherita nails her assignment, belting the Act I anthem with brassy conviction, Pasquale and Firlik mirror their movements while dancers envelop the duo in an avant-garde depiction of the formative experience. It's a stunning sequence that entrancingly navigates the treasured and toxic aspects of that complicated recollection.[22]

Throughout the number, the women activate long lines with their bodies flowing between elongated movements and accented tambourine hits. More and more ensemble join the escapade with their unique choreography scores, occasionally meeting in synchronicity aimed at the Guidos. They are not just periphery, in angelic white, they are active participants who will live on in Guido's memory, affecting his life forever.

A unique addition to Blankenbuehler's *Nine,* takes form through a necessary shift, but albeit small alteration of the script, reimagining the character Our Lady of the Spa. *Hamilton* ensemble star Sasha Hutchings takes on a new Puck-like spirit character named Asa Nisi Masa. "Asa Nisi Masa" is a phrase from Fellini's *8½* that has become in many ways synonymous with soul, spirit, or memory. She guides Guido throughout the show, conducting both the ensemble in choreography and occasionally the orchestra in music. Her power through the show is omniscient, as often is a Blankenbuehler ensemble. His choice to develop this ensemble-based character as a vital component of the revised dramaturgical perspective. As Loria argues, " … whether in his mind or in real life, Guido realizes that it's the women who are truly in charge, and the message of female empowerment remains strong throughout … "[23] Activating Asa Nisi Masa as an ever-present power over the show is a constant reminder to the audience of where the power ultimately lies, with the women. The ensemble's *Hamilton,* Greek-chorus-like, framing of *Nine* provide audiences with a lens through which they are viewing Guido's decisions and their impacts. At the end of the show, Adult Guido watches as Young Guido sings "Getting Tall." The number culminates in all of the ensemble women balletically reappearing in an innocent and playful dance with Young Guido. Guided by Asa Nisi Masa, they take their exists. Young Guido gives goodbye hugs to his mother and to Saraghina before hugging Adult Guido—in many ways repairing his perspective on his past and on his future. Young Guido and his mother reunite one final time as Asa Nisi Masa gently raises her arms to bring the entire cast back on stage to a reprise of "Be Italian." They surround Adult Guido in a circle on the stage allowing him to have one final encounter with each of the women in his life before he is left alone in a spotlight onstage.

CHAPTER 6
BEYOND BLANKENBUEHLER: COLLABORATION AND STEPHANIE KLEMONS

Just as there is far more of Blankenbuehler's work to analyze, there are more conversations to be had regarding his collaborators, especially when considering how his methodology is influencing the industry. He frequently references his collaborators as opening him up to more possibilities and helping him when he feels trapped in linear thought. One such collaborator is longtime associate Stephanie Klemons. Klemons is, without a doubt, an under-discussed voice in this project. Not only is she actively responsible for much of the work that Blankenbuehler stages, but, as the associate choreographer for *Hamilton,* it is her job to take his work and continue to teach it to new performers. Blankenbuehler and Klemons have developed an unbelievably tight-knit partnership. He frequently praises how she finishes his thoughts, elaborates on what he really means when he dictates what a move is to look like, and she pushes him to do better and consider all voices as he works. I had the honor of sitting in on callback auditions for the at the time work in progress called *Only Gold* and can emphatically assert that this is an accurate sentiment about their relationship. Klemons was acting as a Rolodex of Blankenbuehler movements and meanings, remembering when he forgot, translating when he was unclear.

Reflecting on the day she and Blankenbuehler connected, Klemons remembers her audition for *In the Heights*:

> One of my favorite moments when I feel like Andy and I like mind-melded and I was like, "Oh my god, we see each other's thoughts," was the final callback … at the end of each combination, he was like, watch these two people do it. And he called me every time. Like I was one of the two people every time … And he decided to teach us the opening because they were in the middle of doing the workshop … So he was like, I just choreographed the opening number, I'm going to teach you guys a section. And then at the end of this section

> during the "when the lights go down, I lost my radio," there's like this little choreo thing. And he, me, and Rosie Fiedelman were going and he decided to jump in with us when we did it ... And he and I, I like, I don't know why in my brain, I like went the opposite direction at the end to make like this choreo pattern. It was like, I don't even know what came over me. And that choreo pattern ended up in the final version of the show. From then on, I was always in the room with him creating and being a part of, you know, the conversation, so to speak, when he was building things all the way up until I sort of took over managing *Hamilton*.[1]

Klemons credits much of who she is as a collaborator and as a choreographer to the work she has done with Blankenbuehler—that his collaborative style allowed her to develop a voice that is often difficult to have in rehearsal rooms.

> I think that that's the type of thing that, that a great collaboration does, because like, I want you to zip up my loose end. And I want to zip up yours, like we met something, something got lost in translation there, something got lost in translation here.

Figure 8 Blankenbuehler and Klemons set up UK *Hamilton*. Photo courtesy of Andy Blankenbuehler.

> And that is a huge thing I learned from him, that like, collaboratively speaking, that I know if a number doesn't, you know, I always know, and I don't know that Andy has this exact experience. But I do know, like, when he choreographs on the treadmill, like, that's his thing. I have found recently that I can almost only choreograph, like, I can see it in my head. But if I'm not walking, I can't pull it out of my head into my body. So that's been something that I've taken from him, because that has been working for me recently. But, you know, learning that, like, if you don't see the piece in your head, it's not you, it's them.
>
> It's because if the piece is right, thematically, intentionally, first and foremost, from the writers, and then secondarily, musically speaking, if the piece is right, it choreographs itself. And your job is to just pull as much information that you can see in your head out and translate, right, that's back to the translation issue of like, how do you make it recreatable. But having, having the bravery to say, sometimes about a great song, this song is great, but I can't see it. So, something's missing, like, and it might be something so tiny, it might be like a lead in line, it might be that it is hugely from him.[2]

Frequently, Klemons has worked on other projects and has been asked to make something more like Blankenbuehler or has been asked for advice on why a piece of choreography is not working. On many such occasions, she met with resistance, often due to a variety of challenges the industry faces with regards to who has power or creative control in a rehearsal room. She mused:

> Everyone just wants to be as good as him without actually listening to how he did it. And so, I find that to be frustrating because a lot of times it feels like a lack of collaboration in rooms. It's just always so fascinating because I've been in rooms where it's all men and you're just like, okay. But then it's also the hierarchy of, okay, I'm just the choreographer. And you're like, but you know, I know.
>
> Andy never speaks to me like that. Look, he's tough on me because he expects me to be carrying out his work, but he never, ever looks down at me. He never thinks, oh, you're less smart than me. I've never been treated like that by him. Which is really hard because you get used to that and then you start getting treated a different way. And you're like, "Oh, this isn't fun. This isn't fun for me at all." I throw out ideas and Andy never says to me, that's a dumb idea or no, we're not

> going to do that, ever. Even if it's a bad idea, he'll go, "well, let's 'yes, and' the idea" always. And he does that with everybody. He never, even though he's smarter than everyone, he never makes anyone feel like they're dumber than him. And it's truthful. He's not trying. He's just humble. And he knows, but he also knows that he's only as good as the people in the room. He's so good at doing that.
>
> And the other thing is like you end up in this situation in the industry where it becomes hard to waste your time working on things, you know, so it's just, it's a gift. It's a real gift to work with him and learn with him and to take the things that he's taught me.[3]

Klemons once reflected that she is "far more interested in authenticity" than staging dance.[4] She emphasized that in her own work she takes the heart of a moment or concept and encourages the individuals in the ensemble to help that moment grow. Even when she is teaching new cast members of *Hamilton* the choreography, she takes the overall structure of the piece, but ensures that there is space for the individual to own their character. Klemons firmly advocated that "the ensemble reflects the choreographer's soul."[5] Her own work points to Blankenbuehler's propagating influence.[6] Future studies could certainly consider how the ensemble, ensemble body, and choreography are shifting and developing throughout the industry in light of the work of Blankenbuehler, Klemons, and their associates, performers, and students. How are their methodologies influencing other choreographers, directors, and creators? How might the epistemology regarding the ensemble body serve practitioners and scholars alike?

CONCLUSION: BLANKENBUEHLER AND THE ENSEMBLE (BODY)

Andy Blankenbuehler's choreographic vocabulary for *In the Heights*, *Bring It On: The Musical*, *Hamilton*, all of his subsequent projects uniquely revolve around heightened-gesture as a given. He makes pedestrian, everyday movements look interesting while giving precedence to the communication of ideas to an audience. Although Blankenbuehler blends ballet, jazz, Robbins, Fosse, hip-hop, and other typical "musical theatre" dance styles with his use of pedestrian movement and gesture, he prioritizes narrative over virtuosity. Only when he needs virtuosic moments to draw focus or convey specific emotions, concepts, or subtext does he activate them—for example, the stunts in *Bring It On: The Musical*. His Blankenbuehlerized dance, drawing from anything and everything, has opened up a vast physical dictionary from which he can tell stories.

Perhaps more important than his distinctive Blankenbuehlerized dance is how he advanced the potential for the ensemble and the ensemble body to function as vital elements within a production. His emphasis on how characters must communicate real-life through dance, the notion that the dance must come out of the text rather than be something decorative or accessorized onto the text, has elevated the possibility for that dancing character to function more broadly. What happens when we understand a chorus body to be an ensemble body—a dramaturgical body, bringing to the stage its lived experiences alongside the scripted conceptions of a generalized background character? How can this ensemble body walking in a heightened, pantomimic way inform the viewer about the psychology of the principal character onstage? How can a group of ensemble bodies engaging in individualized movements shed light on their socioeconomic positionality?

Historically, the dancing body, the chorus body, and the chorus have morphed and developed in concert with transitions in sociocultural thought and praxis. In the twenty-first century, where conversations regarding racism, sexism, and equitability are coming to the forefront of our sociocultural/sociopolitical consciousness, Blankenbuehler's shift toward the recognition of the individuality and embodied knowledge within the chorus/ensemble has created a link between a production and the audience that promotes sociological metanarratives beyond the show itself. In her piece "Reinstating Corporeality: Feminism and Body Politics," Janet Wolff posits: "the body operates as a symbol of society across cultures, and the rituals, rules, and boundaries concerning bodily behavior can be understood as the functioning of social rules and hierarchies."[1] Whether the ensemble body is presenting the community of (staged) Washington Heights, marginalized students of Jackson High School, or (non) citizens of the Caribbean, it becomes a microcosmic metaphor for society, historically or contemporarily.

Blankenbuehler's emphasis on the ensemble as the lens for a piece positions the individual ensemble bodies within the generalized group of supporting characters as each being important for an audience to encounter and understand a show. The audience receives information either implicitly or explicitly through his augmentation of their significance. For *In the Heights* the audience gains access to a complex social world by bearing witness to the individual ensemble bodies communicating the effects of, response to, and resistance toward processes of gentrification and homogenization. Enjoying spectacular high-flying cheerleading stunts, during *Bring It On: The Musical*, enacted by white virtuosic cheerleading ensemble bodies juxtaposed to hip-hopping ensemble bodies of color circulates a more nuanced dialogue regarding economic disparities concerning race and the practices of cheerleading and hip-hop. Uniting the diverse individual ensemble bodies as a collective voice in *Hamilton* promotes a narrative of inclusivity and ubiquity linking the past and the present to reflect the production's overall concept of revolutionizing Broadway and historiography. Following a production of *Hamilton* President Barack Obama spoke:

> Part of what's so powerful about this performance is it reminds us of the vital, crazy, kinetic energy that's at the heart of America—that people who have a vision and a set of ideals can transform the world. [...] Every single step of progress that we've made has been based on this notion that people can come together, and ideas can move like electricity through them, and a world can change.[2]

The bringing together of people through kinetic energy, through Blankenbuehler's choreography of the individual and collective ensemble bodies, creates a theatrical and social environment that can inspire change.[3]

Dance and choreography's ability to frame the ensemble (body) functioning as the lens of a piece can similarly impact how the audience reads the group or the individual enacting the movement. In today's world, ballet renders a highbrow aura as it distances itself from quotidian gesticulation. Giving precedence to athleticism and virtuosity, incorporating ballet into the piece of theatre frames the ensemble (body) in a way that aggrandize the skill over the individual executing said skill. Theatrical jazz dance—albeit appropriated and somewhat distant from its Black American roots—can promote a quality of sensuality, permissiveness, and expressivity. Hip-hop conjures histories of resistance to oppressive forces on minoritarian groups while pointing to notions of ambition and futurity. Blankenbuehlerized dance—combining these genres and more—elevates a sense of humanity suggesting recognizable gesture and emotion. Blankenbuehler activates his syncretic dance style in a way that shapes the ensemble (body) according to what mood, idea, subtext, nuance, a show calls for in any given moment.

NOTES

Preface

1. Andy Blankenbuehler, interview by Amanda Olmstead. September 17, 2024. Pittsburgh, PA.
2. *Hamilton: An American Musical,* music and lyrics by Lin-Manuel Miranda, choreo. Andy Blankenbuehler. Benedum Center for Performing Arts. Pittsburgh, PA, September 18, 2024.

Introduction

1. Lin-Manuel Miranda and Jeremy McCarter, *Hamilton: The Revolution: Being the Complete Libretto of the Broadway Musical, with a True Account of Its Creation, and Concise Remarks on Hip-Hop, the Power of Stories, and the New America*, 1st ed., ed. Lin-Manuel Miranda and Jeremy McCarter (New York, NY: Grand Central Publishing, 2016), 119.
2. Ibid., 1
3. Andy Blankenbuehler, interview by Amanda Olmstead. December 2, 2024. New York City, NY.
4. Ibid.
5. I use the root of "affect" intentionally in this moment. Effect suggests a thing that is done. "Affect" suggests an action, a presence. In a production, the chorus is actively impacting moments.
6. Andy Blankenbuehler and Sarah L. Kaufman, "Fresh Steps," Symphony Space and Words on Dance, New York City, NY, October 21, 2019.
7. Miranda and McCarter, *Hamilton: The Revolution,* 134.
8. Andy Blankenbuehler, interviewed by Amanda Olmstead. May 1, 2018. Also considered is added context from Blankenbuehler, interview by Amanda Olmstead. December 2024.
9. Blankenbuehler, interview by Amanda Olmstead. December 2024.
10. Ibid
11. Stacy Wolf and Liza Gennaro, "Dance in Musical Theater," in *The Oxford Handbook of Dance and Theater*, vol. 1, ed. Nadine George-Graves (Oxford University Press, 2015), 151.

12. Dennis Waskul and Phillip Vannini, "The Performative Body: Dramaturgy, the Body, and Embodiment," in *The Drama of Social Life: A Dramaturgical Handbook*, ed. Charles Edgley, Phillip Vannini, Simon Gottschalk, and Dennis Waskul (Farnham: Taylor & Francis Group, 2013), 200.
13. Katherine Profeta, *Dramaturgy in Motion: At Work on Dance and Movement Performance* (Madison, WI: The University of Wisconsin Press, 2015), 3.
14. Jonathan Burrows, *A Choreographer's Handbook* (Milton Park, Abingdon, Oxon: Routledge, 2010), 46.
15. Waskul and Vannini, "The Performative Body," 197.
16. Waskul and Vannini, "The Performative Body," 199.
17. This list is inspired by Stacy Wolf and Liza Gennaro's list regarding the functions of dance in musical theatre from their chapter titled "Dance in Musical Theatre" discussed earlier. Wolf and Gennaro, "Dance in Musical Theater," 151.
18. Burrows, *A Choreographer's Handbook*, 4.

Chapter 1

1. Blankenbuehler, interview by Amanda Olmstead. September 2024. *Never Alone* is a ballet Blankenbuehler created in conjunction with the Jacob's Pillow Organization. Written with friend and best-selling author Kate Quinn, the piece tells the story of a disabled British submarine that has been hunted by the German fleet for hours. The crew navigate moments of reprieve, fear, and longing for home as they narrowly escape their enemy.
2. Ibid.
3. Andy Blankenbuehler, "Building Broadway: Hamilton Choreographer Andy Blankenbuehler," Broadway.com, June, 6, 2016, YouTube video, 4:07, https://www.youtube.com/watch?v=R49vKv8f0Wc.
4. Blankenbuehler, interview by Amanda Olmstead. December 2024.
5. Andy Blankenbuehler and Sarah L. Kaufman, "Fresh Steps," Symphony Space and Words on Dance, New York City, NY, October 21, 2019.
6. Ibid.
7. Blankenbuehler, interview by Amanda Olmstead. December 2024.
8. Ibid.
9. Blankenbuehler and Kaufman, "Fresh Steps."
10. **Second position:** the legs are in a parallel standing posture and are just beyond hip-width apart. In ballet the feet are turned out; in jazz the feet are also parallel.
11. **Fourth position:** a standing posture variant where one leg is in front of the other, about a walking step distance apart. In ballet the feet are turned out; in jazz the feet are also parallel.

12. **Sauté:** a jump; both legs leave and return to the ground at the same time.
13. As will be discussed later in this project, he also asserts that this up left to down right diagonal signifies a child-like perspective on life. This is equally true during the moment "New York, New York" he describes.
14. Blankenbuehler and Kaufman, "Fresh Steps."
15. Blankenbuehler, interview by Amanda Olmstead. December 2024.
16. Susan Leigh Foster, *Choreography and Narrative* (Bloomington, IN: Indiana University Press, 1996), 9.
17. Susan Leigh Foster, *Choreographing History* (Bloomington, IN: Indiana University Press, 1995), 3.
18. Susan Leigh Foster, *Reading Dancing: Bodies and Subjects in Contemporary American Dance* (Berkeley, CA: University of California Press, 1986), 188.
19. **Tendu:** one leg stretches along the floor until just the pointed toe touches the floor.
    Devant: in front
    Pas de Bourée: a series of small steps where the legs come together before they reopen. Most commonly the feet move from fifth position (closed) to second position (open wide) to fifth position.
    Arabesque: a body position where the weight is placed over one supporting leg, with the other leg extended behind the body.
    Allongé: stretched or made longer
    Passé: most often used to describe when one leg is bent to look like a triangle with the foot near the supporting leg's knee.
20. **Piqué:** pricking; often used to describe other movements.
    Battement: one leg extends to the front, side, or back of the body.
21. Foster, *Reading Dancing*, 189.
22. **Balancé:** a step that alternates balance between feet, typically in counts of three; the motion often activates a down, up, down pattern.
    En tourant: while turning.
    De côte: to the side.
    Chaîné: a series of short turns that travel across space, typically in a straight line.
    Rond de jambe: when the leg completes a semi-circular motion.
    Plié: knee bend.
23. Blankenbuehler, interview by Amanda Olmstead. December 2024.
24. Ibid.
25. Ibid.
26. Ibid.

Chapter 2

1. Lin-Manuel Miranda and Jeremy McCarter, *Hamilton: The Revolution: Being the Complete Libretto of the Broadway Musical, with a True Account of Its Creation, and Concise Remarks on Hip-Hop, the Power of Stories, and the New America*, 1st ed., ed. Lin-Manuel Miranda and Jeremy McCarter (New York, NY: Grand Central Publishing, 2016), 134.
2. Mark Blankenship, "No Fear of 'Heights': Producers Take Risk on Tyro Talent," *Variety* 405, no. 13 (2007): 55.
3. Linda Winer, "Review: 'In the Heights,' by Lin-Manuel Miranda," *Newsday*, March 10, 2008 (Melville, NY: Tribune Content Agency).
4. "Andy Blankenbuehler- *In The Heights*," MoveTVnetwork.com, Vimeo video, 2:58, February 20, 2012, vimeo.com/37156545.
5. Jayzel Samonte, "Heightened Exposure: *In the Heights*," *Movmnt Magazine*, June 29, 2008, issuu.com/movmnt/docs/movmnt7.
6. In a 1973 article, Dean MacCannell first explored the idea of "staged authenticity" in regards to tourism. Tourists are invited on exclusive tours to see buildings, schools, community gatherings, etc. that have become structured around the schedule and wishes of the tourist. This added layer is one that curates a production that can repeat for the next group of tourists. What was once everyday life has become staged authenticity; what was once "authentic" has become a packaged product altering its original intention.
   See Dean MacCannell, "Staged Authenticity: Arrangements of Social Space in Tourist Settings," *The American Journal of Sociology* 79, no. 3 (1973): 589–603.
7. Andy Blankenbuehler, interviewed by Amanda Olmstead. May 1, 2018. New York City, NY.
8. Lyn Cramer, "Andy Blankenbuehler," in *Creating Musical Theatre: Conversations with Broadway Directors and Choreographers* (London: Bloomsbury Methuen Drama, 2013), 39.
9. Blankenbuehler, interview by Amanda Olmstead. December 2024.
10. Andrew Gans, "Casting Announced for Luis Salgado-Directed In the Heights," *Playbill*, Playbill Inc., March 2, 2017, www.playbill.com/article/casting-announced-for-luis-salgado-directed-in-the-heights.
11. Luis Salgado, interview by Amanda Olmstead. May 6, 2025.
12. Ibid.
13. "*In the Heights:* Chasing Broadway Dreams," PBS Great Performances, video, 54:00, November 10, 2017.
14. Andy Blankenbuehler, "Building Broadway: Hamilton Choreographer Andy Blankenbuehler," Broadway.com, YouTube video, 4:07, June 6, 2016, www.youtube.com/watch?v=R49vKv8f0Wc.

15. Ibid.
16. Stephanie Klemons, interviewed by Amanda Olmstead. June 6, 2018.
17. Ibid.
18. Susan Leigh Foster, *Valuing Dance: Commodities and Gifts in Motion* (New York, NY: Oxford University Press, 2019), 15–16.
19. Blankenbuehler, interviewed by Amanda Olmstead. 2018.
20. Jane Desmond, "Embodying Difference: Issues in Dance and Cultural Studies," in *Meaning in Motion: New Cultural Studies of Dance*, ed. Jane Desmond (Durham, NC: Duke University Press, 1997), 32.
21. Ibid., 43.
22. Foster, 52.
23. Desmond, "Embodying Difference," 41.
24. Mark Franko, *The Work of Dance: Labor, Movement, and Identity in the 1930s* (Middletown, CT: Wesleyan University Press, 2002), 41.
25. Ibid., 2.
26. Quiara Alegría Hudes and Lin-Manuel Miranda, *In the Heights: The Complete Book and Lyrics of the Broadway Musical* (Milwaukee, WI: Applause Theatre & Cinema Books, 2013), 1.
27. Graffiti Pete is dressed in baggy clothing. Reflecting on hip-hop aesthetics and commodified nuances, Carla Stalling Huntington points out, "And forget not the baggy clothes phenomenon that swept the world as a result of jailed African American men who wear loose fitting coveralls represented by rappers on street corners."
    See Carla Stalling Huntington, *Hip Hop Dance: Meanings and Messages* (Jefferson, NC: McFarland, 2007), 141.
28. Charles Isherwood, "From the Corner Bodega, the Music of Everyday Life," *The New York Times*, February 9, 2007, www.nytimes.com/2007/02/09/theater/reviews/09heights.html.
29. Seth Stewart, "Exclusive Interview with Dancer Seth Stewart (*In the Heights* / Madonna)," *I.N-TV*. YouTube video, 7:53, July 6, 2011, www.youtube.com/watch?v=8hoTgDLC4ck.
30. Cramer, "Andy Blankenbuehler," 39.
31. Jeni Tu, "Andy Blankenbuehler," *Dance Teacher* 30, no. 8 (Raleigh, NC: 2008), 96.
32. Quiara Alegria Hudes and Lin-Manuel Miranda, "In the Heights," in *In the Heights: the Complete Book and Lyrics of the Broadway Musical* (Milwaukee, WI: Applause Theatre & Cinema Books, 2013), 3.
33. Lin-Manuel Miranda, interview with Mo Brady, "Writing for Ensembles (*Hamilton, In the Heights*—feat. Lin-Manuel Miranda)," *The Ensemblist*, podcast audio, July 2, 2020, https://www.stitcher.com/show/the-ensemblist/episode/181-writing-for-ensembles-hamilton-in-the-heights-feat-lin-manuel-miranda-63385999.

34. Hudes and Miranda, "In the Heights," *In the Heights*, 3.
35. Andy Blankenbuehler and Sarah L. Kaufman, "Fresh Steps," Symphony Space and Words on Dance, New York City, NY, October 21, 2019.
36. Hudes and Miranda, "In the Heights," *In the Heights*, 3.
37. Ibid., 4.
38. Miranda, *The Ensemblist.*
39. Miranda, *The Ensemblist.*
40. Hudes and Miranda, "In the Heights," *In the Heights*, 4.
41. **Chaîné:** a series of short turns that travel across space, typically in a straight line.
42. Jonathan Burrows, *A Choreographer's Handbook* (Milton Park, Abingdon, Oxon: Routledge, 2010), 40.
43. Miranda, *The Ensemblist.*
44. Burrows, *A Choreographer's Handbook*, 80.
45. Lin-Manuel Miranda, "In the Heights," in *In the Heights*, Vocal Selections (Milwaukee, WI: Williamson Music, Hal Leonard, 2008), 4–9.
46. Hudes and Miranda, "In the Heights," *In the Heights*, 7.
47. Ibid.
48. Ibid.
49. Quiara Alegría Hudes, *In the Heights: The Complete Book and Lyrics of the Broadway Musical* (Milwaukee, WI: Applause Theatre & Cinema Books, 2013), 7.
50. Javier Muñoz was originally cast in the ensemble of *In the Heights* but also doubled as an understudy for Piragua Guy, Sonny, and Usnavi.
51. Melissa Castillo-Garsow and Jason Nichols, "Hip Hop Latinidades: More Than Just Rapping in Spanish," in *La Verdad: An International Dialogue on Hip Hop Latinidades* (Columbus, OH: The Ohio State University Press, 2016), 3.
52. Morgan Marcell, interviewed by Amanda Olmstead. October 21, 2018.
53. Miranda, "In the Heights," *In the Heights*, Vocal Selections, 11.
54. Burrows, 119.
55. Miranda, "In the Heights," *In the Heights*, Vocal Selections, 13.
56. Hudes and Miranda, "In the Heights," *In the Heights*, 12.
57. Andy Blankenbuehler, Michelle Charlesworth, and Harvey Fierstein, "Choreographer Andy Blankenbuehler Talks *In The Heights*," *Broadway Backstage*, ABC7NY, YouTube video, 1:43, May 3, 2008, www.youtube.com/watch?v=IRufwdN5NmQ&t=3s.
58. Hudes and Miranda, "In the Heights," *In the Heights*, 12.

59. **Rond de jambe:** when the leg completes a semi-circular motion.
    À terre: the foot moves on the floor as opposed to en l'air—in the air.
60. **Demi plié:** small bending of the knees.
61. Blankenbuehler, Charlesworth, and Fierstein, "Choreographer Andy Blankenbuehler Talks *In The Heights*."
62. Hudes and Miranda, "In the Heights," *In the Heights*, 12.
63. Foster, 50.
64. Hudes and Miranda, "In the Heights," *In the Heights*, 14.
65. Juliet McMains, "Dancing Latin/ Latin Dancing: Salsa and DanceSport." In *Ballroom, Boogie, Shimmy Sham, Shake: A Social and Popular Dance Reader*, ed. Julie Malnig (Urbana: University of Illinois Press, 2009), 306.
66. Ibid.
67. Hudes, *In the Heights*, 117.
68. John Charles Chasteen, *National Rhythms, African Roots: The Deep History of Latin American Popular Dance*, 1st ed. (Albuquerque, NM: University of New Mexico Press, 2004), 12.12.
69. Lin-Manuel Miranda, "Carnaval Del Barrio," in *In the Heights: The Complete Book and Lyrics of the Broadway Musical* (Milwaukee, WI: Applause Theatre & Cinema Books, 2013), 121.
70. "Carnaval del Barrio- *In the Heights* OBC," YouTube, video, 8:07, https://www.youtube.com/watch?v=Omu3afOVNiQ. "*In the Heights* 2.5 // 'Carnaval del barrio' sub español," YouTube, video, 8:09, June 5, 2020, https://www.youtube.com/watch?v=6Qk7S_Z1EVw.
71. Miranda, "Carnaval Del Barrio," *In the Heights,* 121.
72. Jayna Brown, *Babylon Girls: Black Women Performers and the Shaping of the Modern* (Durham, NC: Duke University Press, 2008), 15.
73. Miranda, "Carnaval Del Barrio," *In the Heights,* 124.
74. Ibid., 126–127.
75. Blankenbuehler and Kaufman, "Fresh Steps."
76. Cramer, "Andy Blankenbuehler," 34.

Chapter 3

1. Kase Wickman, "*Bring It On*: The Complete Oral History," August 6, 2015, http://www.kasewickman.com/?p=2748.
2. I first started cheerleading in 2003. Nearly all of our tryout routines and even competition routines were set to music from the *Bring It On* soundtrack. As my "career" progressed, the dance style within cheerleading began to acquire more

and more hip-hop aesthetics. It could potentially be argued that the *Bring It On* film directly influenced what the form looks like today.

3. Wickman, "*Bring It On*: The Complete Oral History."
4. Patrick Hinds, "Episode 14: *Bring It On: The Musical*," *Broadway Backstory*, TodayTix, November 7, 2017, https://www.todaytix.com/broadway-backstory/episodes/bring-it-on-the-musical.
5. Ibid.
6. Antwan Bethea, interview with Amanda Olmstead. June 13, 2020.
7. Heléne Yorke was originally cast as Campbell in the out of town try outs. During this development process the lead actors were learning how to do professional cheerleading in gymnasiums, challenging stunts and tumbling included. The night before tech rehearsals, Yorke broke her foot attempting a standing back tuck and had to leave the production. A prime example of why Blankenbuehler decided not to try and train actors how to do cheerleading.
8. Jonathan Burrows, *A Choreographer's Handbook* (Milton Park, Abingdon, Oxon: Routledge, 2010), 76.
9. Ibid., 77.
10. Burrows, *A Choreographer's Handbook*, 76.
11. Jeff Whitty, Tom Kitt, Lin-Manuel Miranda, and Amanda Green, *Bring It On: The Musical* (New York, NY: Music Theatre International, 2012), 64.
12. Hinds, "Episode 14: *Bring It On: The Musical*."
13. Ibid.
14. Whitty, Kitt, Miranda, and Green, *Bring It On*, 20.
15. "What I Was Born to Do," Whitty, Kitt, Miranda, and Green, 1; "We Ain't No Cheerleaders," Whitty, Kitt, Miranda, and Green, 20.
16. Whitty, Kitt, Miranda, and Green, *Bring It On*, 1.
17. Burrows, *A Choreographer's Handbook*, 37.
18. Ibid., 76.
19. *The Princess Diaries,* Walt Disney presents a Brownhouse production, a Garry Marshall film; produced by Whitney Houston, Debra Martin Chase, Mario Iscovich; screenplay by Gina Wendkos; directed by Garry Marshall (Burbank, CA: Walt Disney Home Entertainment; Distributed by Buena Vista Home Entertainment, 2001).
20. This statement comes with a few exceptions depending on the night of the performance, due to the use of swings within the ensemble.
21. *Bring It On*, directed by Peyton Reed, writer Jessica Bendinger (Santa Monica, CA: Beacon Pictures, Wonderworks Films; Distributed by Universal Pictures, 2000).
22. Whitty, Kitt, Miranda, and Green, *Bring It On*, 3.

23. *Bring It On: The Musical,* (Videorecording), St. James Theatre, December 14, 2012, Theatre on Film and Tape Archive, NYPL Performing Arts Library, New York, New York.
24. Antwan Bethea, *TwanBringItOn.com,* https://www.twanbringiton.com.
25. Bethea, interview with Amanda Olmstead.
26. Ibid.
27. Ibid.
28. "Bring It On: The Musical" Program, St. James Theatre, July 12, 2012 (New York: NY, Playbill), 7, https://www.playbill.com/playbillpagegallery/inside-playbill?asset=00000150-aea8-d936-a7fd-eefc733a0002&type=InsidePlaybill&slide=5.
29. André Lepecki, *Exhausting Dance: Performance and the Politics of Movement* (New York, NY: Routledge, 2006), 74.
30. Ibid.
31. Lyn Cramer, "Andy Blankenbuehler," in *Creating Musical Theatre: Conversations with Broadway Directors and Choreographers* (London: Bloomsbury Methuen Drama, 2013), 33–34.
32. All of the Truman High School related numbers have a distinct pop music sound and utilize dance aesthetics rooted in ballet, jazz, and cheerleading. The numbers for Jackson High School are more of a hip-hop hybrid combining hip-hop music with pop, and hip-hop dance with jazz. Arguably this hybrid form acclimates the sensitivities of a typical Broadway audience to the genre, still not yet common place in Broadway musicals.
33. Hinds, "Episode 14: *Bring It On: The Musical.*"
34. Ibid.
35. Thomas F. DeFrantz, "The Black Beat Made Visible: Hip Hop Dance and Body Power," in *Of the Presence of the Body: Essays on Dance and Performance Theory,* ed. André Lepecki (Middletown, CT: Wesleyan University Press, 2004), 71
36. Mohanalakshmi Rajakumar, *Hip Hop Dance* (Santa Barbara, CA: Greenwood Press, 2012), xvi.
37. Whitty, Kitt, Miranda, and Green, *Bring It On*, 45.
38. Ibid., 33.
39. Ibid., 22.
40. Ibid.
41. Susan Leigh Foster, *Valuing Dance: Commodities and Gifts in Motion* (New York, NY: Oxford University Press, 2019), 100.
42. Ibid.
43. DeFrantz, "The Black Beat Made Visible," 51.
44. Burrows, *A Choreographer's Handbook*, 32.

45. It is noteworthy that the understudy for the character La Cienga, included in this group of dancers, was white for the Broadway show. However, La Cienga's position as a transgender character keeps her in a marginalized status.
46. Whitty, Kitt, Miranda, and Green, *Bring It On*, 36.
47. **Battement:** one leg extends to the front, side, or back of the body.
48. Whitty, Kitt, Miranda, and Green, *Bring It On*, 36.
49. Ibid., 44.
50. Ibid.
51. Ibid.
52. Hinds, "Episode 14: *Bring It On: The Musical*."
53. Ibid.
54. Laura Mulvey, "Visual Pleasure and Narrative Cinema," in *Media and Cultural Studies KeyWorks*, ed. Meenakshi Gigi Durham and Douglas Kellner (Malden, MA: Blackwell Publishers, 2001), 346.
55. Ibid., 348.
56. Ibid.
57. Andy Blankenbuehler, interview with Gillian Pensavalle, "Episode 218," *The Hamilcast*, Podcast audio, May 4, 2020, https://www.thehamilcast.com/andy-blankenbuehler/.
    This will be further discussed in Chapter Four.
58. Whitty, Kitt, Miranda, and Green, *Bring It On*, 45.
59. Ibid.
60. Ibid., 42.
    It is noteworthy that the Truman High School's mascot is a parrot, a symbol of high class and nobility. Jackson High School's mascot is the Irish. The notion that a formally Irish neighborhood is now home to impoverished people of color is significant. Additionally, the very idea that the non-white school's namesake, Andrew Jackson, historically owned slaves and the students at the school are hailed as "the Irish" adds an additional layer of complicated racial performativity within the text. In the original *Bring It On* film there was also a hint toward such Irishness as the inner-city school was the East Compton Clovers.
61. Rajakumar, *Hip Hop Dance*, xxiii–xxix.
62. Whitty, Kitt, Miranda, and Green, *Bring It On*, 45.
63. Ibid., 47.
64. Ibid.
65. Ibid., 50.
66. Ibid., 63.
67. Ibid., 64.

68. Ibid.
69. Ibid., 66.
70. Susan Leigh Foster, *Corporealities: Dancing, Knowledge, Culture, Power* (London: Routledge, 1996), 6.
71. Whitty, Kitt, Miranda, and Green, *Bring It On*, 69.
72. Ibid.
73. Ibid., 69–70.
74. "Bring It On: The Musical" Program.
75. Whitty, Kitt, Miranda, and Green, *Bring It On*, 71.
76. Andy Blankenbuehler and Sarah L. Kaufman, "Fresh Steps," Symphony Space and Words on Dance, New York City, NY, October 21, 2019.
77. Bethea, interview with Amanda Olmstead.
78. Ibid.
79. Among these movements are:
    High V: arms straight up in the air making a "V," hands in fists, thumbs tucked, with palms directed down.
    Low V: arms straight down by the sides making a "V," hands in fists, thumbs tucked, with palms angled in.
    T: arms straight out from the shoulders, hands in fists, thumbs tucked, with palms directed down.
    Table Top or Daggers: arms bent into the body with elbows pointing down and hands by the shoulders, in fists, thumbs tucked, palms directed inward.
    Left Punch Up: Right-arm bent, hands in a fist, thumb tucked, on the right hip. Left-arm straight up in the air near the ear, hand in a fist, thumb tucked, palm directed inward.
80. Ann Cooper Albright, *Choreographing Difference: The Body and Identity in Contemporary Dance* (Middletown, CT: Wesleyan University Press, 1997), 3–4.
81. "UCA School and Open Rec Rules & Regulations," Universal Cheerleaders Association, UCA High School Cheerleading Championship, 2021, https://www.varsity.com/uca/wp-content/uploads/2020/08/20-21_uca_competition_schoolrules.pdf.
82. Whitty, Kitt, Miranda, and Green, *Bring It On*, 109.
83. Ibid.
84. Ibid., 110.
85. **Uniform Guidelines:** All participant uniforms must cover midriff when standing at attention. Hair for all athletes does not have to be worn the same but must be secured off the face with a simple style that considers all diversities [This is a recent addendum to the rules].
    See "UCA School and Open Rec Rules & Regulations."
86. Cooper Albright, *Choreographing Difference*, 3–4.

87. Whitty, Kitt, Miranda, and Green, *Bring It On*, 111.
88. Ibid., 112.
89. **Competition Performance Area:** Boundary for the NHSCC [National High School Cheerleading Championship]–Any team member stepping outside or touching outside the performance area will cause the squad to receive a.5 penalty per occurrence. The white line is considered a warning mark. See "UCA School and Open Rec Rules & Regulations."
90. Whitty, Kitt, Miranda, and Green, *Bring It On*, 114.

Chapter 4

1. Lin-Manuel Miranda and Jeremy McCarter, *Hamilton: The Revolution: Being the Complete Libretto of the Broadway Musical, with a True Account of Its Creation, and Concise Remarks on Hip-Hop, the Power of Stories, and the New America*, 1st ed., ed. Lin-Manuel Miranda and Jeremy McCarter (New York, NY: Grand Central Publishing, 2016), 116.
2. *Hamilton,* produced by Walt Disney Pictures, 5000 Broadway Productions, Nevis Productions, Old 320 Sycamore, Radical Media; directed by Thomas Kail written by Lin-Manuel Miranda; distributed by Disney+, Walt Disney Studios Motion Pictures, July 3, 2020, New York, NY.
3. "70th Annual Tony Awards 'Hamilton,'" *YouTube*, BroadwayInHD, October 15, 2016, www.youtube.com/watch/b5VqyCQV1Tg.
   In, Merl, "[1280x720] Grammys 2016 Watch Lin Manuel Miranda and the Cast of Hamilton Perform—The Verge," *Vimeo*, March 14, 2018, vimeo.com/260119105.
4. Jeremy McCarter, *Hamilton: The Revolution: Being the Complete Libretto of the Broadway Musical, with a True Account of Its Creation, and Concise Remarks on Hip-Hop, the Power of Stories, and the New America*, 1st ed., ed. Lin-Manuel Miranda and Jeremy McCarter (New York, NY: Grand Central Publishing, 2016), 113.
5. It is important to note that Paul Tazewell is one of just three African American costume designers to be nominated for a Tony Award for Best Costume Design (play or musical). He is the only one to win—for *Hamilton.*
6. Rob Weinert-Kendt, "Rapping a Revolution," *The New York Times*, February 5, 2015, www.nytimes.com/2015/02/08/theater/lin-manuel-miranda-and-others-from-hamilton-talk-history.html.
7. McCarter, *Hamilton: The Revolution*, 10.
8. Sasha Hutchings, interview with Mo Brady, "The History of the Ensemble: Hamilton (Feat. Neil Haskell, Sasha Hutchings)," *The Ensemblist*, podcast audio, July 1, 2020, http://www.theensemblist.com/podcasts. See Lin-Manuel Miranda, "Non-Stop," in *Hamilton: The Revolution: Being the Complete Libretto*

of the Broadway Musical, with a True Account of Its Creation, and Concise Remarks on Hip-Hop, the Power of Stories, and the New America, 1st ed., ed. Lin-Manuel Miranda and Jeremy McCarter (New York, NY: Grand Central Publishing, 2016), 142.

9. Hutchings was one of the original Broadway ensemble cast members of *Hamilton*. This idea of "third girl from the right" comes from a reference she makes about herself in the podcast *The Ensemblist*—it is not necessarily her "role."
10. Hutchings, *The Ensemblist*.
11. Ibid.
12. Liz Mineo, "Correcting 'Hamilton,'" *Harvard Gazette*, Harvard Gazette, July 7, 2020, news.harvard.edu/gazette/story/2016/10/correcting-hamilton/.
13. Tracy Clayton, (@borkeymcpoverty), 2020, "im late w the hamilton criticism stuff & im clearly biased but.. i really like that this conversation is happening. hamilton the play and the movie were given to us in two different worlds & our willingness to interrogate things in this way feels like a clear sign of change," Twitter, July 5, 2020, 2:32 PM EST, https://twitter.com/brokeymcpoverty/status/1279845518227787777?lang=en.
14. Rachel Cargle, (@rachel.cargle), 2020, Instagram, June 29, 2020, https://www.instagram.com/p/CCByOMJnhNq/.
15. Daniella Cheslow, "Parents Are Bringing Their Children to Black Lives Matter Plaza for a 'Once in a Lifetime Experience,'" *DCist*, WAMU 88.5—American University Radio, June 17, 2020, dcist.com/story/20/06/11/parents-are-bringing-their-children-to-black-lives-matter-plaza-for-a-once-in-a-lifetime-experience/.
16. Lin-Manuel Miranda, "Dear Theodosia," in *Hamilton: The Revolution: Being the Complete Libretto of the Broadway Musical, with a True Account of Its Creation, and Concise Remarks on Hip-Hop, the Power of Stories, and the New America*, 1st ed., ed. Lin-Manuel Miranda and Jeremy McCarter (New York, NY: Grand Central Publishing, 2016), 128.
17. Abby Phillip, "Confederate Symbols Are Coming down, despite Donald Trump's Ire—CNN Video," *CNN*, Cable News Network, June 12, 2020, www.cnn.com/videos/politics/2020/06/12/confederate-monument-symbols-military-bases-pkg-phillip-ebof-vpx.cnn.
18. Lin-Manuel Miranda, "Yorktown (The World Turned Upside Down)," in *Hamilton: The Revolution: Being the Complete Libretto of the Broadway Musical, with a True Account of Its Creation, and Concise Remarks on Hip-Hop, the Power of Stories, and the New America*, 1st ed., ed. Lin-Manuel Miranda and Jeremy McCarter (New York, NY: Grand Central Publishing, 2016), 122.
19. Lin-Manuel Miranda, *Hamilton: The Revolution: Being the Complete Libretto of the Broadway Musical, with a True Account of Its Creation, and Concise Remarks on Hip-Hop, the Power of Stories, and the New America*, 1st ed., ed.

Lin-Manuel Miranda and Jeremy McCarter (New York, NY: Grand Central Publishing, 2016), 22.

20. Susan Leigh Foster, *Valuing Dance: Commodities and Gifts in Motion* (New York, NY: Oxford University Press, 2019), 100.
21. Susan Leigh Foster, *Choreographing Empathy: Kinesthesia in Performance* (London: Routledge, 2011), 184.
22. Miranda, *Hamilton: The Revolution,* 22.
23. Neil Haskell, interview with Mo Brady, "The History of the Ensemble: Hamilton (Feat. Neil Haskell, Sasha Hutchings)," *The Ensemblist*, podcast audio, July 1, 2020, http://www.theensemblist.com/podcasts.
24. Carla Stalling Huntington, *Hip Hop Dance: Meanings and Messages* (Jefferson, NC: McFarland, 2007), 60.
25. Ron Chernow, *Alexander Hamilton* (New York: Penguin Press, 2004), 7–27.
26. Chernow, *Alexander Hamilton*, 33.
27. Andy Blankenbuehler, interview with Gillian Pensavalle, "Episode 217," *The Hamilcast*, Podcast audio, May 4, 2020, https://www.thehamilcast.com/andy-blankenbuehler/.
28. Lin-Manuel Miranda, "Alexander Hamilton," in *Hamilton: The Revolution: Being the Complete Libretto of the Broadway Musical, with a True Account of Its Creation, and Concise Remarks on Hip-Hop, the Power of Stories, and the New America*, 1st ed., ed. Lin-Manuel Miranda and Jeremy McCarter (New York, NY: Grand Central Publishing, 2016), 16.
29. Ibid.
30. Ibid.
31. Blankenbuehler, "Episode 217," *The Hamilcast.*
32. Miranda, "Alexander Hamilton," *Hamilton: The Revolution,* 16.
33. Blankenbuehler and Kaufman, "Fresh Steps."
34. Ibid.
35. Miranda, "Alexander Hamilton," *Hamilton: The Revolution,* 16.
36. Blankenbuehler and Kaufman, "Fresh Steps."
37. André Lepecki, "Choreopolice and Choreopolitics: Or, the Task of the Dancer," *TDR: Drama Review* 57, no. 4 (December 1, 2013): 20.
38. Anusha Kedhar, "'Hands Up! Don't Shoot!': Gesture, Choreography, and Protest in Ferguson," *The Feminist Wire*, October 6, 2014, thefeministwire.com/2014/10/protest-in-ferguson.
39. Rodney Diverlus, "Black Lives Matter Toronto: Urgency as Choreographic Necessity," *Canadian Theatre Review* 176 (Fall 2018): 66.
40. Miranda, "Alexander Hamilton," *Hamilton: The Revolution,* 16.
41. Ibid.
42. Chernow, *Alexander Hamilton*, 19.

43. Blankenbuehler and Kaufman, "Fresh Steps."
44. It is also noteworthy that Thayne Jasperson later plays British loyalist Samuel Seabury (as well as understudies King George III).
45. Miranda, "Alexander Hamilton," *Hamilton: The Revolution,* 16.
46. Ibid.
47. Blankenbuehler and Kaufman, "Fresh Steps."
48. Hutchings also plays Rachel in a later moment of the production. In an article for *Dance Magazine,* when asked about a notable ensemble role she said, "Twice in the show they talk about Hamilton's dead mother, and I get lifted up, and then at the end I'm waiting for him. Andy's created a lot of images so you can see what Hamilton is thinking about." Suzannah Friscia, "Hamilton's Dance Revolution," *Dance Magazine* 90, no. 6 (June 1, 2016): 26.
49. Miranda, "Alexander Hamilton," *Hamilton: The Revolution,* 16.
50. Chernow, *Alexander Hamilton*, 9.
51. Ann Cooper Albright, *Choreographing Difference: The Body and Identity in Contemporary Dance* (Middletown, CT: Wesleyan University Press, 1997), 3.
52. Blankenbuehler and Kaufman, "Fresh Steps."
53. Ibid.
54. Chernow, *Alexander Hamilton*, 26.
55. Ibid., 27.
56. I will be using Ephraim Sykes here as he was the *performer* in the Disney+ recording. Sykes later plays George Eacker, the man who killed Philip Hamilton, and understudied Hercules Mulligan/James Madison. He is currently most known for his roles Seaweed J. Stubbs in the NBC Live production of *Hairspray Live* (2016) and David Ruffin in *Ain't Too Proud* (2017).
57. Amy Louise Wood, *Lynching and Spectacle: Witnessing Racial Violence in America, 1890–1940* (Chapel Hill, NC: University of North Carolina Press, 2009), 85.
58. Betsy Struxness was in the Original Broadway Cast. Hope Easterbrook was Struxness's replacement featured in the Disney+ film.
59. Blankenbuehler, "Episode 217," *The Hamilcast.*
60. Miranda, "Alexander Hamilton," *Hamilton: The Revolution,* 16.
61. Foster, *Choreographing Empathy,* 175.
62. Miranda, *Hamilton: The Revolution,* 17.
63. Miranda, "Alexander Hamilton," *Hamilton: The Revolution,* 17. See Chernow, *Alexander Hamilton*, 31.
64. Chernow, *Alexander Hamilton*, 32.
65. Terry Gross, "'The Past Isn't Done with Us,' Says 'Hamilton' Creator Lin-Manuel Miranda," *NPR*, June 29, 2020, www.npr.org/2020/06/29/884592985/the-past-isn-t-done-with-us-says-hamilton-creator-lin-manuel-miranda.

66. Jayna Brown, *Babylon Girls: Black Women Performers and the Shaping of the Modern* (Durham, NC: Duke University Press, 2008), 15.
67. Miranda, "Alexander Hamilton," *Hamilton: The Revolution,* 17.
68. Ibid.
69. Haskell, *The Ensemblist.*
70. Miranda, "Alexander Hamilton," *Hamilton: The Revolution,* 17.
71. Ibid.
72. Jonathan Burrows, *A Choreographer's Handbook* (Milton Park, Abingdon, Oxon: Routledge, 2010), 91–92.
73. Miranda, "Alexander Hamilton," *Hamilton: The Revolution,* 17.
74. Ibid.
75. Ibid.
76. Ibid.
77. Ibid.
78. Ibid.
79. Ibid.
80. Ibid.
81. Blankenbuehler and Kaufman, "Fresh Steps."
82. Randy Martin, *Critical Moves: Dance Studies in Theory and Politics* (Durham, NC: Duke University Press, 1998), 109.
83. Ibid.
84. I am choosing to use the terminology "social ballroom" to refer to traditional partner dances that are non-competitive. Their primary function is for social engagement, but there is a formality associated with their structure. In many cases, they were often performed in a ballroom-style location as a mode of patriarchal courtship.
85. James McMaster and Liz Whittaker Chapman, "Why Hamilton Is Not the Revolution You Think It Is," *HowlRound Theatre Commons*, February 23, 2016, howlround.com/why-hamilton-not-revolution-you-think-it.
86. Ibid.
87. Patrick McMillan and Shirley Rushing, *Ballroom Dance American Style: Smooth, Rhythm, Latin* (Dubuque, IA: Eddie Bowers Pub., Incorporated, 1997), 4.
88. Janet Wolff, "Reinstating Corporeality: Feminism and Body Politics," in *Meaning in Motion: New Cultural Studies of Dance*, ed. Jane Desmond (Durham, NC: Duke University Press, 1997), 97.
89. However, in the scene preceding, "Right Hand Man," the female ensemble members *also* have on the Continental Army jacket.
90. McCarter, *Hamilton: The Revolution*, 68.

91. Chernow, *Alexander Hamilton*, 128.
92. Lin-Manuel Miranda, "Helpless," in *Hamilton: The Revolution: Being the Complete Libretto of the Broadway Musical, with a True Account of Its Creation, and Concise Remarks on Hip-Hop, the Power of Stories, and the New America*, 1st ed., ed. Lin-Manuel Miranda and Jeremy McCarter (New York, NY: Grand Central Publishing, 2016), 71.
93. Ibid.
94. "**Closed position:** partners facing each other separated by a small space. Shoulders are parallel, woman slightly to the right of the man, man's right hand placed on woman's shoulder blade, her left hand placed on his right biceps. Man's left hand holds her right hand in an extended position."
    See McMillan and Rushing, *Ballroom Dance American Style*, 12.
95. "**Cuddle position:** woman is on man's right, both facing the same direction. With a double hand hold man's right hand holds woman's left hand at waist level. His left hand holds her right hand at waist level."
    Parallel position: man and woman stand beside each other, left shoulders adjacent for left parallel, right shoulders adjacent for right parallel.
    Promenade position: man and woman are side by side. Man's right hip is adjacent to the woman's left hip and upper torsos form a "V" in smooth dances, a straight line in rhythm dances.
    Sweetheart position: facing the same direction with the woman on the man's right side, his right hand holds her right hand over her right shoulder. His left hand holds her left hand in front at waist level."
    See McMillan and Rushing, *Ballroom Dance American Style*, 12–13.
96. Jane Desmond, "Embodying Difference: Issues in Dance and Cultural Studies," in *Meaning in Motion: New Cultural Studies of Dance*, ed. Jane Desmond (Durham, NC: Duke University Press, 1997), 32.
97. Ibid.
98. *How to Dance Through Time, Vol. IV: The Elegance of Baroque Social Dance*, directed by Carol Téten. Dancetime Publications, 2003, https://video.alexanderstreet.com/watch/how-to-dance-through-time-vol-iv-the-elegance-of-baroque-social-dance-2.
99. Andy Blankenbuehler, interview with Gillian Pensavalle, "Episode 218," *The Hamilcast*, Podcast audio, May 4, 2020, https://www.thehamilcast.com/andy-blankenbuehler/.
100. "**Spot dance:** a dance that is executed in one area of the floor (swing) as opposed to moving in the line of dance."
    See McMillan and Rushing, *Ballroom Dance American Style*, 13.
101. Miranda, "Helpless," *Hamilton: The Revolution,* 71.
102. Shelly Ronen, "Grinding on the Dance Floor: Gendered Scripts and Sexualized Dancing at College Parties," *Gender & Society* 24, no. 3 (June 1, 2010): 361.
103. Ibid., 367.

104. Ibid., 362–367.

105. Betsy Struxness, interviewed by Amanda Olmstead. October 16, 2018.

106. Chernow, *Alexander Hamilton*, 130.
See "From Alexander Hamilton to Margarita Schuyler, [February 1780]," *Founders Online*, National Archives, https://founders.archives.gov/documents/Hamilton/01-02-02-0613. [Original source: *The Papers of Alexander Hamilton*, vol. 2, *1779–1781*, ed. Harold C. Syrett, New York, NY: Columbia University Press, 1961, pp. 269–271].

107. "**Line of dance:** (LOD, also known as line of direction) counter-clockwise direction in which the dancers move around the dance floor."
See McMillan and Rushing, *Ballroom Dance American Style*, 13.

108. "**Loop turn:** woman's inside turn to the left (counter-clockwise)."
See McMillan and Rushing, *Ballroom Dance American Style*, 13.

109. Blankenbuehler, "Episode 218," *The Hamilcast.*

110. Ibid.

111. Lin-Manuel Miranda, "Satisfied," in *Hamilton: The Revolution: Being the Complete Libretto of the Broadway Musical, with a True Account of Its Creation, and Concise Remarks on Hip-Hop, the Power of Stories, and the New America*, 1st ed., ed. Lin-Manuel Miranda and Jeremy McCarter (New York, NY: Grand Central Publishing, 2016), 80.

112. Blankenbuehler, "Episode 218," *The Hamilcast.*

113. Miranda, "Satisfied," *Hamilton: The Revolution*, 82.

114. Ibid.

115. Ibid., 83.

116. Ibid.

117. "**Loop turn:** woman's inside turn to the left (counter-clockwise)."
See McMillan and Rushing, *Ballroom Dance American Style*, 13.

118. It is perhaps noteworthy here that Angelica Schuyler was actually married to businessman (and eventual English parliament member) John Barker Church three years prior to meeting Alexander Hamilton.

119. Blankenbuehler, "Episode 218," *The Hamilcast.*

120. Friscia, Suzannah, "*Hamilton's* Dance Revolution," *Dance Magazine* 90, no. 6 (2016): 26–30.

121. Morgan Marcell, interviewed by Amanda Olmstead. October 21, 2018.

122. McCarter, *Hamilton: The Revolution*, 113.
The ensemble is seen wearing these jackets throughout the first act. However, this is the first time they *all* have the formal, full-sleeved coats on.

123. Miranda, "Yorktown (The World Turned Upside Down)," *Hamilton: The Revolution*, 121.

124. Foster, *Choreographing Empathy*, 71.

125. Miranda, "Yorktown (The World Turned Upside Down)," *Hamilton: The Revolution*, 121.
126. Ibid.
127. Ibid.
128. Ibid.
129. Andy Blankenbuehler and Stephanie Klemons, "'Hamilton' Choreographer Breaks Down His Moves," photographed by Cassandra Giraldo, *The Wall Street Journal*, Dow Jones & Company, 4:22, May 23, 2016, www.wsj.com/video/hamilton-choreographer-breaks-down-his-moves/8F716467-E023-4900-B149-D6BB3A40B66E.html.
130. Blankenbuehler, "Hamilton' Choreographer Breaks Down His Moves."
131. Ibid.
132. Ibid.
133. Miranda, "Yorktown (The World Turned Upside Down)," *Hamilton: The Revolution*, 121.
134. Ibid.
135. Blankenbuehler, "Hamilton' Choreographer Breaks Down His Moves."
136. Miranda, "Yorktown (The World Turned Upside Down)," *Hamilton: The Revolution*, 121.
137. Ibid.
138. Blankenbuehler, "Hamilton' Choreographer Breaks Down His Moves."
139. Ibid.
140. Ibid.
141. Ibid.
142. Chernow, *Alexander Hamilton*, 163.
143. Miranda, "Yorktown (The World Turned Upside Down)," *Hamilton: The Revolution*, 121.
    Fifth position: both arms are raised up over the head with a slight bend in the elbow and shifted forward slightly. The hands are typically open.
144. Guy Trebay, "The Clowning, Rump-Shaking,: How a Dance Called Krumping Took Over an Inner-City Neighborhood," *New York Times (1923-Current File),* June 19, 2005.
    Krumping evolved from a dance called "clowning" arguably invented by Thomas Johnson, affectionately known as Tommy the Clown. Clowning is a milder version involving face make up and a more entertainment-oriented goal as opposed to a cathartic one.
145. "Krumping," *The Oxford Dictionary of Dance*, Oxford University Press, 2010.
146. Blankenbuehler, "Episode 217," *The Hamilcast.*

147. **Pencil turn:** a stationary turn where the body is completely straight; the non-supporting leg remains down, close to the turning leg.
148. Miranda, "Yorktown (The World Turned Upside Down)," *Hamilton: The Revolution*, 122.
149. Ibid.
150. Blankenbuehler, "Episode 217," *The Hamilcast.*
151. McCarter, *Hamilton: The Revolution,* 113.
     The ensemble is seen wearing these jackets throughout the first act. However, this is the first time they *all* have the formal, full-sleeved coats on.
152. Foster, *Choreographing Empathy,* 184.

Chapter 5

1. Although he was not discussed in this project, Alex Lacamoire was also a part of these three productions serving as the orchestrator.
2. Blankenbuehler also thanks *In the Heights* and *Hamilton* director Tommy Kail for allowing him to use the ensemble as much as he does in these productions. See Andy Blankenbuehler, "*Hamilton* Choreographer Andy Blankenbuehler on the Broadway Q&A," interviewed by Danny George, *Playbill* and The Growing Studio, YouTube video, 1:02:35, June 15, 2020, https://www.youtube.com/watch?v=jnP7GvN9MhI.
3. Blankenbuehler, "*Hamilton* Choreographer Andy Blankenbuehler on the Broadway Q&A."
4. Blankenbuehler, interview by Amanda Olmstead. December 2024.
5. Ibid.
6. Richard Oberacker and Robert Taylor, *Bandstand: The New American Musical* (New York, NY: Samuel French, 2018), 69.
7. Andy Blankenbuehler and Sarah L. Kaufman, "Fresh Steps," Symphony Space and Words on Dance, New York City, NY, October 21, 2019.
   Grand jeté: a big leap where the dancer takes off from the ground on one foot to land on the other; one leg is stretched forward and the other is stretched backward, behind the body.
   Pirouette: a turn or spin on one foot, often completed with the non-supporting leg bent with the foot touching the supporting leg.
8. Blankenbuehler and Kaufman, "Fresh Steps."
9. Oberacker and Taylor, *Bandstand: The New American Musical*, 83.
10. Kate Nash, "Paris," *My Best Friend Is You*, Fiction Records and Geffen Records, 2010.
11. *Only Gold*, Playbill, November 7, 2022, https://playbill.com/production/only-gold-off-broadway-the-robert-w-wilson-mcc-theater-space-2022.

12. Jesse Green, "Review: In 'Only Gold,' Each Move Is Worth 1,000 Words." *The New York Times*, 2022.
13. Sylviane Gold, "Refining Gold: Andy Blankenbuehler Opens up about the Making of Only Gold, the Weight of Creating Post-Hamilton and the Road Ahead," *Dance Magazine*, Vol. 97, Dance Magazine, Inc, 2023.
14. *Only Gold*, Directed by Andy Blankenbuehler, MCC Theater, New York, NY, November 26, 2022.
15. Ibid.
16. Blankenbuehler, interview by Amanda Olmstead. December 2024.
17. Gold, "Refining Gold."
18. Keith Loria, "Review: Women Show Their Might in a Mesmerizing Revival of *Nine*," *TheaterMania*, August 6, 2024, https://www.theatermania.com/news/review-women-show-their-might-in-a-mesmerizing-revival-of-nine_1746850/.
19. Blankenbuehler, interview by Amanda Olmstead. December 2024.
20. *Nine*, "Ti Voglio Bene/Be Italian," performed by Kathi Moss and the original Broadway company at the 36th Annual Tony Awards, directed by Tommy Tune. Video posted by Matt Hagmeier Curtis on YouTube, March 22, 2020, https://www.youtube.com/watch?v=aGp-x3HErEg.
21. Arthur Kopit, "Ti Voglio Bene," *Nine*, music and lyrics by Maury Yeston (New York: Samuel French, 1983), 49–50.
22. Thomas Floyd, "This Musical Looks Like Death (in a Stylish Way)," *The Washington Post (Washington, D.C. 1974. Online)*, 2024.
23. Loria, "Review: Women Show Their Might."

Chapter 6

1. Stephanie Klemons, interviewed by Amanda Olmstead. July 1, 2025. Pittsburgh, PA.
2. Ibid.
3. Ibid.
4. Stephanie Klemons, interviewed by Amanda Olmstead. July 20, 2019.
5. Ibid.
6. Several ensemble members who have worked with Blankenbuehler can also be seen on social media teaching dance classes using his distinctive movement style. They all employ language to suggest emotions, feelings, or ideas in a way similar to Blankenbuehler and Klemons.

Conclusion

1. Janet Wolff, "Reinstating Corporeality: Feminism and Body Politics," in *Meaning in Motion: New Cultural Studies of Dance*, ed. Jane Desmond (Durham, NC: Duke University Press, 1997), 83.
2. Lin-Manuel Miranda and Jeremy McCarter, *Hamilton: The Revolution: Being the Complete Libretto of the Broadway Musical, with a True Account of Its Creation, and Concise Remarks on Hip-Hop, the Power of Stories, and the New America*, 1st ed., ed. Lin-Manuel Miranda and Jeremy McCarter (New York, NY: Grand Central Publishing, 2016), 284.
3. As was discussed in Chapter 3, there is certainly debate over how revolutionary the show as a whole actually is; but there is no question that the work of the ensemble is fundamental to its success.

BIBLIOGRAPHY

"70th Annual Tony Awards 'Hamilton.'" *YouTube*, BroadwayInHD. October 15, 2016. www.youtube.com/watch/b5VqyCQV1Tg.

Albright, Ann Cooper. *Choreographing Difference: The Body and Identity in Contemporary Dance*. Middletown, CT: Wesleyan University Press, 1997.

"Andy Blankenbuehler- *In The Heights*." MoveTVnetwork.com, Vimeo video, 2:58. February 20, 2012. vimeo.com/37156545.

Bethea, Antwan. Interview with Amanda Olmstead. June 13, 2020.

Bethea, Antwan. *TwanBringItOn.com*. https://www.twanbringiton.com.

Blankenbuehler, Andy. "Building Broadway: Hamilton Choreographer Andy Blankenbuehler." Broadway.com, YouTube video, 4:07. June 6, 2016. www.youtube.com/watch?v=R49vKv8f0Wc.

Blankenbuehler, Andy. "*Hamilton* Choreographer Andy Blankenbuehler on the Broadway Q&A." Interviewed by Danny George. *Playbill* and The Growing Studio, YouTube video, 1:02:35. June 15, 2020. https://www.youtube.com/watch?v=jnP7GvN9MhI.

Blankenbuehler, Andy. Interview with Gillian Pensavalle. "Episode 217." *The Hamilcast*. Podcast audio. May 4, 2020. https://www.thehamilcast.com/andy-blankenbuehler/.

Blankenbuehler, Andy. Interview with Gillian Pensavalle. "Episode 218." *The Hamilcast*. Podcast audio. May 4, 2020. https://www.thehamilcast.com/andy-blankenbuehler/.

Blankenbuehler, Andy. Interviewed by Amanda Olmstead. May 1, 2018. New York, NY.

Blankenbuehler, Andy. Interviewed by Amanda Olmstead. September 17, 2024. Pittsburgh, PA.

Blankenbuehler, Andy. Interviewed by Amanda Olmstead. December 2, 2024. New York, NY.

Blankenbuehler, Andy, and Sarah L. Kaufman. "Fresh Steps." Symphony Space and Words on Dance. New York City, NY. October 21, 2019.

Blankenbuehler, Andy, and Stephanie Klemons. "'Hamilton' Choreographer Breaks Down His Moves." Photographed by Cassandra Giraldo, *The Wall Street Journal*, Dow Jones & Company, 4:22. May 23, 2016. www.wsj.com/video/hamilton-choreographer-breaks-down-his-moves/8F716467-E023-4900-B149-D6BB3A40B66E.html.

Blankenbuehler, Andy, Michelle Charlesworth, and Harvey Fierstein. "Choreographer Andy Blankenbuehler Talks *In The Heights*." *Broadway Backstage*, ABC7NY, YouTube video, 1:43. May 3, 2008. www.youtube.com/watch?v=IRufwdN5NmQ&t=3s.

Blankenship, Mark. "No Fear of 'Heights': Producers Take Risk on Tyro Talent." *Variety* 405, no. 13 (2007): 55.

Bring It On. Directed by Peyton Reed, writer Jessica Bendinger. Santa Monica, CA: Beacon Pictures, Wonderworks Films; Distributed by Universal Pictures, 2000.

"Bring It On: The Musical" Program. St. James Theatre. July 12, 2012. New York: NY, Playbill. https://www.playbill.com/playbillpagegallery/inside-playbill?asset=00000150-aea8-d936-a7fd-eefc733a0002&type=InsidePlaybill&slide=5.

Bring It On: The Musical, (Videorecording). St. James Theatre. December 14, 2012. Theatre on Film and Tape Archive, NYPL Performing Arts Library, New York, New York.

Brown, Jayna. *Babylon Girls: Black Women Performers and the Shaping of the Modern*. Durham, NC: Duke University Press, 2008.

Burrows, Jonathan. *A Choreographer's Handbook*. Milton Park, Abingdon, Oxon: Routledge, 2010.

Cargle, Rachel. (@rachel.cargle). 2020. Instagram. June 29, 2020. https://www.instagram.com/p/CCByOMJnhNq/.

"Carnaval del Barrio- *In the Heights* OBC." YouTube, video, 8:07. https://www.youtube.com/watch?v=Omu3afOVNiQ.

Castillo-Garsow, Melissa, and Jason Nichols. "Hip Hop Latinidades: More Than Just Rapping in Spanish." In *La Verdad: An International Dialogue on Hip Hop Latinidades*. Columbus, OH: The Ohio State University Press, 2016: 3–16.

Chasteen, John Charles. *National Rhythms, African Roots: The Deep History of Latin American Popular Dance*, 1st ed. Albuquerque, NM: University of New Mexico Press, 2004.

Chernow, Ron. *Alexander Hamilton*. New York, NY: Penguin Press, 2004.

Cheslow, Daniella. "Parents Are Bringing Their Children to Black Lives Matter Plaza for a 'Once in a Lifetime Experience.'" *DCist*, WAMU 88.5 - American University Radio. June 17, 2020. dcist.com/story/20/06/11/parents-are-bringing-their-children-to-black-lives-matter-plaza-for-a-once-in-a-lifetime-experience/.

Clayton, Tracy. (@borkeymcpoverty). 2020. "im late w the hamilton criticism stuff & im clearly biased but.. i really like that this conversation is happening. hamilton the play and the movie were given to us in two different worlds & our willingness to interrogate things in this way feels like a clear sign of change." Twitter. July 5, 2020 2:32 PM EST. https://twitter.com/brokeymcpoverty/status/1279845518227787777?lang=en.

Cramer, Lyn. "Andy Blankenbuehler." In *Creating Musical Theatre: Conversations with Broadway Directors and Choreographers*. London: Bloomsbury Methuen Drama, 2013: 25–50.

DeFrantz, Thomas F. "The Black Beat Made Visible: Hip Hop Dance and Body Power." In *Of the Presence of the Body: Essays on Dance and Performance Theory*, edited by André Lepecki. Middletown, CT: Wesleyan University Press, 2004: 64–81.

Desmond, Jane. "Embodying Difference: Issues in Dance and Cultural Studies." In *Meaning in Motion: New Cultural Studies of Dance*, edited by Jane Desmond. Durham, NC: Duke University Press, 1997: 29–54.

Diverlus, Rodney. "Black Lives Matter Toronto: Urgency as Choreographic Necessity." *Canadian Theatre Review* 176 (2018): 66.

"Dramaturgy." *Merriam-Webster.com Dictionary* s.v. accessed February 18, 2021. https://www.merriam-webster.com/dictionary/dramaturgy.

Floyd, Thomas. "This Musical Looks like Death (in a Stylish Way)." *The Washington Post (Washington, D.C. 1974. Online)*. 2024.

Foster, Susan Leigh. *Choreographing Empathy: Kinesthesia in Performance*. London: Routledge, 2011.

Foster, Susan Leigh. *Choreographing History*. Bloomington, IN: Indiana University Press, 1995.

Foster, Susan Leigh. *Choreography and Narrative*. Bloomington, IN: Indiana University Press, 1996.

Foster, Susan Leigh. *Corporealities: Dancing, Knowledge, Culture, Power*. London: Routledge, 1996.

Foster, Susan Leigh. *Reading Dancing: Bodies and Subjects in Contemporary American Dance*. Berkeley, CA: University of California Press, 1986.

Foster, Susan Leigh. *Valuing Dance: Commodities and Gifts in Motion*. New York, NY: Oxford University Press, 2019.

Franko, Mark. *The Work of Dance: Labor, Movement, and Identity in the 1930s*. Middletown, CT: Wesleyan University Press, 2002.

Friscia, Suzannah. "*Hamilton's* Dance Revolution." *Dance Magazine* 90, no. 6 (2016): 26–30.

"From Alexander Hamilton to Margarita Schuyler, [February 1780]." *Founders Online*, National Archives. https://founders.archives.gov/documents/Hamilton/01-02-02-0613. [Original source: *The Papers of Alexander Hamilton*, vol. 2, *1779–1781*, edited by Harold C. Syrett. New York, NY: Columbia University Press, 1961, pp. 269–271].

Gans, Andrew. "Casting Announced for Luis Salgado-Directed *In the Heights*." *Playbill*, Playbill Inc. March 2, 2017. www.playbill.com/article/casting-announced-for-luis-salgado-directed-in-the-heights.

Gold, Sylviane. "Refining Gold: Andy Blankenbuehler Opens up about the Making of Only Gold, the Weight of Creating Post-Hamilton and the Road Ahead." *Dance Magazine*. Vol. 97. Dance Magazine, Inc. 2023.

Green, Jesse. "Review: In 'Only Gold,' Each Move Is Worth 1,000 Words." *The New York Times*. 2022.

Gross, Terry. "'The Past Isn't Done with Us,' Says 'Hamilton' Creator Lin-Manuel Miranda." *NPR*. June 29, 2020. www.npr.org/2020/06/29/884592985/the-past-isn-t-done-with-us-says-hamilton-creator-lin-manuel-miranda.

Hamilton. Produced by Walt Disney Pictures, 5000 Broadway Productions, Nevis Productions, Old 320 Sycamore, Radical Media. Directed by Thomas Kail. Written by Lin-Manuel Miranda. Distributed by Disney+, Walt Disney Studios Motion Pictures. New York, NY. July 3, 2020.

Hamilton: An American Musical, music and lyrics by Lin-Manuel Miranda, choreo. Andy Blankenbuehler. Benedum Center for Performing Arts. Pittsburgh, PA. September 18, 2024.

Haskell, Neil. Interview with Mo Brady. "The History of the Ensemble: Hamilton (Feat. Neil Haskell, Sasha Hutchings)." *The Ensemblist*, podcast audio. July 1, 2020. http://www.theensemblist.com/podcasts.

Hinds, Patrick. "Episode 14: *Bring It On: The Musical*." *Broadway Backstory*, TodayTix. November 7, 2017. https://www.todaytix.com/broadway-backstory/episodes/bring-it-on-the-musical.

How to Dance through Time, Vol. IV: The Elegance of Baroque Social Dance. Directed by Carol Téten. Dancetime Publications. 2003. https://video.alexanderstreet.com/watch/how-to-dance-through-time-vol-iv-the-elegance-of-baroque-social-dance-2.

Hudes, Quiara Alegría, and Lin-Manuel Miranda. *In the Heights: The Complete Book and Lyrics of the Broadway Musical*. Milwaukee, WI: Applause Theatre & Cinema Books, 2013.

Huntington, Carla Stalling. *Hip Hop Dance: Meanings and Messages*. Jefferson, NC: McFarland, 2007.

Hutchings, Sasha. Interview with Mo Brady. "The History of the Ensemble: Hamilton (Feat. Neil Haskell, Sasha Hutchings)." *The Ensemblist*, podcast audio. July 1, 2020. http://www.theensemblist.com/podcasts.

In, Merl. "[1280x720] Grammys 2016 Watch Lin Manuel Miranda and the Cast of Hamilton Perform - The Verge." *Vimeo*. March 14, 2018. vimeo.com/260119105.

In the Heights. (Videorecording). Richard Rodgers Theatre. October 10, 2008. Theatre on Film and Tape Archive, NYPL Performing Arts Library, New York, New York.

"*In the Heights* 2.5 // 'Carnaval del barrio' sub español." YouTube, video, 8:09. June 5, 2020. https://www.youtube.com/watch?v=6Qk7S_Z1EVw.

"*In the Heights*: Chasing Broadway Dreams." PBS Great Performances, video, 54:00. November 10, 2017.

Isherwood, Charles. "From the Corner Bodega, the Music of Everyday Life." *The New York Times*. February 9, 2007. www.nytimes.com/2007/02/09/theater/reviews/09heights.html.

Kedhar, Anusha. "'Hands Up! Don't Shoot!': Gesture, Choreography, and Protest in Ferguson." *The Feminist Wire*. October 6, 2014. thefeministwire.com/2014/10/protest-in-ferguson.

Klemons, Stephanie. Interviewed by Amanda Olmstead. June 6, 2018. Pittsburgh, PA.

Klemons, Stephanie. Interviewed by Amanda Olmstead. July 20, 2019. Pittsburgh, PA.

Klemons, Stephanie. Interviewed by Amanda Olmstead. July 1, 2025. Pittsburgh, PA.

Kopit, Arthur. *Nine*. Music and lyrics by Maury Yeston. New York, NY: Samuel French, 1983.

"Krumping." *The Oxford Dictionary of Dance*. Oxford University Press, 2010.

Lepecki, André. "Choreopolice and Choreopolitics: Or, the Task of the Dancer." *TDR: Drama Review* 57, no. 4 (December 1, 2013): 13–27.

Lepecki, André. *Exhausting Dance: Performance and the Politics of Movement*. New York, NY: Routledge, 2006.

Loria, Keith. "Review: Women Show Their Might in a Mesmerizing Revival of *Nine*." *TheaterMania*. August 6, 2024. https://www.theatermania.com/news/review-women-show-their-might-in-a-mesmerizing-revival-of-nine_1746850.

MacCannell, Dean. "Staged Authenticity: Arrangements of Social Space in Tourist Settings." *The American Journal of Sociology* 79, no. 3 (1973): 589–603.

Marcell, Morgan. Interviewed by Amanda Olmstead. October 21, 2018.

Martin, Randy. *Critical Moves: Dance Studies in Theory and Politics*. Durham, NC: Duke University Press, 1998.

McMains, Juliet. "Dancing Latin/ Latin Dancing: Salsa and DanceSport." In *Ballroom, Boogie, Shimmy Sham, Shake: A Social and Popular Dance Reader*, edited by Julie Malnig. Urbana, IL: University of Illinois Press, 2009: 302–322.

McMaster, James, and Liz Whittaker Chapman. "Why Hamilton Is Not the Revolution You Think It Is." *HowlRound Theatre Commons*. February 23, 2016. howlround.com/why-hamilton-not-revolution-you-think-it.

McMillan, Patrick, and Shirley Rushing. *Ballroom Dance American Style: Smooth, Rhythm, Latin*. Dubuque, IA: Eddie Bowers Pub., Incorporated, 1997.

Mineo, Liz. "Correcting 'Hamilton.'" *Harvard Gazette*, Harvard Gazette. July 7, 2020. news.harvard.edu/gazette/story/2016/10/correcting-hamilton/.

Miranda, Lin-Manuel. "In the Heights." In *In the Heights*, Vocal Selections. Milwaukee, WI: Williamson Music, Hal Leonard, 2008.

Miranda, Lin-Manuel. Interview with Mo Brady. "Writing for Ensembles (*Hamilton*, *In the Heights* - feat. Lin-Manuel Miranda)." *The Ensemblist*, podcast audio. July 2, 2020. https://www.stitcher.com/show/the-ensemblist/episode/181-writing-for-ensembles-hamilton-in-the-heights-feat-lin-manuel-miranda-63385999.

Miranda, Lin-Manuel. "Lin Manuel Miranda '02." *Wesleyan University*. www.wesleyan.edu/admission/videos/linmanuel.html.

Miranda, Lin-Manuel, and Jeremy McCarter. *Hamilton: The Revolution: Being the Complete Libretto of the Broadway Musical, with a True Account of Its Creation, and Concise Remarks on Hip-Hop, the Power of Stories, and the New America*. First edition. New York, NY: Grand Central Publishing, 2016.

Mulvey, Laura. "Visual Pleasure and Narrative Cinema." In *Media and Cultural Studies KeyWorks*, edited by Meenakshi Gigi Durham and Douglas Kellner. Malden, MA: Blackwell Publishers, 2001: 342–352.

Nash, Kate. "Paris." *My Best Friend Is You*. Fiction Records and Geffen Records, 2010.

Nine. "Ti Voglio Bene/Be Italian," performed by Kathi Moss and the original Broadway company at the 36th Annual Tony Awards, directed by Tommy Tune. Video posted by Matt Hagmeier Curtis on YouTube. March 22, 2020. https://www.youtube.com/watch?v=aGp-x3HErEg.

Oberacker, Richard, and Robert Taylor. *Bandstand: The New American Musical.* New York, NY: Samuel French, 2018.

Only Gold. Directed by Andy Blankenbuehler. Performed at MCC Theater, New York, NY. November 26, 2022.

Only Gold. Playbill. November 7, 2022. https://playbill.com/production/only-gold-off-broadway-the-robert-w-wilson-mcc-theater-space-2022.

Phillip, Abby. "Confederate Symbols Are Coming down, despite Donald Trump's Ire - CNN Video." *CNN*, Cable News Network. June 12, 2020. www.cnn.com/videos/politics/2020/06/12/confederate-monument-symbols-military-bases-pkg-phillip-ebof-vpx.cnn.

Profeta, Katherine. *Dramaturgy in Motion: At Work on Dance and Movement Performance.* Madison, WI: The University of Wisconsin Press, 2015.

Rajakumar, Mohanalakshmi. *Hip Hop Dance.* Santa Barbara, CA: Greenwood Press, 2012.

Ronen, Shelly. "Grinding on the Dance Floor: Gendered Scripts and Sexualized Dancing at College Parties." *Gender & Society* 24, no. 3 (June 1, 2010): 355–377.

Salgado, Luis. Interview by Amanda Olmstead. May 6, 2025.

Samonte, Jayzel. "Heightened Exposure: *In the Heights*." *Movmnt Magazine.* June 29, 2008. issuu.com/movmnt/docs/movmnt7.

Stewart, Seth. "Exclusive Interview with Dancer Seth Stewart (*In the Heights* / Madonna)." *I.N-TV.* YouTube video, 7:53. July 6, 2011. www.youtube.com/watch?v=8hoTgDLC4ck.

Struxness, Betsy. Interviewed by Amanda Olmstead. October 16, 2018.

The Princess Diaries. Walt Disney presents a Brownhouse production, a Garry Marshall film. Produced by Whitney Houston, Debra Martin Chase, Mario Iscovich. Screenplay by Gina Wendkos. Directed by Garry Marshall. Burbank, CA: Walt Disney Home Entertainment; Distributed by Buena Vista Home Entertainment, 2001.

Trebay, Guy. "The Clowning, Rump-Shaking,: How a Dance Called Krumping Took Over an Inner-City Neighborhood." *New York Times (1923–Current File).* June 19, 2005.

Tu, Jeni. "Andy Blankenbuehler." *Dance Teacher* 30, no. 8. Raleigh, NC: 2008: 96.

"UCA School and Open Rec Rules & Regulations." Universal Cheerleaders Association, UCA High School Cheerleading Championship. 2021. https://www.varsity.com/uca/wp-content/uploads/2020/08/20-21_uca_competition_schoolrules.pdf.

Waskul, Dennis, and Phillip Vannini. "The Performative Body: Dramaturgy, the Body, and Embodiment." In *The Drama of Social Life: A Dramaturgical Handbook*, edited by Charles Edgley, Phillip Vannini, Simon Gottschalk, and Dennis Waskul. Farnham: Taylor & Francis Group, 2013: 197–210.

Weinert-Kendt, Rob. "Rapping a Revolution." *The New York Times.* February 5, 2015. www.nytimes.com/2015/02/08/theater/lin-manuel-miranda-and-others-from-hamilton-talk-history.html.

Whitty, Jeff, Tom Kitt, Lin-Manuel Miranda, and Amanda Green. *Bring It On: The Musical.* New York, NY: Music Theatre International, 2012.

Wickman, Kase. "*Bring It On*: the Complete Oral History." August 6, 2015. http://www.kasewickman.com/?p=2748.

Winer, Linda. "Review: 'In the Heights,' by Lin-Manuel Miranda." *Newsday*. Melville, NY: Tribune Content Agency. March 10, 2008.

Wolf, Stacy, and Liza Gennaro. "Dance in Musical Theater." In *The Oxford Handbook of Dance and Theater*. Vol. 1, edited by Nadine George-Graves. Oxford University Press, 2015: 148–168.

Wolff, Janet. "Reinstating Corporeality: Feminism and Body Politics." In *Meaning in Motion: New Cultural Studies of Dance*, edited Jane Desmond. Durham, NC: Duke University Press, 1997: 81–100.

Wood, Amy Louise. *Lynching and Spectacle: Witnessing Racial Violence in America, 1890–1940*. Chapel Hill, NC: University of North Carolina Press, 2009.

INDEX